Censorship and the Permissive Society

Censorship and the Permissive Society

BRITISH CINEMA AND THEATRE
1955–1965

Anthony Aldgate

CLARENDON PRESS · OXFORD

1995

Oxford University Press, Walton Street, Oxford OX2 6DP

Oxford New York

Athens Auckland Bangkok Bombay
Calcutta Cape Town Dar es Salaam Delhi
Florence Hong Kong Istanbul Karachi
Kuala Lumpur Madras Madrid Melbourne
Mexico City Nairobi Paris Singapore
Taipei Tokyo Toronto

and associated companies in
Berlin Ibadan

Oxford is a trade mark of Oxford University Press

Published in the United States
by Oxford University Press Inc., New York

British Library Cataloguing in Publication Data
Data available

Library of Congress Cataloging in Publication Data
Aldgate, Anthony.
Censorship and society : British cinema and theatre, 1955–1965 /
Anthony Aldgate.
Includes bibliographical references and index.
1. Motion pictures—Censorship—Great Britain—History.
2. Theater—Censorship—Great Britain—History—20th century.
I. Title.
PN1995.65.G7A43 1995   94–30668
363.3'1—dc20

ISBN 0–19–811241–6
ISBN 0–19–818352–6 (Pbk)

1 3 5 7 9 10 8 6 4 2

Typeset by Graphicraft Typesetters Ltd., Hong Kong

Printed in Great Britain
on acid-free paper by
Bookcraft Ltd., Midsomer Norton, Avon

For Hannah and Jane

Acknowledgements

I should like to thank the following individuals and institutions for the exceptional help and kindly assistance they showed in providing support, sources, or information: the Arts Faculty and A42X Course Team at the Open University; BBC Written Archives Centre, Caversham; Roy Boulting; the British Film Institute Library; Sally Brown (British Library, Manuscript Collections); Julie Christie; David Edgar; Clive Emsley; James Ferman (British Board of Film Classification); Alison Gunn; Robert Hands; Sue Harper; Angela Jamieson; Arthur Marwick; Andrew Patrick (formerly British Film and Television Producers Association Ltd.); Guy Phelps (British Board of Film Classification); Jeffrey Richards; the late Tony Richardson; Wendy Simpson; John Titman (Lord Chamberlain's Office); and Sir John Woolf.

Theatre stills appear by permission of the British Library and film stills by permission of the British Film Institute Stills, Posters, and Designs department. Stills from *Spare the Rod* appear by courtesy of Bryanston Films Ltd.; from *Room at the Top* by courtesy of Romulus Films Ltd.; and from *Look Back in Anger*, *The Entertainer*, *Saturday Night and Sunday Morning*, *The Loneliness of the Long Distance Runner*, and *A Taste of Honey* by courtesy of Woodfall Films. Several people helped considerably in securing permission to use them: John Henderson, Natasha Richardson, and Brian Sammes.

My greatest debt of gratitude, however, is owed to the late John Trevelyan who aided the research immensely at a very early stage of development and, in effect, set it all in motion.

Contents

Abbreviations

BBFC	British Board of Film Censors
BFI	British Film Institute
BFPA	British Film Producers Association
FBFM	Federation of British Film Makers
LC	Lord Chamberlain's Office, Play Censorship Correspondence, held in the British Library Manuscripts Collection

1 The Twilight Zone

'The 1990s', I read a while back, 'are looking more to the insights of the sixties than the values of the eighties'. It was a bold judgement to advance at the outset of the decade. Certainly, the pop record charts are frequently invaded by 'golden oldies' from the period, albeit usually borne on the back of myriad television commercials. Ageing rock stars still 'hit the road' with considerable success or pack out Wembley Stadium for comeback concerts. Advertising agencies herald the advent of a 'second sixties' in which 'the key values' of the era—'peace', 'love', and 'equality'—are being 'reborn for the nineties as a reaction to what existed in the eighties'. Journalistic clichés are dutifully trotted out and much is promised. It remains to be seen, however, whether the 'sixties revival' is merely another passing fad and voguish fancy or offers anything of substance. Whether, as the forecasters predict: 'The nineties will be a period when concern with the problems of others rises.'

Not so long ago, after all, it was usually more in order to damn the legacy of the 1960s. 'We are reaping what was sown in the sixties', Margaret Thatcher announced in March 1982. 'The fashionable theories and permissive claptrap set the scene', she argued, 'for a society in which the old virtues of discipline and restraint were denigrated.' What were once dubbed with hyperbole 'the swinging sixties' were subsequently maligned with equal vehemence as 'sick and self-indulgent'. Others followed in her wake and jumped on the same bandwagon. So much so that the playwright and film-maker, David Hare, was prompted to complain in June 1989: 'It is the fashion now to denigrate the sixties. . . . We are told that the deep-rooted problems of British life stem from the sixties . . . [as] trendy right wing politicians, in hollow affectation, pretend to trace this country's ills to those days.'[1]

For Hare, as for fellow playwrights David Edgar, Howard Barker, Howard Brenton, and Trevor Griffiths, the decade should better be judged

1

as progressive and liberalizing. All sought to offer corrective rejoinders to jaundiced Thatcherite views as they revalued the 1960s in the themes and concerns of several distinctly impressive pieces of drama or discourse. David Edgar in particular heartily condemned 'the demonisation of the 1960s' as perpetrated by the New Right. He fiercely contested its grim vision and elaborated the reasons why the decade could not easily be written off. The Left, he believed, proved 'uniquely radical and creative' in its politics—'rejecting the traditional eurocentrism of the Old Left, and more or less inventing the notion of a left politics of personal life'—and was 'strikingly successful', both in achieving specific goals such as the ending of American participation in Vietnam and in its legacy.

This legacy consisted in an extensive vocabulary of protest, not least in the cultural sphere, from community theatre to poster, badge, and T-shirt art, and in the creation of a network of novel organizational forms 'from community resource centres and publishing collectives to consumer co-operatives and free schools'. The Left's work also bore fruit in a number of new political movements whose roots had been put down in the 1960s, from environmentalism to feminism, which 'although provoked by the worst of the 60s, was undoubtedly enabled by the best of it'. Crucially, Edgar concludes, 'the social gains of the period (including the setting up of the Race Relations Board, and its successors, the passing of the Abortion Act, and the abolition of hanging) have remained, despite considerable pressure, stubbornly intact'.[2]

Against the Thatcherite revisionist tendency, Edgar contends, it is worth reaffirming that the 1960s proved a time when substantial advances were made. The emblematic central figure of his 1987 play *That Summer*, Howard ('early 40s, a university lecturer'), remembers the era in fondly affectionate and heavily nostalgic terms, yet offers a spirited defence of the real gains achieved by way of racial desegregation, growing disgust with the Vietnam war, the rise of feminism, and the like. His key speech—highly personalized and occasionally rhapsodic, though by no means improbable—culminates with an anecdote:

A story. The University of Edinburgh. Where I taught social anthropology, from 1966 to '69. The students' union, divided, men and women. A girl I knew, who had got really pissed off with this situation. So, one Saturday, she dolled herself up in what I think is called a cocktail dress, she went down to the men's union, on her own, and entered the great bar—no doubt among the longest in the western world—and strolled up to the counter bold as brass and inquired if they could furnish her with one small g and t. And the barman said, 'I'm sorry, madam, I can't serve you'. And by now, of course, it being Saturday, not only had her presence been observed, and commented upon, indeed, but by now there was a fearful catcalling, and whistling, and stamping in the gallery; and having asked again, and having been refused again, she began the long walk back, towards the door. And you can imagine both the manner and the matter of the catcalling, and what courage, and indeed what perspicuity, for her to turn back, at the door, to look across that sea of bloated, drunken, student faces, smile a withering smile, and drop—one—shoulder strap. And turn, and go. (*Pause*) In 1967. That time, when young Americans were lying down in front of troop trains. Che Guevara fighting his doomed battles in the hills. Mohammed Ali saying, 'Hell no, I won't go.' That time. That summer.[3]

Nor is the debate over the 1960s confined to playwrights and politicians: social historians have been carefully, stringently redrawing the contours of the era. While there is inevitably much dispute about its true radical import, nevertheless, it is said, there was assuredly a lot that was new and vital. Although the significance and novelty of the time are easily exaggerated, it remains essentially correct to suggest that a break did occur. When considering whether there was a 'Cultural Revolution', for example, Arthur Marwick suggested in 1988:

Mrs Thatcher, indeed, was right, if for the phrase 'the old virtues of discipline and restraint were denigrated' we substitute 'the social controls established by the Victorians were overthrown'. Whatever today's radical initiatives towards privatization and marginalizing the state, this was a revolution which will not easily be reversed since, in fact, it had little to do with the state and everything to do with society

'The key acts of the period', Marwick reiterates, 'were not part of some political blueprint for transforming society but resulted from pressures generated from within society.' Hence there was the Betting and Gaming Act in 1960; in 1967, the Abortion Act, National Health Service (Family Planning) Act, and the Sexual Offences Act; the Theatres Act in 1968; the Representation of the People and the Divorce Reform Acts of 1969; and, in 1970, the Matrimonial Property Act, Equal Pay Act, and the Chronic Sick and Disabled Persons Act. 'Acts of Parliament must never be mistaken for the reality of social change', he cautions, but 'in fact the reality of change was palpable in the archaeology of everyday life, in attitudes, behaviour and artefacts.' Although he takes great care not to underestimate the undoubted 'sources of tension and deprivation—race relations and high-rise housing for instance', Marwick maintains the 1960s were, if not 'a golden age', still 'a time of release and change'.[4]

Nowhere was there more evidence of release and change, it appears, than in the realms of censorship. British drama, for example, benefited enormously from the process of 'decensorship' which began in the 1960s. Following the 1968 abolition of the Lord Chamberlain's legal powers of control over theatres, which had largely consisted in his office's responsibility for examining play scripts before public performance, the stage enjoyed a new surge of creativity, especially from its blossoming 'fringe'. The younger playwrights like Edgar, Hare, and Griffiths were immediate beneficiaries and produced their first substantial work around this time.[5]

The 'great liberation for printed literature', to borrow John Sutherland's words, occurred almost a decade earlier on 21 July 1959, when the Obscene Publications Act (sponsored by then Labour back-bencher, Roy Jenkins) passed into law. This definitely opened the gates. But real freedom from censorship for literature—'the crucial blow for the freedom of literature and publishing alike'—was decisively won at the outset of the next decade. It came in November 1960 when a jury of three women and nine men returned a verdict of 'not guilty' in the prosecution of Penguin Books for publication of the unexpurgated version of D. H. Lawrence's last novel, *Lady Chatterley's Lover*, and thus made it 'available for the first time to the public in the United Kingdom'. Decensorship, Sutherland argues, played a significant part in the transformations of the 1960s:

The 1960s released all sorts of new energies and dissidence. Television, stage and film chafed against restriction. There was a new charter for the BBC in 1964 and liberal direction under Hugh Carleton Greene (a truly demonic figure, according to Mrs Whitehouse). At the British Board of Film Censors, John Trevelyan liberalized film licensing. It was a gradual process, but in terms of the milestones by which such things are measured, 1966–68 would seem to have been the critical threshold. In November 1966, Kenneth Tynan used the word 'fuck' in a television studio discussion. There was immediate uproar, but the monosyllable could not be unsaid. Threatened prosecution of Edward Bond's *Saved* in 1967 mobilized Parliament at last to get rid of the ludicrous Lord Chamberlain's censorship. And Lindsay Anderson's *If*... (1968) got through to general release with a tuft of female pubic hair visible to the 18-plus British population. As Roy Jenkins put it in a phrase which the *Daily Telegraph* will throw back in his face for ever more— the permissive society was the civilized society. Liberalization was fought every inch, but its tide in the 1960s was irresistible.[6]

Sutherland's case is persuasive and his arguments compelling. But some things are worth reiterating and others require revision. While the 'liberal'-minded Hugh Greene led the BBC to great heights during the 1960s, it was a slow and arduous process. In December 1962, he was enough of a pragmatist to think an apology should be sent to the Prime Minister, Harold Macmillan, for a sketch in the new satirical show, *That Was The*

Week That Was, which he felt 'went beyond reasonable limits'. Moreover, one could easily take issue with the choice of the years 1966–8 as the 'critical threshold' for British cinema; indeed, many important censorship battles had been fought long before the 1968 appearance of Lindsay Anderson's film *If.* . . . Arthur Marwick, when seeking in characteristic fashion 'to pin down as precisely as possible the critical point of change', in fact settles on 1959, and spotlights the appearance of *Room at the Top* in January of that year as crucial in both the process of decensorship and the revitalization of British cinema generally. Though somewhat guarded about exact dates and causes, most commentators agree the years around the start of the 1960s witnessed significant change. 'It is certainly true to say', Janet Thumim states, 'that the characteristic themes treated in popular film underwent marked changes.' The period 1959–63 is distinguished for Stuart Laing, furthermore, because it was 'marked by the appearance (and subsequent sudden disappearance) of a "New Wave" of social realist films which seemed to signal a renaissance of seriousness and contemporary relevance within British cinema'. The roots of change in 1960s British cinema undoubtedly lay in the twilight zone of the 1950s.[7]

Nobody would deny, however, that much remained to be achieved by way of decensorship in the first half of the 1960s. And Sutherland is correct to single out John Trevelyan as a key figure. His role as secretary of the British Board of Film Censors (BBFC), which he took over in July 1958, was paramount. For the epigram of the book he wrote after his resignation, Trevelyan chose: 'Times change and we must change with them.' He described there the kind of relationship he sought to foster with film-makers:

I used to enjoy script discussions. They were not always, as might be supposed, concerned with detail, that is with lines or with visuals that could be censorable, frequently I wanted the film-maker to talk about the people in his film so that I could get to know how he saw them. I often used to ask what he thought their lives had been before what we were to see on the screen, and what he thought happened to them afterwards. A novelist builds up characters in his imagination; so does a film-maker. Sometimes the film-maker develops his characters as he makes his film . . .

Some film-makers . . . used to like me to come to the studio while their films were being shot. I think they realised that by doing this I could get the 'feel' of the production, and that this was important to me. Later I used to see 'rough-cuts' or 'fine-cuts' of their films with them, and we used to have long talks afterwards in which the word 'censorship' was rarely, if ever, used. This, in retrospect, I regard as the greatest compliment that a film-maker could pay me. It implied that

I cared about their films, and that they regarded me more as an adviser or consultant than a censor . . . I am glad to say that most of the fine film-makers working in this country gave me their confidence knowing that I would do all I could to help them, and that I would always give them my honest opinion of their films. I think we had a mutual respect, and for this I am grateful since it made my job possible.[8]

Other observers besides Sutherland have praised Trevelyan's efforts in recognizing and bringing about change, none more so than the film-maker Bryan Forbes, who pin-pointed the dilemmas for the censor and film-makers alike in 1974:

Granted the need for a film censor, a question open to continuing debate, it is doubtful whether anybody could have done the job better than John. Chain-smoking his way through porn and pleasure, his lean and hungry look gave no indication of his true character . . . as he eased into his emperor's clothes he made a genuine effort to remove most of the mystique and was at some pains to earn the confidence of responsible film-makers . . . he used his vast experience of the worst of human nature, to which, within the confines of Wardour Street he was no stranger, to judge whether we had introduced violence or sex for purely spurious effect or whether our intentions had been dramatically honourable. To this extent he was primarily responsible for the growing maturity of British films during the Sixties. There are some who blame John in part for the present permissive society, failing to recognize that change was inevitable. What he did—all he could do—was to give a lead, guiding film-makers and audiences alike in deliberate, easy stages. Emotionally, I am opposed to all and any form of censorship, but I am cynically aware of the commercial profitability of violence and perverted sex and there is no doubt in my mind that had we not had John's restraining hand the flood gates of filth would have opened wide a decade ago. And I do not think it is difficult for men of reason and intelligence to define filth.[9]

Defining 'filth', in truth, was less easy than Forbes credited, even among 'men of reason and intelligence', and there was by no means always mutual agreement over its careful delineation. But Forbes, like Sutherland, is right when referring to the inevitable reaction which beset all moves towards liberalization. It was evident, for example, during the debate in the House of Lords on 22 June 1959, at the Committee Stage of the Obscene Publications Bill. Although the bill did not strictly deal with the mainstream cinema and 'ordinary films', the Lord Chancellor, Viscount Kilmuir, moved an amendment to include the exhibition of films 'in a private house to which the public is not admitted' as a further instance of the publication of 'obscene matter'. His express purpose was 'to catch the dirty man who shows a filthy film in a house or a place in a back street'.

Lord Amwell, 'octogenarian Socialist', took advantage of the moment to expound at length his views on 'filthy films'. He was not seeking to stop approval of the amendment, which passed through easily enough. But he was trying to define 'filth' with regard to cinema, and to expand its horizons accordingly:

I saw a picture at the end of last week, a picture which was last week all over north-west London and this week is all over north-east London, a picture called *Look Back in Anger*. I am not objecting to the picture as such. I think it was 'phoney'; I am getting a little tired of the kind of frustrated psychology which is quite unrealistic in respect of cinema performances; but that is a matter of taste. In the film there were two 'gags' of a description that one cannot just call Rabelaisian, or words of that description; they were pure and unadulterated filth for the sake of it. When people say, 'It will go over the heads of pure-minded people', it simply is not true; it was not intended to go over the heads of any people at all. It was not a double meaning joke or anything of that kind. I am not puritanical in matters of art or literature, or anything of that kind. I can read Sterne's *Sentimental Journey* or the *Decameron* or even the Restoration playwrights without turning a hair. I have no objection to that kind of thing, and I have no objection to *double entendre*. There was plenty of that in the old Victorian music hall and it did not do very great harm because it was straightforward and robust. But the particular 'gags' that I refer to were pure filth of the most unutterable description.

I should like to know just where we stand about things of that kind. Why for the sake of profits should these vast aggregates of finance impose that kind of thing as they please upon the community through this wide and important section of public entertainment? I do not want to criticise the cinema or the stage or anything else. It is the particular case where there is no justification whatever, in wit or anything else, which is more and more being imposed upon the public simply for the purpose of making profits. I should like to know just how we stand in respect of Common Law in a matter of that kind.[10]

Little wonder, perhaps, that the process of decensorship was gradual. It was fought every inch of the way and, though the tide may well have been in its favour, progress proved anything but smooth or untroubled for the cinema as for the theatre. Neither cinema nor theatre could easily escape a system of censorship which depended as much on the exercise of pre-production scrutiny as it did on post-production review.

Moreover, the secretary at the BBFC and the comptroller at the Lord Chamberlain's office regularly informed each other of their respective activities and followed a policy of 'keeping in step'. Lord Cobbold, the Lord Chamberlain from 1963 to 1968, echoed John Trevelyan's sentiments on the need for change during the course of an important parliamentary debate over theatre censorship, which lasted nearly five hours, on 17 February 1966. 'Public opinion', he stated, 'is not static, and my objective is to move . . . with the mood of the times.'[11] Privately, the new generation of British playwrights, including John Osborne, Shelagh Delaney, and Harold Pinter (all of whom saw their stage plays transposed to the screen), experienced considerable difficulties with his office over everything from precise details in the use of language to wider issues regarding theme and content. The customary routine—like the one employed by the BBFC for films—was that managements seeking licences to produce their plays were told of the censors' reservations and misgivings before public presentation, and were expected to amend the works accordingly. The more adventurous and dynamic companies, however, might still encounter censorship problems.

Producer Joan Littlewood, general manager Gerry Raffles, and licensee John Bury were prosecuted in 1958 over the Theatre Workshop's production of Henry Chapman's *You Won't Always Be On Top* at the Theatre Royal, Stratford East. In 1966 summonses were issued to William Gaskill (the director), Greville Poke (secretary of the English Stage Company), and Alfred Esdaile (theatre licensee) over their production of Edward Bond's *Saved* at the Royal Court Theatre. Once more, successful prosecution ensued. The cases were different and proceedings were instigated by successive Lord Chamberlains. But the intention was the same: to warn managements of the error of their ways and to bring them back into line. Joan Littlewood's Theatre Workshop was prosecuted for introducing material, born of her highly improvisatory techniques, which had not been licensed and was felt to be offensive—'vulgar and not in good taste'. George Devine's English Stage Company was prosecuted over the matter of presenting a new stage play under 'club' auspices (done to escape the changes required to 'foul' language and other aspects of Bond's text) before it had been licensed by the Lord Chamberlain. In the latter instance, ironically, things came to a head less than a year after Lord Cobbold had maintained: 'we always think of ourselves as a licensing authority rather than as a censoring authority. The bias is always to give a licence unless there is a very strong ground for objection.' He elaborated upon his office's 'good intentions' and the mutually beneficial working relationship it had evolved with theatre companies in much the same terms that Trevelyan adopted:

Most of the managements have been in touch with the people in my office for years and are on very good terms with them. They write in, and they come in, and explain and ask for reconsideration; and of course one is always ready to look at any arguments that are put up. There is a bit of gamesmanship in all this. Some managements, not all, put in a number of four-letter words and other things they know perfectly well will be cut out, possibly in the hope that we will cut them out and leave one or two borderline things in. And of course there is some advertising value in 'banned by the censor'. So there's a good deal of give and take in this. And very often we arrive at an arrangement which is perfectly proper and suits everyone concerned.

It is doubtful whether Theatre Workshop or the English Stage Company would have agreed with the rosy picture he painted, nor his depiction of the supposedly harmonious state of affairs between managements and his office. Though the fines imposed upon them in 1958 and 1966 were nominal, both incidents lent support to those parties pressing for substantial changes in stage censorship. A Theatre Censorship Reform Committee appeared shortly after Littlewood's altercation. And William Gaskill later said of his run-in with the censors: 'The *Saved* affair had brought to a head the case against the Lord Chamberlain's power of pre-censorship. The following three years were dominated by the fight to break his power, a fight we eventually won.'[12]

Not all theatre managements were so inclined, of course, to buck the system. In some quarters, indeed, there was criticism of the censor for being too lenient and too lax. Henry Sherek, a leading impresario and 'top class purveyor of fine drama', complained bitterly on radio and in the press during 1961 of his 'embarrassment at the filth the Lord Chamberlain allowed to go on in the theatre'. He felt that theatre censorship was proving 'a little too considerate' and argued for some form of differential licence similar to the 'X' certificate for adult films which obtained with regard to the cinema. In the event, his plea got nowhere, although Brigadier Sir Norman Gwatkin, Comptroller of the Lord Chamberlain's office, grasped the opportunity to spotlight the censor's situation:

The Lord Chamberlain cannot, even if he wished to do so, for ever travel in a horse carriage; he is now in a motor car and many people are trying to force him into a spaceship . . . You would probably be surprised to know how much we cut out in words and how much we warn about business, but since the evidence at the trial of *Lady Chatterley* I am beginning to wonder who one is trying to protect.[13]

Gwatkin need not have worried unduly. There were sufficient numbers of people who felt sure they urgently required some protection. As we shall see, his office received a regular postbag from 'disgruntled' members of the public, protesting at the 'filth' they had witnessed for themselves on the stage and seeking its immediate removal. Like Henry Sherek, they would have preferred the Lord Chamberlain to abandon altogether the age of the motor car and fully revert to the conditions which obtained in the days of horse and carriage. They did not wish to see any loss in steering power, however, and sought instead increased control of the reins.

By the same token, there were plenty of people who felt certain that whatever protection the censors afforded remained as vital for the cinema as for the theatre, if not more so. While the advocates of greater control were clearly disappointed when the 1968 Theatres Act finally removed the Lord Chamberlain's powers, they were consoled by the fact that in the cinema, at least, censorship remained ever-present. The customary dictates of the film-making process saw to it that there were numerous pitfalls awaiting the film-makers of the day. Whether these were manifested in the pressures traditionally applied by the BBFC, despite Trevelyan's enlightened stewardship, or in an inherently hidebound and conservative-minded film industry, there were hurdles in abundance to overcome before any film was produced and put on public exhibition. Furthermore, the experiences of that band of British 'new wave' film-makers and the difficulties they encountered in bringing to the screen the works of John Braine, John Osborne, Alan Sillitoe, and Shelagh Delaney among others, bear fulsome testimony to the forces aligned against the liberalizing tendency. To understand the predicament they faced in their relations with the BBFC, with the wider censorship process, and with the film industry generally, is better to understand the debate over the permissive or progressive aspects of the changes affecting British society from the 'doldrums era' of the 1950s to the 'swinging sixties'. The ten years from 1955 to 1965 constitute a crucial period in forging a new sense of openness in the cinematic and theatrical exploration of key 'problematic' subjects. They also highlight the social, ideological, and political forces at work within the shifting terrain of the 'permissible'.

Notes

1 The London advertising agency Foote, Cone, and Belding coined the phrase 'Second Sixties' for its 1990 campaign 'The times they are a-changin' which of course harked back to the 1965 Bob Dylan hit record with the same title, while the Henley Centre for Forecasting noted the shift in values towards greater 'concern' in its 1989/90 *Planning for Social Change*. Margaret Thatcher's remarks were reported in the *Guardian*,

28 Mar. 1982. For David Hare's comments see 'Cycles of hope and despair', *Weekend Guardian*, 3–4 June 1989.

2 David Edgar's arguments are briefly outlined in 'It wasn't so naff in the 60s after all', *Guardian*, 7 July 1986, and elaborated at length in his collection of essays, *The Second Time as Farce: Reflections on the Drama of Mean Times* (London, 1988). For further comment on Thatcher's cultural views see Howard Barker, 'The triumph in defeat', *Guardian*, 22 Aug. 1988, and Howard Brenton, 'The art of survival', *Guardian*, 29 Nov. 1990.

3 David Edgar, *That Summer* (London, 1988), 75.

4 Arthur Marwick, 'The 1960s: Was there a "Cultural Revolution"?', *Contemporary Record*, 2/3 (1988), 18–20. But see esp. his books *British Society since 1945*, 2nd edn. (Harmondsworth, 1990) and *Culture in Britain since 1945* (Oxford, 1991). A less 'optimistic' account can be found in Kenneth Morgan, *The People's Peace: British History 1945–1989* (Oxford, 1990). For a decidedly 'pessimistic' rendering see William Williamson, *The Temper of the Times: British Society since World War II* (Oxford, 1990).

5 For the impact of 1968 on Trevor Griffiths in particular see the useful introduction, 'Intervening in Society's Life', to Mike Poole and John Wyver, *Powerplays: Trevor Griffiths in Television* (London, 1984), 6–7.

6 John Sutherland, *Offensive Literature: Decensorship in Britain, 1960–1982* (London, 1982), 2. Also invaluable over the question of decensorship in literature is H. Montgomery Hyde (ed.), *The Lady Chatterley's Lover Trial* (London, 1990). For theatre, see the contemporary account by Richard Findlater, *Banned: A Review of Theatrical Censorship in Britain* (London, 1967), as well as the more recent survey by John Johnston, a former comptroller in the Lord Chamberlain's office, *The Lord Chamberlain's Blue Pencil* (London, 1990).

7 See 'PM sanguine over Frost's satire show', *Guardian*, 2 Jan. 1993; Arthur Marwick, '*Room at the Top*, *Saturday Night and Sunday Morning*, and the "Cultural Revolution" in Britain', *Journal of Contemporary History*, 19/1 (1984), 129, 149; Janet Thumim, 'The "Popular", Cash and Culture in the Postwar British Cinema Industry', *Screen*, 32/3 (1991), 249; Stuart Laing, *Representations of Working Class Life, 1957–1964* (Basingstoke, 1986), 109.

8 John Trevelyan, *What the Censor Saw* (London, 1973), 208–9.

9 Bryan Forbes, *Notes for a Life* (London, 1974), 343. See also Penelope Houston, *The Contemporary Cinema, 1945–1963* (Harmondsworth, 1963), 120, where she stated: 'Trevelyan's tenure . . . has opened paths which only a few years ago would have remained firmly barred'. Alexander Walker, *Hollywood, England: The British Film Industry in the Sixties* (London, 1974), 43–4, said he 'helped to create the atmosphere in which a new kind of cinema could flourish'. John Hill, *Sex, Class and Realism: British Cinema 1956–1963* (London, 1986), 48, agreed that he demonstrated 'increasing leniency'. James C. Robertson, *The Hidden Cinema: British Film Censorship in Action, 1913–1972* (London, 1989), 161, believed Trevelyan epitomized 'radical permissiveness'. The more recent books on British cinema, including James Park, *British Cinema: The Lights That Failed* (London, 1990), 106, also mention his 'openness'.

Guy Phelps, *Film Censorship* (London, 1975), 43–5, is the one writer who has enjoyed unrestricted access to BBFC files at the time of researching his account. While he acknowledges that Trevelyan overturned the BBFC tradition of 'maximum secrecy and minimum publicity', he has significant reservations: 'In general, Trevelyan's policies are characterised more by caution than by the swashbuckling liberalisation with which he is sometimes credited.' Phelps, crucially, emphasizes the degree of continuity between Trevelyan's regime and those of his two immediate predecessors as BBFC secretary. Phelps's excellent and subtle reading of the Trevelyan years has gone largely unheeded by commentators. Only Robertson, *The Hidden Cinema*, also first-rate, notes the extent to which Trevelyan simply accelerated policies introduced by others, though he does not deal at all with the 'new wave' cinema.

10 *Parliamentary Debates (Lords)*, ccxvii. 73–9, 22 June 1959.

11 Johnston, *Blue Pencil*, 183, 195, 219–24. Also Findlater, *Banned*, 205.

12 Cobbold's comments were made in interview with J. W. Lambert for the *Sunday Times*, 11 Apr. 1965, and repr. verbatim in Johnston, *Blue Pencil*, 272–7. Johnston also outlines the events surrounding *Saved*, 213–16, where he quotes from Gaskill's own account of the proceedings, as well as giving details of *You Won't Always Be On Top* (*Blue Pencil*, 164).

13 The correspondence is quoted in Johnston, *Blue Pencil*, 164–5.

2 The Times they are A-changin'

In the spring of 1954, director Ronald Neame was considering his next project. A lighting cameraman in the 1930s, he had been associated during the 1940s with David Lean, first as director of photography and then as producer on such outstanding films as *Great Expectations* and *Oliver Twist* before becoming a director himself in 1947. Neame, like Lean and many other British film directors, invariably turned to literary sources for his inspiration. At the outset of the 1950s he transferred Arnold Bennett's *The Card* and Mark Twain's *The Million Pound Note* to the screen. Jill Craigie's screenplay and Geoffrey Unsworth's Technicolor camerawork undoubtedly contributed to the appeal of the latter. But both films were genuinely acknowledged as polished and accomplished efforts, albeit strikingly lacking in personal style, a charge that stuck thereafter. Though Neame won critical acclaim with Joyce Cary's *The Horse's Mouth* in 1959 and a measure of popular success in the 1960s with films of James Kennaway's *Tunes of Glory* and Muriel Spark's *The Prime of Miss Jean Brodie*, the criticism that he displayed decent craftsmanship but little else besides may perhaps explain his increasing disillusion with 'Art House type' cinema, and his resort in the 1970s to expensive international productions, backed by American money, and avowedly aimed at the commercial market.[1]

In March 1954, however, Neame's attention fell upon Michael Croft's recently published novel, *Spare the Rod*. An immediate best seller, it was reprinted twice in that year alone. Croft, subsequently director of the National Youth Theatre from 1956 until his death in 1986, drew upon his experience as a teacher to tell the tale of an enthusiastic newcomer to the profession, John Sanders, who struggles to control the young hooligans in a badly equipped secondary modern school. He is loath to resort to the harsh methods employed to maintain discipline which are practised by most of his colleagues and sadistically relished by one of them in particular, Gubb. Sanders succeeds, but in the process is driven to side with the

13

children against his colleague and compelled finally to resign. A 'fine teacher', with the promise of good references, he transfers to another school.

The book was a simple account, hardly original, but somewhat sensational by virtue of its overt attack on corporal punishment. An author's note emphasized that Worrell Street was 'an imaginary school', and that the conditions described were 'not universal in reality'. Yet they were 'sufficiently prevalent in certain districts to justify the picture I have given'. Croft's purpose was to 'draw attention to the grave and complex problems facing many teachers at the present time whose work I have tried to describe sympathetically and faithfully'. Despite his good intentions, the leading teachers' unions were far from pleased and expressed considerable disapproval and anger in the pages of their professional journals. This did not prevent Neame, 'a director of rare integrity', from engaging Croft to prepare the screen version of his novel.[2]

The fruits of their collaborative venture appeared within four months and were presented for pre-production scrutiny to the BBFC at the beginning of October 1954. That was the procedure, after all. Although filmmakers were not obliged to submit a script before commencement of production, fully 80 per cent of them regularly did so. The purpose, quite simply, was to ascertain the BBFC script-readers' reactions to likely areas of controversy in theme or subject and to pinpoint possible problems in depiction or treatment before shooting began. Once completed, of course, a film had to be formally tendered for classification anyway, since without the award of a BBFC certificate no film could be exhibited in public cinemas. But this was a further piece of 'voluntary' censorship and something of an early warning system designed to alert producers and censors alike to potentially troublesome aspects.

This informal process was especially useful after 1951, when the 'X' certificate was introduced, by indicating whether a script or scenario might be placed in that category. An 'X'-certificate film could be shown to persons over 16 years old, whereas an 'A' film could be shown to persons under that age, provided they were accompanied by an adult, and a 'U' film was passed for universal exhibition.[3] The pitfalls for production companies were obvious. Film distributors and exhibitors were a notoriously conservative lot. They favoured the notion of 'family entertainment' and were less inclined either to finance, release, or show 'X'-rated films, which were increasingly associated with the seamier realms of continental production or with the horror genre. The large cinema circuits of the day were especially sensitive in this regard and often did not book them.

Decisions on the likely award of an 'X' certificate were crucial in film industry thinking during the 1950s.

The pre-production script for *Spare the Rod* was not well received at the BBFC from the start. John Trevelyan, previously a schoolmaster and chief education officer before landing the job of part-time censor in 1951 (and finally, in 1958, the key post of BBFC secretary), set the ball rolling with some fierce criticisms of the project:

The book came out recently and was well reviewed in the Sunday newspapers. The author of the book wrote this screenplay, which is like the book as a house built with bricks but no mortar would be like the same house with mortar added. All the most important scenes are there, but the mass of detail and analysis which holds the thing together has had to be omitted, to the detriment of the subject. I do not know enough about contemporary State schools to say whether any of them are in such a plight as this. Even if they are, the choice of this story for a film is most impolitic. Everyone knows that we are short of good school buildings and good teachers and *not* short of slow-witted children from undisciplined homes. It is dispiriting to the teaching profession and deplorable in its probable effect on children in a cinema audience that such a thing should be debated on the screen. And who is going to be entertained by it? I haven't come across a script for months that it would give me greater pleasure to see dropped. But I doubt if we can ban it. And to make a film about classroom life 'X' would be fearful in its implications. Besides, what are they doing that is 'X'? They aren't committing any crimes: even the sadistic Gubb is an angel compared with Jack Palance in a western. (As to the milk bottle incident, it spoils one's appetite for the next meal, so it would not be proper to include it even in an 'X' film.) So presumably all we can do is tidy up details and make it an 'A'. If I am wrong and we can be harsher, I shall be most delighted and relieved. But I think they've got us cornered. In which case all we can do is to be very firm on details, of which I have a number.

A second reader, Audrey Field, felt much the same. She concluded that 'Trevelyan's detailed observations 'correspond almost exactly with my own'. Moreover, she recommended that the president and secretary of the BBFC 'should certainly read this script'. Not least since 'Mr Neame (whom we have recently had occasion to obstruct in his project of making a comic film about a trial marriage by a boy and girl of about 20) is a very pertinacious man and one of the Rank group of film-makers so our line, whatever it is, will have to be taken with some conviction if it is to be held'.[4] The president, Sir Sidney Harris, did indeed read it and he too shared 'J. T.'s natural indignation'. It was 'a monstrous script', he asserted, and, 'If made into a film it would give justifiable offence to every local education authority in the country and the NUT, as well as to most decent parents, and it would be unfit for any children to see.'

1. 'Treat 'em rough. Come down on 'em hard. Show 'em who's boss'—Gregory (*Geoffrey Keen*) and Worrell Street's head, Jenkins (*Donald Pleasance*), belong to the same school of teaching and agree on their philosophy. (*Spare the Rod*)

The dilemma was obvious and very much as Trevelyan had indicated. The story would have to be 'modified substantially' to pass the film as 'A'; yet it did not really warrant an 'X', and even to contemplate this would have 'fearful implications' and set a bad precedent for future films about 'classroom life'. To help matters along, however, Harris offered a few practical suggestions as to how the script might be revised. He was willing, for instance, to allow 'a *weak* headmaster' who is unable to properly control either the staff or boys, but not one who deliberately encourages corporal punishment or brutality. The advantage here was that it would make it easier to paint one of the masters as an out-and-out bully, as proposed, who is 'a bit of a brute and enjoys using the cane'. The new young, idealistic master would therefore be a foil who starts well but breaks down, for a time, under the strain. Still, he must not be allowed to resign finally, as written, or leave with the solace and promise of promotion to a better school. Furthermore, the drabness of the story must be relieved by the newcomer succeeding at the last and influencing, by

2. John Sanders (*Max Bygraves*) prefers to spare the rod and teach by gentler means. A 'modern educationalist' and 'bright-eyed progressive' with 'new-fangled ideas', Sanders seeks to win his pupils' confidence. (*Spare the Rod*)

example, the whole staff for the benefit of all and sundry: 'The headmaster is the one to go.' Hence, everything would be suitably resolved. These were the proposals put forward by Harris to ameliorate the present and unfortunate condition of the plot. How, though, to impress them upon the director? 'As a matter of tactics', Harris added, the best course would be 'to make a list of all the objections raised by the examiners.' Such a list would 'no doubt bring Mr Neame along post haste and our objections in principle could then be elaborated'.[5]

So it proved. A letter was forwarded within a week, on 14 October 1954, and a meeting with the then secretary, Arthur Watkins, arranged for 18 October. In the interim, plainly, the BBFC's objections appreciably hardened and their resolve stiffened. Enough opinions had been canvassed now to merit forcing the issue. It was necessary, therefore, to take a definite stand and compel a 'harsher' line in regard to the threat of an 'X' category. Neame was told in no uncertain terms of the strength of BBFC feeling against his proposed film. He was informed by Watkins at their meeting: 'it was the view of the Board, backed by expert opinion amongst the Examiners, that the script presented a completely distorted picture and that no responsible producer would be justified in launching such a film on the public, having regard to the effect it would have on parents and teachers and education authorities.' Neame responded by referring to Croft's own experiences in order to argue that the conditions depicted plainly existed in at least one school to their certain knowledge. But Watkins replied that 'even if this were so, which we found difficult to believe, conditions such as these existing in one school would not justify a film which would certainly suggest to the public that the trouble was more widespread'. Neame lost the argument and 'put up very little resistance against the case for an "X" (although he did not relish the prospect of an "X" certificate)'. He agreed at the last to go away and think the whole matter over before deciding whether he was willing to continue on the basis of an 'X'-certificate award. In the event, he chose not to do so and dropped the project. By such means were BBFC fears assuaged and relief guaranteed, at least for a short while.[6]

Ronald Neame, predictably, was not pleased with the outcome. Though he dropped the idea of this film, he was certainly not finished with the BBFC. He proceeded to raise the whole matter of the difficulties he had encountered at a meeting of the British Film Producers Association. The BFPA promoted the interests of the production side of the industry, and its membership included representatives of the major producing companies and the leading studios. It thereby comprised companies which accounted for almost 75 per cent of British first feature films. Neame was a member. He outlined his complaints at a council meeting on 5 January 1955 in a long speech which summarized film-makers' problems with the BBFC while also aiming a few well-chosen barbs at other realms of the industry:

Mr Ronald Neame said that he had asked for this matter to be brought to the attention of the Executive Council as he felt very strongly that the 'X' certificate was no longer serving the purpose for which it was originally intended. The British Board of Film Censors had stated at the outset that it was intended to encourage the production of films for adult audiences. In fact, however, the 'X' certificate was being wrongly exploited and was assisting considerably wider distribution of Continental films in this country than might otherwise be possible whilst, at the same time, attempts by British producers to make films suitable for adult audiences had, more often than not, failed. This was due mainly to the fact that both the Odeon and Gaumont circuits, in addition to a number of independent exhibitors, were reluctant to include 'X' films in their programmes. The production, therefore, of a film likely to be given an 'X' certificate immediately became an uneconomical proposition.

Continuing, Mr Neame said there was a further difficulty in that it had been the custom in this country for some time for scripts to be submitted to the Censor prior to the commencement of production. In many cases the Censor, after examination of the script, had indicated that the resulting film would be almost certain to be allocated an 'X' certificate, whereas it was quite possible that after examination of the completed film the Censor might grant it an 'A' certificate. Because of the risk involved, however, producers were disinclined to proceed with the making of a film which, at the script stage, had been regarded by the Censor as an 'X' rather than an 'A' film.

During the discussion which followed it was suggested that enquiries might be made as to whether a similar procedure in regard to scripts was followed by American companies, and it was also pointed out that there was no compulsion on producers to submit a script to the Censor. On the other hand, the President said that if scripts were not submitted, there might be difficulty in obtaining a distributor's guarantee or a bank loan, and in any case, the National Film Finance Corporation was unlikely to lend its support.

Mr Neame said that his chief complaint was that if, after examination by the Censor, a script was considered to merit an 'X' certificate, it was almost impossible for it to be made, whereas he was strongly of the opinion that a number of pictures made by American companies in this country had somehow overcome this obstacle and had been allocated an 'A' certificate where, had the script been submitted to the Censor, he would undoubtedly have expressed the view that the film would be given an 'X' certificate.

The BFPA meeting of 5 January 1955 unanimously agreed a twofold resolution. First, members were invited to submit their written views to the Association about 'their experiences of difficulties concerning the "X" certificate', the intention plainly being to accumulate as much detailed information as possible with which to confront the BBFC. Secondly, it was agreed that an *ad hoc* committee of executive council members would seek an interview with the BBFC 'to discuss all aspects of the effect of the "X" certificate on British film production'. The committee chosen to represent their interests included, inevitably, the senior officers of the Association, but also in its ranks was John Woolf of Remus Films—a significant addition in view of subsequent events regarding his production of *Room at the Top* in 1958.[7]

1955 began then on a distinctly unhappy note for the BBFC. The fracas over *Spare the Rod* had undoubtedly lit a fuse within the BFPA and matters proceeded to get worse on several fronts. Arthur Watkins, the BBFC secretary, found that some local authorities were imposing onerous regulations of their own regarding the exhibition of 'X'-certificate films. In Blackburn, for instance, the authority was refusing to allow any 'X'-rated film to be shown at all until it had also been approved locally. Certain towns would not allow them on Sundays. The BBFC's role was clearly being seriously questioned and its system undermined. Though Watkins could confidently claim that 'none of the industry's critics had suggested a good alternative to the "X" category', he was also obliged to announce that 'the whole question of censorship classification' was being reviewed by an advisory sub-committee (under John Trevelyan's chairmanship) of the Cinema Consultative Committee.[8]

By 3 March 1955, moreover, Watkins and Harris had the BFPA delegation on their doorstep. It comprised the president, Robert Clark, director-general Sir Henry French, the general secretary, Peter Taylor, and key film producers John Woolf, Arthur Dent, and Marcel Hellman. They pressed them about several matters, including the detrimental effects of possible 'X' certification on financial backing for films; the reluctance of some cinemas to exhibit them; the submission of scripts in advance; and the lack of an independent or adequate machinery to contest Board decisions regarding classification where, it was noted pointedly, 'this was one of the few countries in the world where no appeals facilities existed'. The delegation duly 'accorded its appreciation' for the Board's 'ready co-operation'. But subsequent discussion among their own ranks made it abundantly clear that many BFPA members felt little had been achieved over pre-production scrutiny or an appeals procedure 'to ensure completely fair and unbiased treatment'. It was resolved that in future all dissatisfied producers would continue to inform the BFPA of their problems and, if required, the Association would institute its own scrutiny and appeals system with a view to approaching the Board 'for reconsideration of its decision'.[9]

Things hardly improved throughout the rest of the year. Indeed, if anything, relations between the two bodies became increasingly strained. Some BFPA members must have wondered whether Arthur Watkins was really the right man to umpire the Variety Club match on 7 July between Tommy Trinder's XI and Peter Wilson's XI. Certainly, the fourteenth annual general meeting of the BFPA held exactly one week later, on 14 July 1955, said enough to remind Watkins of their ongoing complaints. Robert Clark, the retiring president and executive council member representing the Associated British Picture Corporation, used his speech to repeat their various grievances: over script submission in advance of production; about 'that unknown quantity', the 'X' certificate, which threatened scripts intended for adult audiences; the probability that cinemas 'aiming at providing family entertainment will not book films which cannot be shown to anyone under 16 years of age'; the problems of obtaining production finance as a consequence of 'reduced exhibition prospects' and the 'X' classification; the feeling that 'a comparable imported film' would likely be in the 'A' category; and his sense that they were confronted with difficulties 'which did not arise in other countries'. 'It appears', Clark continued, 'that British producers are placed at a disadvantage in the production of films of an adult character as compared with productions in other countries.' The meeting earlier in the year between the BFPA and BBFC, furthermore, had led him to the conclusion that 'there was nothing that could be done about it'. Despite the gloomy outlook, however, the Association decided there was one thing that should be done. They chose to withdraw from the BBFC's Cinema Consultative Committee which jointly represented the interests of licensing authorities and all sections of the film industry.[10]

The BFPA were further alienated when at the end of 1955 the BBFC president, Sir Sidney Harris, declared he was in favour of a proposal forthcoming from the National Council of Women. They wanted facilities for reviewing films which were about to be released in order to compile a monthly report 'with the object of aiding parents in the selection of films suitable for their children'. The BFPA, along with the Cinematograph Exhibitors Association and the Kinematograph Renters Society, were not happy at the prospect and felt 'the industry might be laying itself open to a new form of unwarranted censorship'. Clearly, as events throughout the year had amply demonstrated, there were enough problems in dealing with the censorship that already obtained without inviting more.[11]

If 1955 was a year of difficulties between censors and producers, the next two years saw considerable efforts to build bridges and restore relations. There was indeed a need for this, as the new BFPA president, John Davis, who also represented J. Arthur Rank Productions, made clear in his inaugural address to the fifteenth annual general meeting on 11 July 1956. On that occasion he stressed the desire for 'unity within the industry', and said nothing by way of criticism of the BBFC. Subsequently, the BFPA rejoined the Cinema Consultative Committee. From July, as it happened, the BFPA was heavily engaged in deliberations about its own key personnel. The proposal mooted at its executive council was to appoint a permanent full-time salaried president 'on the grounds that the demands upon the time of anyone taking this job on voluntarily were heavy, and consequently there were few members of the Association who were in a position to spare the time'. A selection committee agreed on 2 January 1957 that the present director-general would be invited to become their first paid president and, crucially, that the BBFC's Arthur Watkins should be appointed vice-president, with a view to his taking over as president at the outset of 1958. It made a good deal of sense, of course. In addition to gaining the benefits of Watkins's undoubted expertise and insider knowledge, the intention, plainly, was that his appointment would help smooth relations between producers and censors. Recruiting Watkins was, to be sure, a clever move. On 23 January 1957, however, the BFPA met again, this time to deliberate how it should react to the news that a competitor producers' body was in the offing, the Federation of British Film Makers (FBFM). The two matters need not have been related, since there had long been criticism that the BFPA was run for the benefit of powerful vested interests and was especially susceptible to 'undue influence being exercised by the Combines'—Rank and ABPC. But, doubtless, some independent-minded producers had not forgotten the troubled times with the censors which had arisen, in the first instance, over *Spare the Rod*.[12]

Nor, indeed, had *Spare the Rod* itself been entirely forgotten. Ronald Neame might have dropped out of the running, but other producers were still interested in it. John Haggarty, for instance, took it over and submitted a draft treatment to the BBFC late in 1956. The situation now, of course, was really very tricky and largely of the BBFC's own making. Audrey Field highlighted what she felt were the strengths and weaknesses of the new proposal, and the pitfalls which confronted the Board as a result of the line taken previously:

In its main outline, this treatment is very similar to the previous script. However, there is the possibility of its being developed along less dangerous lines. And the most objectionable incident—the finding of the piece of excrement in the milk bottle—has been omitted. Instead, the cause of the final showdown between Gubb and Hackett is that someone has tried to poison Gubb's dog and he has strong evidence pointing to Hackett. Another circumstance which is in this treatment's favour is that it begins with shots of the excellent school to which Sanders is appointed after the Worrell Street fiasco, and ends with a scene in the same school. The film is dedicated to the teachers 'who are striving to carry out their interpretation of secondary education'. Whether teachers will appreciate the tribute is still open to grave doubt, but at any rate they are a less unsympathetic lot than the ones in the book—or so it appears, though everything would depend on the development of the shooting script and on the interpretation of the actors. I am pleased to note that Sanders is less concerned to curry favour with his charges and has some sense of responsibility towards the other members of the staff, even if he does have a public fight with Gubb.

The Times they are A-changin'

A difficult question of policy is involved here. We are committed to pass some sort of screen version of this story in the 'X' category. On the other hand, our letter to the previous inquirers tends to imply that we would not pass a screen version of the story in the 'A' category; and, this being so, Mr Neame and Co. might feel aggrieved if we did so now. However, I personally feel that there is a prospect of the present script being developed in such a way that 'inefficient running of a school and moral deterioration of its teachers through their inability to control children' would be too strong a description of the situation. The general impression might be rather one of harassed, overworked, and in some cases unfit or ageing teachers fighting a desperate battle under the handicap of unsuitable buildings, obsolete equipment and unmanageably large forms.

This is not to say that I think the subject is a good one for children. Whatever our critics may profess to think, it is well known to everyone who has even the most casual contacts with teenagers that they are in a little island of their own, cut off alike from young children and grown-ups, and that only other teenagers are 100% real people to them. There is a consequent danger of identification and imitation in films about teenagers which does not apply to the (admittedly very undesirable) 'A' films about Hollywood sex and gangsterdom which are quoted against us. But there are features in the behaviour of Sanders' form which would not be liked, even by quite unruly children: for example, even the sort of boy who would himself mimic Angell, the stutterer, would not think it funny when anyone else did it. And the form bully is put outside the pale for everyone by his attempt to poison the dog. I have a number of details for 'A'. But I do feel that it is better, if at all possible, not to have to put a picture of secondary modern education in this country into a category which protects children under 16 from seeing it. If the picture is hopelessly distorted the better course is to try and lessen the distortion. From what I read of Mr Haggarty's career in films, I should think he would be quite willing, not only to aim at this himself, but also to exert a mollifying influence on the author of the book who appears to be against soft-pedalling . . .

We should not, of course, give any firm decision about an 'A' certificate till we have seen a fully developed shooting script: but I do think we should leave the door open for an 'A' at this stage, not say 'Your film is bound to be "X"'.

P.S. A lot will depend upon how far the behaviour of the form is only tiresome, unruly and generally out of hand, and how far it degenerates into downright insolence and violence. Mr Haggarty may well be able to avoid *The Blackboard Jungle* touch.[13]

Unfortunately, it appears that little of this genuine willingness to compromise extended to the negotiations between Watkins and Haggarty. Once again, clearly, opinion hardened between formulation of the script-reader's report and notification of the BBFC's decision to the producer. If Field was for compromise, Watkins was not. John Haggarty recorded:

Mr Watkins wrote to me that such a film was likely to receive an 'X' certificate because 'the inefficient running of a school and the moral deterioration of its teachers through their inability to control children are not, in our view, subjects to be debated in the presence of children of school age'. In subsequent discussion he made perfectly clear there was no objection to a wholly adult film being made . . . My likely distributors, however, were interested in the film only if it carried an 'A' certificate . . . So it was all that simple. No 'A' certificate, no guarantee of distribution. No guarantee, no film finance. Collapse of project.[14]

Why, though, the repeated insistence by Watkins upon the likelihood of an 'X' certificate when there was plainly a willingness within his own ranks to compromise? As a matter of policy? To save face? Probably both. Perhaps also because of something else to which Audrey Field had alluded in passing—*The Blackboard Jungle*. Evan Hunter's *The Blackboard Jungle* and Michael Croft's *Spare the Rod* were both published in 1954. (Post-1954 reprints of the latter, in fact, advertised it as 'a book that has been described as the English equivalent of America's *The Blackboard Jungle*'.) In that same year, furthermore, MGM's finished film of *The Wild One*, starring Marlon Brando, was presented for BBFC certification. All three shared the theme of teenage hooliganism. There was always, Field had stated, the 'danger of identification and imitation in films about teenagers'. Moreover, her comments on teenagers generally had been endorsed by another script-reader, Newton K. Branch, who had penned 'I do agree' in the margin of her report. With such thinking in evidence, it is little wonder all three films suffered at the hands of the BBFC.

The Wild One, 'a spectacle of unbridled hooliganism', was particularly hard hit. 'Our objection is to the unrestricted hooliganism', said Arthur Watkins; 'Without that hooliganism there can be no film and with it there can be no certificate.' It did not receive a BBFC certificate until November 1967. The script of *Spare the Rod* was the next one to be presented, in October 1954, with the results we have seen. The film of *The Blackboard Jungle* followed in March 1955. Watkins considered it was filled 'with scenes of unbridled, revolting hooliganism' and informed MGM that: 'The Board is not prepared to pass any film dealing with juvenile delinquency or irresponsible juvenile behaviour, whether on the streets or in the classroom.' In fact this film was eventually granted an 'X' certificate on 12 August, but only because substantial MGM pressure had been brought to bear by the personal appearance of the film's producer, Pandro S. Berman, and after great deliberation in the BBFC's ranks. Even then, six minutes'-worth of cuts were required to the film in order to appease all parties.[15] Haggarty, clearly, was no Pandro Berman. Besides, he knew the fate that

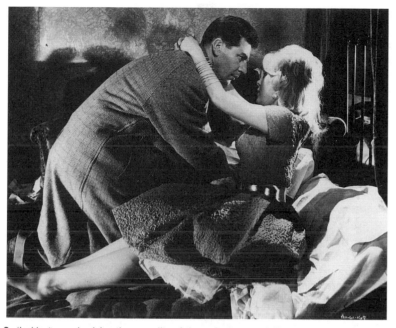

3. 'Incidents emphasising the sexuality of these fourteen and fifteen year olds have been considerably jazzed up . . . several of the girls in Sanders' class have become dirty little things. Something has gone gravely wrong with our country for this is undoubtedly a true picture of the facts.' (*Spare the Rod*)

had befallen Neame. By the time that Croft's novel came round a second time, in December 1956, Watkins was determined to fob him off, as indeed he did.

Spare the Rod was tendered for BBFC consideration yet again in November 1960, during Trevelyan's term as secretary of the Board. Several factors conspired on this occasion to allow it to proceed at long last. For one thing, it was taken on by producer Victor Lyndon as a starring vehicle for the talents of entertainer Max Bygraves, who had shown a strong personal interest in the book. 'He knew the story backwards', commented Croft, 'It was his own schooldays, he said. He believed in the story and he wanted to play a dramatic part.' For another, Croft had little to do with the final script. The director engaged by Lyndon, Leslie Norman, threw out his treatment because it was too 'heavy' and engaged John Cresswell to do the writing instead. Though Croft spoke kindly of his efforts, the results were plain to see.[16] 'The story is basically the same as

25

it always was', commented Audrey Field, but 'details have been much changed':

my impression is that the hooliganism is now less vicious and more childish, that the caning figures rather less prominently, but that the lines and incidents emphasising the sexuality of these fourteen and fifteen year olds have been considerably 'jazzed up' (I am quite certain of this).

I have always felt that this subject should be toned down to a point where it would be possible to give it an 'A' certificate. I do not like films to give the impression, justifiable though it may be, that there are dark doings in some of our secondary modern schools of a kind not merely unsuitable, but actually prohibitive, for other schoolchildren to see and hear; moreover I think that an 'X' certificate would be largely ineffective, since determined 13 year old girls, dressed up in their holiday clothes, can often get into 'X' films, and this subject might well have a particular appeal for them, in which case they would try even harder than usual. Most important, I think that the things in this script which would not do for 'A' would be highly undesirable even for 'X'.

In these lax days, there is a limit to what the censor can do, because of the half-heartedness, and often the opposition, of a large minority of the public. If we dissipate our efforts too much, we may not achieve anything at all. We have got to put first things first and concentrate on them. I feel that the three salient features of contemporary life about which we have to be most wary are:

1. Explicit visual and sound details of brutality and sadism.
2. Vicious hooliganism by boys and youths, especially when accompanied by insolence and crowned with success.
3. Screen presentation and discussion of the sexual corruption of children, particularly of girls (including all those under the age of consent).

This script contains debatable details of all these three kinds. No. 1 does not appear to me to go much too far, and I think it could easily be brought into conformity with an acceptable standard. No. 2 also, I think, though overdone here and there, could easily be changed if the makers of the film would co-operate. The salient dangerous thing is no. 3. We have a lot of lines of dialogue and incidental visuals which make it clear that several of the girls in Sanders' class have become dirty little things. Something has gone gravely wrong with our country, for this is undoubtedly a true picture of the facts (see the recent report on health, with its emphasis on the prevalence of V.D. among children of 12 and over; and see also the attached cutting from a provincial newspaper serving a respectable, reasonably well-off and predominantly rural area of Hampshire, which never has been, and probably is not now, below average in morals).

I do not believe that ventilating the facts in public cinemas will help, I think it will hinder. And the 'X' is not a sufficient safeguard. After all, who gave V.D. to these girls? Presumably not the under-16 boys, or if they did, their own morals are also a cause for public concern. I do think that now, with the lamentable recent report fresh in their minds, the public might support a tough line about sex and children. Be that as it may, we clearly cannot accept a number of the sex details in this script . . .

If it is not felt that the picture stands any chance of an 'A', even with cuts, I think that the sex side would still need some modification, even if not so rigorous— particularly the meaning behaviour of the 14-year-old child with the master alone in the flat.

P.S. Note that I don't mind calf love and silly sentimentality from the girls to Sanders, or even silly, rather sex-conscious larking about between the boys and the girls. But I mind the evidence of corrupt sexual precocity and of too much knowledge too young.[17]

The 'treatment' afforded the sex scenes, then, would be 'all important', but Field felt certain they could be done 'in an acceptable way, particu- larly bearing in mind the strong and wholesome personality of Max Bygraves (who is to be Sanders)'. Trevelyan recounted the outstanding reservations in a letter to Lyndon on 5 December 1960 where, from the outset, he indicated a distinct readiness to consider the film for the 'A' category. Though he conceded that 'The brutality and the sadism in the present script is much less than its predecessors (with which you were not concerned)', he agreed that 'the sex side' now posed undoubtedly 'the most worrying point': 'It was largely, if not entirely, absent from previous scripts. We do not mind evidence of a schoolgirl "crush" on Sanders, even if it is implied that it is based on a precocious sexual knowledge and experience, but we could not have explicit sexual knowledge and experi ence of the kind indicated by the script in the "A" category.'[18]

Lyndon, Norman, and Cresswell obliged by toning their film down to meet the BBFC's needs and a posse of four censors, including Trevelyan, trooped in to view the completed production on 10 February 1961. One censor was reported as feeling that 'the film may increase teachers' prob- lems in some schools' but strenuously sought to correct the impression that he dissented from the majority opinion they reached that day: 'I did not want to give it an "X". I see all the reasons for *not* doing so. What I said was that it was, in my opinion, an "X" film. There is a difference.'[19] The film was passed with an 'A' certificate, first shown at the Odeon, Marble Arch, on 18 May and put on general release from 19 June of that year. How far, though, could the decision to allow the film at long last be attributed to the liberalism of Trevelyan's new regime in adapting to the changed tenor of the times and how far to the compromises which had emerged during production? The publicity material which accompanied *Spare the Rod* inevitably laid great stress on selling it as 'The Film They Tried to Stop', briefly outlining its difficulties with the censors, but promising finally that 'the bite and power of Croft's original story are all there'. Some critics were prompted to agree. James Breen, for example, said in the *Observer*: 'Except in minor details the director, Leslie Norman, does not shirk the terrible problems that Michael Croft's novel helped to expose; in general the sharp edges of the original are only very slightly smoothed.' But most critics found the film disappointing. '*Spare the Rod* isn't, for two-thirds of the way, such a bad little film', William Whitebait commented in the *New Statesman*, 'but its dim status is typical of the British film industry':

Spare the Rod starts off well enough, in a murky corner of State education, with the new master arriving (but in the middle of prayers?) to find a tired headmaster, an atmosphere of the cane and of Hymns Ancient and Modern, and more concern over the lunch money than anything taught in a classroom. The staff are just managing to hold their own against their pupils; this battle, eventually lost, formed the theme of Mr Croft's novel. The film, however, soon getting no further with it and making no attempt to exercise the screen's capacity to push reality out into the streets and homes, begins ladling in the melodrama. Delinquency with a capital D starts to rampage; there's an absurd visit of the new master to the home of a sexy 15 year old girl; the caning old-timer is absurdly locked up in a lavatory all night; an unjust beating leads to a riot; and the radiant end includes Christmas, smiling negroes, the master bully discomfited, and our hero, with a girl on his arm, retreats in blaze of glory. One likes Max Bygraves despite this. Donald Pleasance keeps a spark going in the lowered headmaster, when he doesn't have to cough too much.

Derek Hill, for *Tribune*, continued in the same vein:

Good intentions must also be assumed somewhere behind the production of *Spare the Rod*, especially as Max Bygraves has sunk some £50,000 of his own money into the film. But the old schizophrenia that attacks almost any British film dealing with a contemporary social problem is here so rampant that it wrecks everything. Entertainment *or* social comment? It's an absurd, suicidal way of looking at a subject, but it's an attitude our writers and directors seem unable to avoid. This adaptation of Michael Croft's novel about a progressive East End schoolmaster's difficulties with a school's toughest class introduces melodrama and excitement which have nothing to do with the original. Every situation is hotted up, distorted, exploited for kicks, until the film is as relevant to its subject as *Suzie Wong* to the life of a Hong Kong whore. Director Leslie Norman seems the most guilty, determined on a British *Blackboard Jungle* and clueless at controlling a bunch of actors who act with a capital A. Only the kids come through cleanly. And it's hard to be annoyed at Bygraves's own good-natured incompetence.[20]

4. Trouble flares up because of Gregory's sadistic methods and the whole school riots. (*Spare the Rod*)

Whitebait and Hill must have found it especially galling that *Spare the Rod* turned out as it did, since they had both cited its long-running saga as a *cause célèbre* when seeking to rally support, in July 1960, against the system of censorship exercised by the BBFC. Despite provoking a short-lived flurry of correspondence, however, their efforts came to naught.[21] The completed film of *Spare the Rod*, furthermore, hardly advanced anybody's cause. Trevelyan may have changed his predecessor's intransigent stand somewhat but at the last, it seemed, Croft had been let down most by the hidebound and conservative nature of the mainstream British film industry. The BBFC had hardly been tested. By contrast, the 'new wave' films proved a stiffer test, as the BBFC soon found out.

Notes

1 The extent of Neame's ambition during the 1950s was probably best expressed in his desire that *The Horse's Mouth* would prove 'one of those rare and fortunate films which interests both the intellectual and the average film fan', as reported in

Kinematograph Weekly, 3 Apr. 1958, p. 22. Despite the distinguished presence of Alec Guinness, who starred as novelist Joyce Cary's creation Gulley Jimson, and the paintings of John Bratby, described as the 'angry young man' of British art, it simply did not repay Neame's hopes. Nor did the topicality invested in *Windom's Way* (1958) which again enjoyed a script by Jill Craigie, with some excellent acting from Peter Finch, and dealt with Malaya. The biographical material held on Neame in the BFI Library, London, states that in Britain he was 'always considered an Art House type director'. In the 1970s he made film versions of Paul Gallico's *The Poseidon Adventure* and Frederick Forsyth's *The Odessa File*.

2 Michael Croft, *Spare the Rod* (London, 1954), 5. Two reprints followed in 1954, a paperback edition in 1957, and three subsequent reprints in 1959 and 1961. The outcry which greeted the novel's first appearance is outlined in Croft's article, 'Saga of Censorship', *Observer*, 4 June 1961.

3 The evolution of the BBFC's categories for classification is well explained in Neville March Hunnings, *Film Censors and the Law* (London, 1967).

4 BBFC file on *Spare the Rod*: reader's report, 4 Oct. 1954.

5 Ibid., memorandum by Harris, 7 Oct. 1954.

6 Ibid., memorandum by Watkins, 18 Oct. 1954.

7 BFPA executive council meeting, 5 Jan. 1955, minute 10.

8 *Kinematograph Weekly*, 6 Jan. 1955, p. 3.

9 BFPA council meeting, 6 Apr. 1955, minute 44. See also, *Kinematograph Weekly*, 10 Mar. 1955, p. 7, and Catherine de la Roche, 'Don't Shoot the Censor', *Films and Filming* (Apr. 1955), 12.

10 *Kinematograph Weekly*, 21 July 1958, pp. 6–7; BFPA council meeting, 14 July 1955, minute 101. By the end of the year, *Kinematograph Weekly* had announced that 'British studios are still among the least "X" conscious in the world. They made two "X" certificates during 1955, a 100% rise on the previous year' (29 Dec. 1955, p. 6).

11 See, *inter alia*, minutes of the following BFPA council meetings: 5 Oct. 1955, minute 126; 2 Nov. 1955, minute 140 (iv); and 7 Dec. 1955, minute 151.

12 'Presidential address', annex to the minutes of fifteenth annual general meeting, 11 July 1956; BFPA council meeting, 15 Aug. 1956, minute 313; BFPA council meeting, 2 Jan. 1957, minute 381. The results of the Special meeting of the BFPA executive council which was held to discuss 'the proposed establishment of the Federation of British Film Makers' were extensively summarized in minute 386 of 23 Jan. 1957. Though the FBFM served as a lively pressure-group and lobbying influence from the late 1950s to the mid-1960s, in the event it went the way of many such independent bodies in British cinema and was finally compelled to merge. It joined the BFPA in 1967, though not before members had expressed their continued 'anxieties', yet again, 'about the possibility of domination of any combined body by the Rank organisation and ABC'. My special thanks go to Roy Boulting, who holds the remaining extant papers of the FBFM, for allowing me access to the same.

13 BBFC file on *Spare the Rod*: reader's report, 4 Dec. 1956.

14 John Haggarty, letter to the *New Statesman*, 13 Aug. 1960, p. 216.

15 The problems which beset *The Wild One* and *The Blackboard Jungle* are explored in great detail by Robertson, *Hidden Cinema*, 104–10, 113–16.

16 Michael Croft's role in the final production is outlined in his *Observer* piece, 'Saga of Censorship'. Max Bygraves has nothing whatever to say about the film in his autobiography, *I Wanna Tell You a Story* (London, 1976). For some inexplicable reason, the spelling of Sanders's surname changed to Saunders for the completed film. I have retained the original spelling throughout my text, as used in Croft's novel and the first two treatments.

17 BBFC file on *Spare the Rod*: reader's report, 25 Nov. 1960.

18 Ibid., Trevelyan to Lyndon, 5 Dec. 1960.

19 Ibid., Frank Croft's handwritten amendment to notes on viewing of the completed film prepared by Newton K. Branch, 10 Feb. 1961

20 See the reviews in the *Observer*, 21 May 1961; *New Statesman*, 19 May 1961; and *Tribune*, 26 May 1961; all contained on the microfiche for *Spare the Rod* in the BFI Library, London.

21 Derek Hill, 'The Habit of Censorship', *Encounter* (July 1960), 52–62; William Whitebait, 'This Nanny', *New Statesman*, 9 July 1960, p. 48; and id., 'This Censorship', *New Statesman*, 30 July 1960, pp. 153–4. John Trevelyan, inevitably, replied to their criticisms in *Encounter* (Sept. 1960), 61–4, and *New Statesman*, 16 July 1960, p. 86.

3 **Nothing Succeeds Like 'X'-cess**

Jack Clayton's film, released in January 1959, of John Braine's 1957 best-selling novel, *Room at the Top*, has invariably been much praised. 'In its treatment of class and sex', Arthur Marwick has stated, it was 'so stark and concentrated as to be genuinely revolutionary.' For Stuart Laing, the film helped lift British cinema from the doldrums and escapism that typi-fied the usual run-of-the-mill 1950s fare, and it 'replaced Ealing and Boulting Brothers' comedies with regional/working-class realism as the dominant style in British film-making'. 'The film looked at everyday events and settings of contemporary life', Laing notes, and 'this was innovatory and radical in itself.' Like Marwick, furthermore, Laing elaborates upon the need to place the film in context in order to appreciate its importance: 'The novel and film of *Room at the Top* became situated at the forefront of a considerable cultural trend whose roots lay, in part, in the "Move-ment" novels of Kingsley Amis and John Wain and the "Angry" writers of 1956—John Osborne and Colin Wilson.'[1]

John Trevelyan, too, felt the film should best be seen in context to grasp its full significance, especially since it proved a first major test of his term as secretary to the **BBFC**.

In retrospect one can see that Jack Clayton's *Room at the Top*, made in 1958, was a milestone in the history of British films, and in a way a milestone in the history of British film censorship. Up to this time the cinema, with rare exceptions, had presented a fantasy world; this film dealt with real people and real problems. At the time its sex scenes were regarded as sensational, and some of the critics who praised the film congratulated the Board on having had the courage to pass it. Ten years later these scenes seemed very mild and unsensational. Even in 1958 I found it difficult to understand what had justified the congratulations, and even asked my colleagues at the Board whether we had missed anything. There was no nudity or simulated copulation, but there was rather more frankness about sexual relations in the dialogue than people had been used to.[2]

5. Joe Lampton (*Laurence Harvey*) surveys his provincial roots but aims for life at the top. (*Room at the Top*)

Trevelyan's evident delight at the praise given the BBFC for passing the film is easy to justify and simple to understand. *Room at the Top* was a considerable success, after all. It was the fourth-biggest hit at the British box-office in 1959, following *Carry on Nurse*, *I'm All Right Jack*, and *The Inn of the Sixth Happiness*, and it turned out, according to *Kinematograph Weekly*, a favourite with both 'the intelligentsia and the crowd'.[3] In America, it won two of the 1959 Academy Awards (Oscars) for Simone Signoret's performance and Neil Paterson's screenplay. But it had been given an 'X' certificate. Surely, with this one film, it had been shown beyond doubt that British productions of a distinctly 'adult' nature could be granted an 'X' yet still reap their due rewards from critics and cinema-goers alike? Did this not prove the Board's policy was right?

Some things are certain. Trevelyan was saying less about the circumstances surrounding this film than he knew. And the surprise expressed at both the congratulations heaped upon them and at reported reactions over the sensational nature of the sex scenes masked the knowledge of the genuine difficulties the BBFC had encountered. The point, quite simply, was that *Room at the Top* was presented for the censors' consideration as a completed film on 2 October 1958 and they were given, exceptionally, no opportunity for pre-production scrutiny of the script. It was a calculated move on the producers' part and clearly involved a measure of risk given that the film was always likely to be something of a tricky proposition. Not that John and James Woolf, the producers, were seeking confrontation. Far from it. They were just better equipped than most at knowing how to cope with the censorship system and had in any case done a fair amount to anticipate problems at the post-production stage and to deal with them accordingly. The result, finally, was that agreement was reached with the BBFC on the difficulties that did arise and their film was passed, pretty much in the state they had intended. But the fact that the Woolfs largely achieved their desired objectives by no means heralded the opening of the flood gates, in censorship terms, as other producers were to find. Moreover, it was also due in no small part to events which had befallen the Board earlier that year.

1958 proved as awkward a year for the BBFC as 1955 had been. The Board's relations with producers took a turn for the worse, if anything, though it was somewhat better cushioned to cope with troublesome matters by virtue of Arthur Watkins's position as president of the BFPA, and it demonstrated increasing confidence in handling affairs as a result of key personnel changes of its own. J. Lee Thompson was the initial source of disquiet on this occasion. His complaints arose over the BBFC's objections, fifty in all, to Ted Willis's screenplay for the planned production of *No Trees in the Street*. Lee Thompson chose to air his grievances publicly and forcefully with a campaign that reiterated many of the issues raised in 1955 but which also took account of the film industry's position by 1958.

He began at the Critics' Circle annual dinner with a speech in which he described the BBFC as 'a miserable millstone around the neck of the

6. 'The "shock" appeal of the film rests mainly on the personality of Simone Signoret, who always carries about with her the climate of a sultry foreign "X" to which the patrons of English-speaking "X"s are not accustomed.' (*Room at the Top*)

British film industry'. Inevitably, the trade press reported his demand for 'an appeals panel', to be made up of film critics, 'which would view and consider British productions given "X" certificates or cuts which producers consider unfair', as well as his wider call for 'a much more enlightened and adult approach to censorship in view of the developing competition from censor-free television'. Both the BBFC and the BFPA were plainly taken by surprise. On seeking a response from John Nicholls, the short-lived successor to Watkins as secretary of the Board, *Kinematograph Weekly* was informed that 'the BBFC is unable to comment on the plan at this stage'. Watkins, speaking now on behalf of the BFPA, of course, replied that it was 'not proper to comment in advance of an approach from J. Lee Thompson'.[4]

Neither the BBFC nor the BFPA could stall for long, however, in view of Lee Thompson's evident desire to press his charges home and his subsequent attempts to spread the message further afield. He gave a fifteen-minute talk on BBC radio, for instance, which was broadcast on 15 April

1958 and entitled 'Who shall censor the censor?' His complaints were threefold:

1. The censor makes no allowance for the competition we experience from television.
2. The censor favours foreign films. I accuse him of being more likely, and more ready, to pass adult material in films coming from America and from the continent, than from our own country.
3. There are numerous and glaring inconsistencies in censorship of films of a similar type.

'The censor needs a change', was the clarion-call of numerous articles Lee Thompson wrote immediately thereafter for film magazines and periodicals, such as the one written for *Films and Filming*, under that same banner headline, where he concluded: 'At present the dice are loaded against creative British film-makers. The solution is a film censorship which, like the law, not only sees that justice is done, but in open court makes it apparent to all—film-maker, critic and filmgoer—that justice *is* done.'[5]

Not surprisingly, Lee Thompson gained a measure of support elsewhere in the industry. The Federation of British Film Makers was now in operation and, though recruitment was initially fitful, it soon proved a useful pressure-group for the more vocal members among the producers' ranks. Lee Thompson joined. The scriptwriter, Leigh Vance, another FBFM member, agreed that 'The position of the BBFC should be reviewed in the light of today's changing circumstances.' He promised to press the Screenwriters' Association, of which he was vice-chairman, to support moves to bring about 'an all-industry meeting to discuss the question of censorship' by raising the matter at its next council meeting.[6] One trade paper even reported that a question was to be tabled in the House of Commons. At the same time, the BFPA was urged to consider the issue of 'current relations between members and the BBFC', and to address 'in particular what was thought be the failure on the part of the Board to keep in step with the policy of television as regards suitable public entertainment'. This it did at a council meeting on 2 April 1958. The BFPA accepted an offer from its president, Arthur Watkins, 'to put the views of the council to the officers of the BBFC'.[7]

Little appeared to result directly from any of these moves. Vance's pressure came to naught. The reported promise of a Commons question from the Labour MP, Dingle Foot, to ask 'whether the government will institute an inquiry into the censorship of cinematograph films by the BBFC with a view to legislation on the subject', simply did not materialize:

he posed a question relating solely to the abolition of stage censorship.[8] Watkins, for his part, had a meeting in early May with the BBFC to express 'the producers' concern at some aspects of censorship'. He did not report back to his members, though, until 4 June; the delay is doubtless explained by the more significant events then taking place at the BBFC, with which he was intimately concerned, as we shall see shortly. He dealt quietly with the matter, and requested that 'instances of material being used in UK television which would appear to imply a wide divergence between BBFC and television standards should be brought to his attention'.[9]

The BBFC sought to defuse the situation by taking steps of its own which were aimed at answering, point by point, the detailed complaints originally made by J. Lee Thompson while also taking the opportunity to outline its broader policy regarding film censorship. A spokesman was given the job of responding to Lee Thompson's criticisms and, wherever Lee Thompson appeared, in print or on radio, this spokesman was sure to follow. It was, in short, a public relations exercise. Obviously, it required someone who showed a 'control of public relations techniques' and who was 'well equipped to proselytize for the Board'.[10] The person chosen for the task was John Trevelyan. His broadcast of 13 May 1958 was an accomplished performance which neatly addressed points of general and particular concern while striking a note of honest conviction and sound common-sense. Most of all, it revealed what commentators praised as Trevelyan's undoubted skills in presenting the BBFC's case:[11]

Can the Board's policy be defined? I think it can. I would say that in censoring films the Board tries to reflect intelligent public opinion as far as it can be judged, and tries to avoid the showing on cinema screens of anything that might do positive harm, especially to children and young people, and anything that might be likely to offend or disgust reasonable people . . .

First, this question of television. It's perfectly true that things have been shown on television that would not have been passed in a film to be shown in a public cinema, although I believe that most things have a lesser impact on the small television screen in the home than they would have on the large screens of cinemas with a crowd of people producing a mass response. What Mr Lee Thompson didn't mention was that, as you know, there's been a good deal of criticism, both public and private, of some of the things that have been shown on television. This is one of the ways in which we can test public opinion. We're watching the position closely and steadily adjusting our policy all the time. Public opinion isn't static: it's constantly changing, and we try to reflect these changes. Mr Lee Thompson was right when he said that television can show adult plays, such as *Death of a Salesman*, without the restrictions of external censorship; but such plays are not shown in 'Children's Hour' but at times when most children are in bed.

Nothing Succeeds Like 'X'-cess

Does Mr Lee Thompson really think that *Death of a Salesman* is suitable entertainment for the young? And it's much easier to switch off a television set if there is something you don't want your children to see than to take the children out of a cinema when you've paid for their seats. He complains that adult subjects can only be shown in the cinema under an 'X' certificate. This was the very reason why the 'X' certificate was introduced. Before we had it such subjects could not be shown on the screen at all, except in an expurgated edition suitable for young children to see. Now there is practically no adult subject which could not be considered for an 'X' certificate if treated with sincerity and restraint . . .

Secondly, we are accused of giving more favourable treatment to foreign films, including American films. This is not true, although it may seem so in one respect—behaviour which is characteristic of a foreign country might possibly be accepted in a foreign film when similar behaviour, which is not characteristic of this country, might not be acceptable in a British film . . .

Thirdly, we are accused of inconsistencies. If this means that we sometimes allow an incident or a phrase in one film and refuse it in another, I can only say that this kind of thing may well happen with intelligent censorship. We consider each film individually and we are very much influenced in our decisions by the quality and character of the film, and the sincerity and integrity of its production. Would Mr Lee Thompson prefer us to work to a written code? If so, I can assure him that he would run into much more censorship trouble than he does now . . .

In general, I think I can claim that the film censors in their difficult job have the support of the film industry and the public. No one likes censorship in principle but not even Mr Lee Thompson wants film censorship to be abolished. What we hope is that our reflection of intelligent public opinion at any one time is a fairly true reflection and that film-makers will continue to work closely with us so that censorship will not produce serious problems for them or for us. Perhaps the best testimonial we have to the success of our work is that after nearly fifty years' experience of the working of the present system of censorship, neither the local authorities nor the cinema industry as a whole have shown any desire to remove from their necks what Mr Lee Thompson was pleased to call 'a miserable millstone'.[12]

Despite his complaints, however, J. Lee Thompson was no rebel. His intentions for *No Trees in the Street* made that abundantly clear. 'It was an answer to the angry young men set', he stated, and 'The story maintains that, though perhaps small, social progress has been made in the past 20 years.' While they were inevitably unhappy with the BBFC's strictures over Ted Willis's script, Lee Thompson and his producer, Frank Godwin, were still willing to proceed. They were evocatively described in the trade press as 'the team that reflects life through the steam on the kitchen mirror . . . They make films that examine the problems of ordinary, working-class people and they have determined that this imprint will mark all their productions.' But for all the talk of producing 'a gutsy film that probes', Lee Thompson chose to give this 'essay in slum life in London's East End' a period setting from the late 1930s. It suited their purpose, as he maintained in an interview: 'It's not about youngsters going wrong because of poor social conditions. We aren't making excuses for the Teddy Boys. We've had enough of those films. We are saying, in effect, stop your silly whining, look at what it used to be like.' On completion, it was still given an 'X' certificate, largely because the censor's reservations about a key scene involving a young man ('the boy must not be young, he must be about 18') and a gun ('there must be no emphasis on the power of weapons') had clearly not been resolved to the BBFC's satisfaction. One critic, by no means alone in his opinion, was prompted to describe the finished film as 'a heavy-handed, thick-eared melodrama'.[13]

If nothing else, though, Lee Thompson's eruption had rekindled intense dissatisfaction with the BBFC and provided a stimulus which, allied to the long-running difficulties experienced with producers generally, undoubtedly had some effect on BBFC thinking about its position in regard to the industry. Moreover, the Board was facing a pressing problem within its own ranks: John Nicholls, who had been recruited from the Foreign Office's Cultural Affairs Section to replace Watkins in January 1957, announced at the outset of May 1958 he would quit the job within a month. 'Mr Nicholls's resignation is due to his decision to return to work connected with the fine arts', was the official statement given out by Sir Sidney Harris. 'It is in no way connected with recent criticism of the Board in the press', he continued, 'nor is it the result of any pressure from the film industry.' But such arguments were hardly convincing, especially when the trade press proceeded to report the BBFC statement alongside repetition of J. Lee Thompson's recent charges and announced they would be answered by Trevelyan's forthcoming talk on the radio. The inference was obvious. The industry had indeed become 'fiercely critical of his approach', Guy Phelps has concluded, and 'confidence in the Board declined until it was clear that Nicholls could not continue in office'.[14]

Plainly, something meaningful had to be done to restore faith in the BBFC. Harris was reluctant to make another appointment on his own initiative. He hit upon the novel and surprise idea of inviting various key players in the industry—producers, renters and exhibitors—to join him in choosing Nicholls's successor. It was a wise decision and particularly convenient when the representatives invited to serve on the appointments committee included such experienced people as Arthur Watkins. It was perhaps no surprise when they chose John Trevelyan, who had effectively done Nicholls's job for some months anyway, and who had represented BBFC interests so ably when dealing publicly with criticism from the likes of J. Lee Thompson.

Trevelyan expressed great pride, subsequently, that he was 'the first secretary of the Board who was appointed by a joint committee representing all sections of the film industry, and who was therefore not the personal appointee of the president'. He was also put thereby, as Phelps comments, in 'a position of much greater strength in relation to the president than his predecessors'. It was soon made clear that 'the secretary was now entirely in control of the day-to-day affairs of the Board'.[15] At the same time, however, he must have known full well he had his work cut out to win the grass-roots confidence of the industry in the same way that he had obviously secured the trust of its top echelons. If 1958 proved eventful for the BBFC, so too did it for John Trevelyan.

No sooner had he formally taken over the post in July, furthermore, than he was presented with a twofold dilemma when the pre-production script of John Osborne's *Look Back in Anger* was submitted for consideration, soon to be followed by the completed film of John Braine's *Room at the Top*. The 'angry young men' had apparently arrived at the censor's doorstep in earnest. The fact that he had to consider both the script of *Look Back in Anger* and the film of *Room at the Top* within a month of each other must have concentrated Trevelyan's mind wonderfully. Given what they represented, here was the first test of his intentions as secretary of the BBFC and of his relations with the film industry at large. They provided the means, ironically, whereby he would stamp his own brand of pragmatic and liberal compromise upon both. His reaction to *Room at the Top* was immediately illuminating.

Room at the Top posed special problems for the BBFC. It was, to begin with, a Remus production for Romulus Films. Both companies were owned by John and James Woolf, two highly respected producers. Their father was C. M. Woolf, a renowned and powerful figure in the British cinema of the 1920s and 1930s, and a president of the BFPA until his death in 1943. John Woolf, the business brain in the partnership, was an influential figure at the producers' association in his own right, and served on its executive council in the 1950s and 1960s. He was, in fact, a member of the BFPA delegation to see Watkins at the BBFC in March 1955 over the question of 'X' films and pre-production censorship of scripts. He was also on the selection committee that recommended the appointment of Watkins as future president of the BFPA. James Woolf worked in publicity for Universal in Hollywood before the war and returned to Hollywood at the war's end to join Columbia. He had 'the flair for "production" more commonly found there than in Britain', Alexander Walker comments, and 'he was an obsessional film-maker, loving the wheeling and dealing'. An 'artist' and 'a midwife for talent', to borrow Bryan Forbes's words, James Woolf spotted Laurence Harvey and Heather Sears in early roles and put them both under contract.[16]

The Woolfs had started their own company in 1948. They immediately engaged a roster of burgeoning production-line talent, including Jack Clayton, who was used on six consecutive pictures before being granted his directorial debut with *The Bespoke Overcoat* in 1955. Though a short film, it was given a general release and won an Oscar. The Woolfs' output was varied and eclectic. It ranged from routine domestic comedy employing British directors—Gordon Parry for *Sailor Beware* (from Philip King and Falkland Cary's farce), Maurice Elvey for *Dry Rot* (based on John Chapman's play), and Ken Annakin for *Three Men in a Boat* (from Jerome K. Jerome's novel), all in 1956—to large, expensive co-productions employing Hollywood directors and international actors—two in 1953 with John Huston's *Beat the Devil* and *Moulin Rouge* (starring, respectively, Humphrey Bogart and Jose Ferrer), and one in 1957 from David Miller, *The Story of Esther Costello* (with Joan Crawford and Rossano Brazzi). Several of the Woolfs' productions, furthermore, had encountered considerable problems with the BBFC, notably Henry Cornelius's *I Am A Camera* (1955), because it had intended broaching the homosexual theme evident in its original sources (Christopher Isherwood and John van Druten) and Gordon Parry's *Women of Twilight* (1952), because it was based on Sylvia Raymen's controversial all-woman play about 'baby farming' and unmarried mothers. *Women of Twilight*, indeed, enjoyed the unique distinction of becoming Britain's first film to be granted an 'X' certificate after introduction of the category in 1951.[17]

The Woolfs' experience of the industry, then, was considerable. They were born and bred in the business, unlike many of those running 'new wave' companies like Woodfall Productions, where Tony Richardson and John Osborne were imports from the theatre. And they were shrewd, commercial producers. Though thwarted in their attempts to buy the rights of John Osborne's *Look Back in Anger* in the autumn of 1956, they were plainly intent on exploiting the potentially rich seam of new British writers coming to the fore. John Braine soon proved an obvious candidate. His book *Room at the Top* was published in March 1957. Braine's interview with Woodrow Wyatt on BBC's *Panorama* on 8 April 1957, which reportedly added a further 12,000 copies to sales, was seen by John

Woolf. An abridged serialization of the novel in the *Daily Express* for ten days from 22 April doubtless further enhanced its popular appeal, as did agreement over a book-club edition and the sale of paperback rights to Penguin Books on 15 May. The Woolfs proceeded to acquire the film rights for £5,000. The experienced Scot, Neil Paterson, was bought in as scriptwriter. But much of the production company was recruited in-house, with Jack Clayton being given the director's job. Although at the outset James Woolf apparently favoured using the film as a vehicle for the talents of husband and wife team Stewart Granger and Jean Simmons, the brothers sensibly agreed that Braine's characters needed fleshing out in a different way. In addition, they had their own contract players to consider. Thus, they gave the comparative newcomers, Laurence Harvey and Heather Sears, two of the leading roles as Joe Lampton, the protagonist, and Susan Brown, the industrialist's daughter. Simone Signoret was brought in at Clayton's suggestion for the part of Alice Aisgill, Joe's mistress. In one obvious respect, therefore, changes were immediately required of Braine's original novel as Alice became French and was provided with a new social background. Nevertheless, Clayton promised, when announcing to the trade press that location shooting would start in June 1958, the film 'will remain remarkably true to John Braine's best-selling novel'.[18]

Clayton's promise, allied to the automatic recognition by reviewers that Braine was 'a leading member of the new school of young writers', not to mention the reputation his novel quickly acquired in the popular press for its relatively frank depiction of sex, should have been sufficient to alert the BBFC to the fact there would be problems over the film. Those problems were inevitably compounded, however, when the Woolfs chose not to tender a script for advance scrutiny. Instead, as we have seen, their film was submitted for BBFC consideration close to final cut stage and in pretty much its finished state. Given the troubles encountered at the BBFC before Trevelyan took a firm grasp at the helm, what better time to test new waters? The alternatives posed for the BBFC were obvious. It could reject the film outright, though that was unlikely bearing in mind the costs that had been incurred by the production company (to the tune of £280,000) and the furore such a move would arouse at a time when relations with the industry were already strained. Or it could allow it through virtually untrammelled with the prospect, at best, of a modest amount of amendment here and there to achieve their desired effect. There were risks involved for all parties, to be sure: if the BBFC took any exception to the film and even minor changes were required, the Woolfs must hope they would be technically feasible and relatively straightforward—with no loss in continuity or characterization, for instance, and incurring little further expense; the censors, for their part, must not be seen to lose credibility in the face of such an obvious attempt to present them with a *fait accompli*. Certainly, Trevelyan's latitude in the matter appeared to be severely curtailed. In the event, he made the most of a distinctly tricky situation and turned it to advantage.

What the censors viewed, then, on Thursday 2 October 1958, was a copy of *Room at the Top* at 'fine cut' stage (with separate picture and magnetic soundtrack, to accommodate last-minute editing before marrying the two into a final show print). Little wonder, perhaps, that the producers got away with as much as they did—not least, as Arthur Marwick has observed, 'with rather more "language" than the Board of Censors would have wished for'.[19] Nevertheless, the BBFC was adamant about several things which were subsequently expressed in meetings and correspondence. Some were easy to effect, others proved more difficult. Thus, the word 'lust' in the line 'Don't waste your lust', and 'bitch' in 'You're an educated and moral bitch' were changed respectively to 'time' and 'witch' by the simple expedient of having the actors re-dub the words for the soundtrack. (The audience could hardly be expected to spot the fleeting lack of exact lip synchronization and even now, with the extra benefit of slow playback facilities on video, for instance, one has to look carefully to spot the discrepancies.) Similarly, the word 'scalped' was deleted, finally, from the reported description of Alice Aisgill's death in a car crash and a new line substituted, voice over, albeit after considerable discussion about how graphic the dialogue could still be. Trevelyan's reservations on this score were made clear in a letter of 13 October:

We still feel that the lurid descriptions of Alice's death are overdone and hope that some way can be found of reducing them. Most of the description is spoken off-screen when Joe's head and shoulders alone are visible, so cutting should not be difficult. Unfortunately, what we regard as the worst lines—Raymond Huntley's line 'She was scalped' and '. . . then the steering wheel . . .' are spoken when the camera is showing Joe's hand holding the glass. I hope, however, that some way can be found of shortening or transposing the soundtrack. Incidentally, we all thought that some reduction in this verbal description would be an artistic improvement, but you may think differently.

John Woolf's reply the very next day revealed the extent to which they had sought to accommodate the censors' expected misgivings in advance by simply having Alice's death reported and not actually shown:

I must say that I am concerned that Alice's death in the film should not be toned down too much. Dramatically, it is of course terribly important and I should have thought too that the fact that she met a violent end is morally right from the censorship point of view. As I mentioned to you, we had at one time thought of shooting the scene itself but when we decided against that, it certainly did not occur to us that just having it talked about by other characters would be likely to raise censorship problems.

The biggest problem, finally, concerned a post-coital scene between Joe Lampton and Mavis, a working-class girl with whom he enjoys a brief, flirtatious encounter in a woodyard scene towards the end of the film. The scene required changes to alter the 'implication'—so that it 'gets rid of the idea that he has made love to her'; revised dialogue to make it altogether more 'acceptable'; and, clearly, some measure of reshooting.[20]

At the end of the day, however, all parties declared themselves satisfied with the results and the film was given an 'X' certificate. 'They will take an "X" ', Trevelyan noted. It came as no surprise and advertising for the film announced 'A Savage Story of Lust and Ambition—The Film of John Braine's Scorching Best Seller'. The meetings and correspondence between the producers, director, and BBFC secretary had proved nothing if not harmonious, after all, even distinctly amicable. 'It is a great pleasure to me to meet someone with the sensitivity not to allow the dramatic content of a scene to be destroyed by purely arbitrary rules of censorship', Jack Clayton wrote on 6 November 1958; 'I am happy that we have found a solution to all the original objections which is mutually agreeable.' Trevelyan replied on 2 February 1959, congratulating Clayton on 'the outstanding success' of the film and urging him to get on and make more. 'It was a pleasure to discuss things with you because you so readily took the point of my comments', he continued, then added: 'Some reviewers seem to be rather surprised we should have passed the film as it was without cuts, but we still think that it is perfectly acceptable for the "X" category, and indeed the sort of film that we would like to see in this category.' It was a revealing statement. 'I have been enthusiastically praising your whole attitude to films to every journalist or interested person that I have met', Clayton replied, on 13 February 1959, while passing yet more compliments: 'I believe it is a wonderful thing for our industry to have a Censor who wishes to help and encourage the making of adult films.'[21]

Despite the mutual congratulations, however, Trevelyan obviously had doubts over *Room at the Top*, not least since he knew how far he had been something of a hostage to circumstances and the producers. He decided

7. 'The love-making was certainly fairly hot for those who are not accustomed to foreign "X"s . . . I'm glad we allowed the frankness and the visuals to go no further.' (*Room at the Top*)

therefore to send two BBFC examiners along to early public screenings, to observe audience response—an innovation introduced by Arthur Watkins in the early 1950s but rarely used. In addition to providing an insight into contemporary class attitudes, their reports reveal how carefully, if impressionistically, the BBFC monitored cinemagoers' reactions. They constituted, in short, a modest attempt at market research. Trevelyan, of course, now had to answer for BBFC policy. It helped him a lot to have some idea what audiences thought. It helped a lot more when the film in question turned out, as this did, to be a considerable popular success. One examiner saw the film at an afternoon showing in the Plaza cinema within a week of its release on 22 January 1959, and reported:

Balcony packed, so stalls probably ditto. On the whole, a silent, sensible audience of real adults, not Teddy Boys. But there was the inevitable odd burst of inane laughter at some of the more outspoken lines. One man hurried out in the middle and said to the attendant at the balcony exit 'This is a disgusting film', which made several people giggle. I thought it was a good film—except the end, which was shockingly overdone, and the inevitable loading of the dice against the people with money. (For instance, Jack Wales wasn't quite the 'public-school type' but he was too near it for such nasty little 'gamesmanship' ploys as calling Our Hero 'Sergeant' every time he spoke to him.) I think the 'shock' appeal of the film rests mainly on the personality of Simone Signoret, who always carries about with her the climate of a sultry foreign 'X', to which the patrons of English-speaking 'X's are not accustomed. People were probably also interested to hear the words 'whore', 'bitch' and 'bastard' which still has the charm of novelty for the cinemagoing public. The love-making was certainly fairly hot for those who are not accustomed to foreign 'X's, but it looked to me fairly easy to defend. I expect the film will produce a few cross letters in its passage round the provinces, but there was nothing in it that I personally was surprised or worried to see or hear in an 'X' film.

Another examiner viewed the film on 4 February 1959 and commented:

I saw this at the Carlton. I should say that in a packed house, about 80% of the audience were people of 30 or over—many from 'the provinces'. The youngest I saw were about 19, an Espresso bar couple with duffel coats and pony tail. I have seldom seen an audience more gripped by or more sympathetic to any other British film (except possibly *Kwai*). This was partly due to the extraordinary but unobtrusive realism of the photography and to a high standard in direction. Simone Signoret's performance deserves an Oscar. She has never been so good.

I am not surprised that people have talked about the frankness of the dialogue—certainly the most 'adult' we have ever allowed in a non-continental film. But I thought the visuals were discreet enough. It is interesting to note that after most of the tricky scenes, i.e. the seduction of Susan, there were little touches of wry or ironical humour which made the audience chuckle and helped to remove any think or offence which the audience might otherwise have felt.

I only heard one lot of female gasps. That was when Wolht referred to Signoret as 'that old whore'. This, I think, was partly due to the unexpectedness of the remark and partly because I think most of the women in the audience were so much in sympathy with Signoret's predicament (the tragically ageing face etc.).

There can be no question that, at least from the sort of audience that goes to the Carlton, the Board has done the right thing with this film. But I'm glad we allowed the frankness and the visuals to go no further. How easy it would be if all tricky scripts were made by such a good technical team.[22]

Not everybody, however, was enamoured of *Room at the Top*. When it came before the Commonwealth Film Censorship Board, for instance, the chief censor in Sydney wrote enquiring of the BBFC 'whether the version sent to Australia may possibly vary somewhat from that passed by your Board'. He queried several matters which had raised a few eyebrows among his members, including lines of dialogue which still remained in

8–10. His love affair over, Joe is beaten up and punished for his transgressions, before he settles finally for marriage to the local millionaire's daughter. (*Room at the Top*)

the film, such as 'You constipated bitch', 'You bastard, you bastard, you filthy rotten bastard', and 'I'll slit your bloody gizzard'. Trevelyan affirmed that it was the same version and that the BBFC had allowed the lines. 'The dialogue in this film is admittedly strong', he continued, 'but the Board considered it was acceptable for the "X" category in a film that was clearly made with sincerity.' His concluding sentence, nevertheless, laid down an important caveat: 'Such dialogue would not necessarily be accepted in other films.'[23] There were still limits to what would be permitted in 'new wave' cinema and they applied, principally though not exclusively, to 'language'. Given that British 'new wave' cinema was rooted in stage and literary adaptations for the most part, with only an occasional original screenplay in evidence, it is no surprise that this turned out to be a major cause of concern for the censors.

For all the reservations expressed by the Australian censors, Jack Clayton and John Trevelyan had every reason to feel pleased. *Room at the Top* was a box-office hit and revealed, according to most reviewers, that British 'adult' films had arrived. 'Whether they praised its realism, or condemned its sordid qualities', Arthur Marwick has pointed out, 'the critics were unanimous in recognising *Room at the Top* as something new and stunning in British film-making.' 'Critical reaction was by no means universally favourable', Robert Murphy concurs, 'but there was general agreement on the film's sincerity.' Among contemporary critics, for instance, Frank Jackson singled out the importance of the film's 'sincerity' (first advocated by Trevelyan, of course) when writing in *Reynolds's News*: 'At long last a British film which is truly adult. *Room at the Top* has an "X" certificate and deserves it—not for any cheap sensationalism but because it is an unblushingly frank portrayal of intimate human relationships'. While Dilys Powell spoke for many critics at the time of the film's release, when she stated in the *Sunday Times*: 'It gives one faith all over again in a renaissance of the British cinema.'[24] Trevelyan, for his part, shared in the praise for allowing the film but was credited most with settling an issue that had been paramount in BBFC thinking since the 'X' category was introduced and had long proved the source of much concern in relations with the industry—how best to promote British adult films of 'quality'. The criteria applied by Trevelyan to *Room at the Top* substantially set the parameters in this respect and helped to determine the critical consensus that existed across the industry when judging 'quality' cinema thereafter.[25]

What, then, constituted 'quality' cinema and how to measure Trevelyan's achievement? The notion of 'quality' is notoriously elusive, of course. It is perhaps better understood for British cinema between 1955 and 1960 by distinguishing those features which the industry and censors alike plainly agreed it did *not* entail. 'Sensationalism', for instance, which was often seen as the obverse of 'sincerity' and usually associated with 'exploitation', was a key debilitating factor. The BFPA noted as much when discussing a 'resolution concerning exploitation in films of themes of brutality and violence' on 2 February 1955, less than one month after it had debated the complaints laid by Ronald Neame in the matter of the 'X' certificate:

The General Secretary referred to a letter which he had received . . . concerning a resolution passed at the 1953 [Trades Union] Congress deploring the increased exploitation in films of themes of brutality and violence for the purposes of sensationalism. The General Secretary added that a similar letter had been addressed to the Cinematograph Exhibitors Association and that apart from noting its contents, it was understood that no action had been taken by the CEA General Council. The General Secretary was directed to reply . . . stating that the Executive Council had noted the contents and sympathised with the action taken by local Trade Councils in giving effect to the resolution[26].

If, on that occasion, the BFPA was content merely to sit back and endorse, albeit sympathetically, another body's fears and concerns, by 3 December 1958 the Association was all for taking direct ameliorative action to be rid of, or at least marginalize, the overtly 'sensationalist' and 'exploitative' films emanating from within the industry's ranks:

At the request of a member the Council discussed the current vogue for horror films and the danger of its bringing the industry into disrepute. Criticisms in the press and from private individuals were read to the meeting and emphasis was laid on the importance of the family business to the industry. It was noted that the Kinematograph Renters Society had set up a censorship committee of its own to deal with doubtful posters. After discussion it was agreed . . . that the British Board of Film Censors should be requested to consider the reinstatement of an 'H' certificate for horror films in addition to the existing 'U', 'A' and 'X' certificates.[27]

At the time when the BBFC was asked to deal with the BFPA's request, however, Trevelyan had been in post as secretary for several months and was well into his stride. He was also increasingly convinced, of course, that more would be achieved by promoting the right kind of adult 'quality' film than by hiving off any despised 'exploitative' products into a hastily revived category. He felt certain that the prospects which awaited the former course of action would doubtless also hasten the natural demise of 'exploitative' films. The commercial and critical success which instantly greeted the release of *Room at the Top* in January 1959 must have reinforced this conviction and strengthened his resolve enormously. The short-term outlook already appeared to be distinctly promising for Trevelyan's strategy.

In keeping with his new 'open door' policy, Sir Sidney Harris, the BBFC president, initiated a consultation process with several bodies to deal with the BFPA's request, and it was agreed the matter would also come before the Cinema Consultative Committee. Since Harris was its chairman, Trevelyan must have felt pretty confident when lodging an opinion and defending his position. Moreover, the Cinema Consultative Committee embarked upon its deliberations just as *Room at the Top* opened to general acclaim. Predictably, the film was cited during discussions. The outcome of their deliberations was also equally predictable, as *Kinematograph Weekly* reported on 14 May 1959:

The Cinema Consultative Committee has decided not to support a BFPA recommendation that the 'H' certificate be brought back to cover horror films. A report of the decision was received by the BFPA General Council at its meeting last week. The recommendation, said President of the Association, Arthur Watkins, at last Thursday's press conference, was made so that horror films could be identified separately. He added: 'The objective was that the "X" certificate could stand for truly adult films. This was always the hope of the BBFC'. *Room at the Top*, he thought, was an example of a good 'X' picture because of its 'adult approach'.

Mr Watkins said he was not criticising horror films—'They have their public and they have a right to that public'. But a belief that the 'X' meant something horrific and sensational was becoming current and he thought that reintroduction of the 'H' certificate would put pictures of that nature in their own category. The Cinema Consultative Committee, however, felt this would not be a good thing. And as it appeared that the spate of horror films was in decline, it was decided to take no action that might later prove unnecessary.[28]

It was fortunate for Trevelyan that the debate over reinstatement of the 'H' certificate was largely settled when it was, during the opening months of 1959. Had it arisen exactly a year later, the final decision could well have been very different. For one thing, Sir Sidney Harris resigned on 5 April 1960 and was replaced on 1 June by Lord Morrison of Lambeth, the first former Home Secretary to serve as president of the BBFC since Edward Shortt in the late 1920s. The 'high mutual regard and cordial working relationship' which had so marked Harris and Trevelyan's term together, as James Robertson observes, was noticeably lacking in relations between Morrison and Trevelyan, where 'tension', 'friction', and 'clashes' were all too evident. Morrison was never the natural or friendly ally to Trevelyan's cause that Harris had been.[29]

By the spring of 1960, anyway, there was less reason for believing that 'the spate of horror films was in decline'. It is doubtful, in fact, whether there were ever good grounds for such optimism. If there were, every-body's expectations were certainly confounded in the opening months of 1960 with the appearance of one film, Michael Powell's *Peeping Tom*, that sorely tested censors and industry alike. *Peeping Tom* confronted all the prevailing tenets over 'quality' and 'taste' which constituted the critical consensus. Trevelyan instantly recognized its potential—for better and worse—when first presented with a script in September 1959, and sought to steer Powell away from his intended project. It was 'well written' and 'might make a good film', he stated, but 'there is every indication that it . . . would fall into the "X" category'. After carefully outlining several detailed points for revision, Trevelyan emphasized that his strong sense of unease stemmed from the feeling that: 'This is an interesting script but its morbid concentration on fear and on the infliction of fear might be done in such a way as to make it an essay in sadism. This we would certainly be unhappy about. If you can make it into a straight thriller with a psy-chological background it should be agreeable.'[30] Since Michael Powell was plainly reluctant to make changes if they could be avoided, Trevelyan thereafter reiterated his concerns at great length. He invited the director along for private interview during February 1960, once the film was com-pleted, and followed up their discussions with copious correspondence. His comments were invariably painstaking and perceptive, especially when highlighting features which would soon prove the basis for considerable criticism:

it seems to me that your picture is capable of conveying impressions that you had no intention of conveying and I think that it would be in your interests as well as ours if you re-edited the picture with this in mind. Somehow it should be made clear that the killings are not sex killings but that the boy has, in his pathological condition, a revulsion against the physical forms of sex.

As I suggested, I think you should in the first instance make the following cuts:

The scene in which the prostitute is murdered, as seen through the viewfinder of the camera, should be reduced so that we see no more than the beginning of her terror. If there is any way of indicating more clearly that she is frightened because she knows that she is going to be killed rather than afraid because she knows that she is about to have an unpleasant sexual assault it would be better, but this may not be possible.

Delete the shot of Mark's reaction as he rises at the end of the film projection. As I explained, this gives the mistaken impression that he was having a sexual reaction.

Delete the two shots of the nude girls in the album.

Delete as far as possible references to the girl's bruises and the camera's concentration on them. It would be as well to avoid any inference of sexual sadism.

Delete all except the first shot of the girl's disfigured face and re-edit the scene as far as possible so as to make it even more clear that the boy has no sexual interest in his work as a photographer of art studies. In particular, you should be careful to avoid any suggestion that he gets sexual satisfaction from a facial disfigurement.

In the murder of the dancer at the studio remove as far as possible emphasis on the tripod spike, particularly when this touches, or is held against, her throat. This is an unpleasant weapon and the less emphasis there is on it the better . . .

You should consider whether Helen's question 'What did you do to those girls?' conveys a wrong impression by suggesting that she is referring to sexual assault of a normal or abnormal type.

I think that it might be desirable to remove the shot in which Helen's face is seen in the reflector in a distorted way. Somehow it makes the whole thing even more unpleasant.

Reduce the sequence of Mark's suicide removing as far as possible the emphasis on the tripod spike. I appreciate that you cannot remove this completely but the scene is very harrowing and unpleasant.

The most important thing is that you should remove the impression that Mark is a sexual sadist. I know that you had no intention of presenting him as such but the impression is there. For instance . . . he says to the dancer 'Just to kill isn't enough for me'. In the light of the all too common murders for sexual motivation we have to be careful about this kind of thing. Anything which could emphasise that Mark's pathological condition produces a revulsion against physical sex will help.

I hope that you will find it possible to remove the farcical elements from the scene when the psychologist comes to the studio. In the context, this seems in rather bad taste and I do not think it contributes to the film.[31]

Trevelyan finished by expressing his 'every confidence that in your re-editing you will make the picture acceptable'. It was wishful thinking, in the main, as he may well have realized. What else, though, could be done? He could easily have left the film-makers to their fate, of course, let them proceed to final completion, and then simply banned their film from exhibition. There were compelling reasons for going to such extremes, after all. *Peeping Tom* obviously threatened to thwart his plans for the 'X' certificate. It might also possibly rekindle the dreaded debate over horror films and the 'H' category. Instead, to his credit, Trevelyan persevered with the task of advising the film-maker to the last. He was plainly motivated by three factors: his recognition that Powell was a 'distinguished film-maker'; a feeling that having allowed the project at script stage, the

BBFC was duty bound to pass the finished film in one category or another; the knowledge that if *Peeping Tom* was rejected it would only attract unwarranted publicity for being 'banned by the censor' and so still find exhibition outlets. Liberalism and pragmatism carried the day. In consequence, Trevelyan continued counselling Powell about suggested deletions until 10 March 1960—exactly three weeks before the film's planned trade show. And he was still viewing contentious scenes and reels as late as 15 March 1960.[32]

Powell reciprocated by making some revisions to the film—albeit by shortening scenes Trevelyan had recommended for re-editing rather than attempting anything more substantial. *Peeping Tom* ended up essentially as its director had intended, in short, and therefore received an 'X' certificate. The trade show which followed on 31 March 1960 opened the floodgates for a torrent of critical abuse. It was nothing if not vitriolic. William Whitebait, for instance, reported in the *New Statesman*:

For some weeks an Eye has been staring out of newspapers and from buses: now, with *Peeping Tom* at the Plaza, it is upon us. 'Do you know what the most FRIGHT-ENING thing in the world is . . . ?' 'Please, sir. Chap with a cinecamera on a tripod, and he comes nearer the girl, photographing her, and then he puts out the tripod front, and there's a knife on the end, and then there's a distorting mirror she must look into, and then he—' ''I'hat's enough, Whitebait: don't give away the plot.'

Peeping Tom stinks more than anything in British films since *The Stranglers of Bombay*. Of course, being the work of Michael Powell, it has its explanation, its excuse. But so had *The Stranglers*; it was 'history', you remember. *Peeping Tom* is 'psychology'. Why does the murderer with the cinematic itch and the skewering tripod do as he does? Because his father was a famous psychologist who specialised in Fear and kept a cinematic record of his son's fear as he reacted to bright light at night, a lizard dropping on the bed, and lovers embracing on a seat. Mama's death-bed provided him with a real family album shot.

So no wonder his son went in for taking feelthy pictures in Soho (though, really, these were exceedingly prim); and went up to street-women after dark with his camera purring under his coat. Marvellous camera: it gets perfect tones in a dark street and in ill-lit interiors, is noiseless, and though bulky, invisible: the envy of any cine-club.

But with the tripod idea he gets more ambitious. And then the girl downstairs grows curious about him; and so does her blind mother, sensing wrong . . . such wrong that in the end, with girls getting wary and inspectors on his tail, he does himself in on the spike of his tripod, staring into the distorting mirror.

But what worries me is that anyone at all could entertain this muck and give it commercial shape. The combination of the two is peculiarly nauseous; and it is odd to reflect that the last film of Mr Powell's we saw was *Battle of the River Plate*.

True, before that, A *Canterbury Tale* and A *Matter of Life and Death* more than hinted at morbidity.

Derek Hill harped upon much the same theme for his review in *Tribune*. Most of the invective was reserved for Powell's film, once again, though he also took the opportunity of including a few well-chosen gibes at the BBFC's expense. Despite his subsequent much-publicized criticism of the BBFC's role generally, however, Hill was more guarded in this instance, clearly preferring not to lay the blame at the censors' door in granting a certificate, and hoping rather, doubtless very much as Trevelyan hoped, that cinema-goers' reactions would see the film off. That was the response he invoked and in no uncertain terms:

The only really satisfactory way to dispose of *Peeping Tom* would be to shovel it up and flush it swiftly down the nearest sewer. Even then the stench would remain.

Every now and again we're assured by industry representatives, the British Board of Film Censors or some equally suspect authority, that the boom in horror films is over. The truth is that there has been little if any decline in the number produced . . .

Obviously there's a legitimate place in the cinema for genuine psychological studies. But this crude, sensational exploitation merely aims at giving the bluntest of cheap thrills. It succeeds in being alternately dull and repellant . . .

Last week Powell explained on the radio, in the first of a BBC series unbelievably called 'Artist at Work', that the author of the original story and script, Leo Marks, had been shocked when *Peeping Tom* had been suggested as a title. 'He thought it might attract the wrong people', said Powell. Marks himself was upset that the film had suffered several censor cuts 'including the parts which appealed most to me' . . .

The immediate answer to trash like *Peeping Tom* is not more censorship, for that could only worsen a position growing rapidly impossible. The box office is the real test—and not the West End box office where anything that causes a stir in the press stands a chance of attracting a queue, but the provincial and suburban box office. And that's where you come in—or rather, I hope, where you don't.[33]

Hill, at least, was sensibly restrained about advocating that the BBFC's powers be enlarged to deal with films like *Peeping Tom*. Plainly, he would never have denied it a certificate. Others were less certain. Flintshire County Council, for instance, was one body which would clearly have preferred the film not to have reached the screen in the first place. Trevelyan strove hard to mollify Flintshire's Cinematograph Committee and to convince them of the reasons for his adopted course of action:

I am interested, and not surprised, to hear the reactions of the Cinematograph Committee to the film *Peeping Tom*. I must, however, make it clear that in making its decision this Board is not influenced by the fact that films showing violence and brutality are great box office attractions. Our work of censorship is more concerned with this subject than with any other and we are faced with it in various forms week by week. Until recently we have not had much trouble with British film production, but now that British films can get a wide showing in the U.S.A., and have an extended world market generally, producers are tending to put more of this kind of thing into their films. I take every opportunity of impressing our views on producers and we are keeping the situation reasonably under control.

I feel sure that your Committee would immediately say this was not borne out by our giving a certificate to *Peeping Tom*. I would reply that in dealing with this film we were faced with real difficulties. First, we had given our views on the script, which was well written and which could have been made into a very different kind of picture, and we were then faced with a completed picture which emphasised the unpleasant aspects rather than the more serious and reasonable aspects of the story. Secondly, we know from experience that if we entirely rejected this film it would be sent to a large number of local authorities and would have been passed by quite a number of them; thus getting exploitation value as a banned film. We made a considerable number of cuts in the film before giving it a certificate and we were not happy about the final result but we felt that in the circumstances this was the wiser course.

Comparatively few local authorities appear to be interested or concerned about these matters. Your authority, I am glad to say, is an exception. For this reason I would like to have an opportunity at some time of meeting your Committee so that I may discuss these problems with them. I would be glad to hear what they had to say and I would be able to explain some of the problems with which we are faced. If you think this would be a good plan perhaps you will let me know. In the meantime let me assure you that your letter will receive serious consideration here.[34]

In the event, Trevelyan and Hill were vindicated. *Peeping Tom* was a commercial failure, which is perhaps no surprise given the critical mauling it had received and the widespread opprobrium it had attracted. If there were lessons to be learned from the *Peeping Tom* débâcle, as indeed there were, the industry was hardly interested and soon turned its back on the matter. In September 1960, the executive council of the BFPA resorted yet again to bland pronouncements urging members to engage principally in the production 'for general release of films of family entertainment value', and stressing the need for 'the avoidance of themes and incidents which, though possibly sensational and of great impact, are offensive to the reasonable tastes and standards of those whose patronage is necessary to the health and future of the industry'.[35]

While the BFPA advocated adherence to familar, if increasingly hollow, maxims about the need for 'family entertainment', however, Trevelyan knew full well that film-makers required endless cajoling and prompting, and, most of all, that they responded best to commercial success. Ever the realist and pragmatist, he continued to place his faith in the immediate benefits to be gleaned from promoting 'new wave' films as the means of rehabilitating 'X'-rated cinema.

Notes

1 Marwick and Laing provide the best analyses of *Room at the Top*. See e.g. Marwick's essay, *'Room at the Top*: The Novel and the Film', in id. (ed.), *The Arts, Literature, and Society* (London, 1990), 249–79, and Laing, *'Room at the Top*: The Morality of Affluence', in Christopher Pawling (ed.), *Popular Fiction and Social Change* (Basingstoke, 1984), 157–84.

2 Trevelyan, *What the Censor Saw*, 106.

3 *Kinematograph Weekly*, 17 Dec. 1959, p. 6.

4 Ibid., 20 Mar. 1958, p. 3. Josh Billings, in the same paper, had already called upon the BBFC to 'Wake up, Rip Van Censor' and urged: 'Let there be more light in 3, Soho Square.' See the 'Your Films' column, *Kinematograph Weekly*, 20 Feb. 1958, p. 11.

5 *Talking of Films*, 15 Apr. 1958, script held in BBC Written Archives, Caversham; *Films and Filming* (June 1958), 8.

6 *Kinematograph Weekly*, 10 Apr. 1958, p. 3.

7 BFPA council meeting, 2 Apr. 1958, minute 623.

8 *Kinematograph Weekly*, 8 May 1958, p. 3; *Parliamentary Debates (Commons)*, dlxxxvii. 1414, 8 May 1958.

9 BFPA council meeting, 4 June 1958, minute 654.

10 This description comes from Phelps's assessment of Trevelyan in *Film Censorship*, 50. Similar comment can be found in Forbes, *Notes for a Life*, 343.

11 See e.g. David Robinson's contemporary opinion in his article, 'Trevelyan's Social History: Some Notes and a Chronology', *Sight and Sound*, 40/2(1971), 70, where he notes: 'To an extent the brilliance of Trevelyan's own work at the BBFC has been a beautiful conjuring trick, dazzling enough to distract us, most of the time at least, from the essential anomaly of the Board, its peculiar division of function between censorship and classification, its uncertainty between protection of minors and moral guardianship of adults. Previous censors shunned publicity, thus adding an air of secrecy to the already mistrusted activities of the Board. Trevelyan revels in the limelight, has publicly defended the Board's work before a packed Royal Festival Hall, is always available and articulate and informative; and almost persuades you that the Board has today no secrets.'

12 Trevelyan's ripostes to J. Lee Thompson were delivered in *Talking of Films*, 13 May 1958, script held in BBC Written Archives, Caversham, and 'Censored: How and Why

We Do It', *Films and Filming* (July 1958), 8. The article followed, almost verbatim, the same lines as the broadcast.

13 'Three in search of the common touch', *Kinematograph Weekly*, 10 Apr. 1958, p. 29; *Daily Herald*, 6 Mar. 1959. Ted Willis's recollections of his work with J. Lee Thompson, their encounters with the censor, and the critical reaction afforded their films together are usefully outlined in his autobiography, *Evening All* (London, 1991).

14 Trevelyan, *What the Censor Saw*, 69–70; *Kinematograph Weekly*, 8 May 1958, p. 3; Phelps, *Film Censorship*, 42. Interestingly, Phelps quotes the minutes of a meeting held as early as 6 Nov. 1957 between the BBFC and the Kinematograph Renters Society in which the latter put forward their criticisms of Nicholls's approach. They include two of the points subsequently made by J. Lee Thompson: there was an 'arbitrary categorisation of films', and the Board was taking no account of 'developments in the type of material . . . now considered permissible on television'. In fact the post had been discreetly advertised in *The Times* as early as 31 Mar. 1958.

15 The details of Trevelyan's appointment, from which these quotes are taken, are well outlined in *What the Censor Saw*, 68–71, and Phelps, *Film Censorship*, 41–3.

16 Walker, *Hollywood, England*, 51–2; Forbes, *Notes for a Life*, 306. There is much on James Woolf in the two biographies of Laurence Harvey: Des Hickey and Gus Smith, *The Prince* (London, 1975), and Paulene Stone with Peter Evans, *One Tear is Enough* (London, 1975). Also, for the considerable help afforded Terence Stamp's film career until James Woolf's death in 1966, see the many entries in the third part of Stamp's autobiography, *Double Feature* (London, 1989). Jean Shrimpton adds, for her part, that Stamp 'never made a career move without Woolf's advice' and that 'He had a Svengali effect on Terry', in *An Autobiography* (London, 1991), 111.

17 For a brief outline of Clayton's work with the Woolfs, see G. M. A. Gaston, *Jack Clayton: A Guide to References and Resources* (Boston, Mass., 1981), 2–4; Huston describes his collaborative ventures with them and Clayton in John Huston, *An Open Book* (London, 1981), 187, 205, 215–16, 246, 248. *Women of Twilight* was a joint Romulus–Daniel Angel Productions venture.

18 *Kinematograph Weekly*, 20 Feb. 1958, p. 21; Walker, *Hollywood, England*, 51–5; Marwick, *Arts, Literature and Society*, 233, Harry Ritchie, *Success Stories: Literature and the Media in England, 1950–1959* (London, 1988), 36–7. While Walker, *Hollywood, England*, 52, and Gaston, *Jack Clayton*, 10, agree that Simone Signoret was cast on Clayton's suggestion, Robert Murphy, by contrast, in *Sixties British Cinema* (London, 1992), 304–5, believes she was brought into the production at the suggestion of Peter Glanville, the Woolfs' alternative choice for the director of *Room at the Top*.

19 See Arthur Marwick, 'Room at the Top', 133, where he scrupulously analyses the full extent of the changes required. Marwick is spot-on in concluding generally: 'It is quite wrong to envisage a conflict between potentially revolutionary film-makers on one side and an establishment-minded censorship on the other.' But in the case of *Room at the Top*, especially, there was plainly more behind the ensuing negotiations than he allows.

20 BBFC file on *Room at the Top*: Raymond Anzarut to BBFC, 1 Oct. 1958; exception form No. 15540, 2 Oct. 1958; action taken, 5 and 6 Oct. 1958; Trevelyan to John Woolf, 13 Oct. 1958; Woolf to Trevelyan, 14 Oct. 1958; Woolf to Trevelyan, 20 Oct. 1958.

21 Ibid., Clayton to Trevelyan, 6 Nov. 1958; Trevelyan to Clayton, 2 Feb. 1959; Clayton to Trevelyan, 13 Feb. 1959.

22 Ibid., Audrey Field, note from examiners, 29 Jan. 1959; Newton K. Branch, note from examiners, 5 Feb. 1959. For an outline of the more innovative aspects introduced during Watkins's period, including visits to film performances by examiners, see Trevelyan, *What the Censor Saw*, 49–51, 54, and Robertson, *The Hidden Cinema*, 99, 102.

23 BBFC file on *Room at the Top*: letter from C. J. Campbell, Dept. of Customs and Excise, Commonwealth of Australia, to Trevelyan, 2 Apr. 1959; Trevelyan's reply, 7 Apr. 1959.

24 See Marwick, '*Room at the Top*', 140, and Murphy, *Sixties British Cinema*, 15. Murphy is virtually alone among more recent commentators in acknowledging, correctly in my opinion, Trevelyan's 'attempt to rehabilitate the "X" certificate' and in noting Trevelyan's astuteness in seeing *Room at the Top* as 'an ideal opportunity to re-establish its respect-ability'. For contemporary critical reaction, see Frank Jackson, *Reynolds's News*, 25 Jan. 1959, and Dilys Powell, *Sunday Times*, 25 Jan. 1959, as well as all other reviews on the microfiche for the film held at the BFI Library, London.

25 Much has been written damning what are now construed as the detrimental char-acteristics of the 'critical consensus' which dominated the late 1950s and early 1960s, and which espoused the cause of 'new wave' films at the expense of more expressive cinema. Ian Christie, for example, talks ironically of 'a highly selective, though familiar, picture of British cinema sunk in torpor before the arrival of the Angry Young Men (or Northern Realists), who would transform it into a world-class contender in the early sixties', *Arrows of Desire* (London, 1985), 101–2.

Andy Medhurst is equally unhappy about 'the adulation given to the social realist, angry-young-men films . . . [and] their being acclaimed as some kind of artistic renais-sance'. He is scathing about the nature of 'The critical consensus, with its prescriptive commitment to a narrowly realist aesthetic serving as a vehicle for a vapidly liberal social awareness', and feels 'that hegemony also helps to explain the hostility towards particular other areas of production expressed by the same critics who rushed to welcome the naturalistic impulse'. See '*Victim*: Text as Context', *Screen* 25/4–5 (1984), 28–9.

Both commentators rightly agree this dominant consensus explains the distinctly hostile reception afforded e.g. Michael Powell's 1960 film of *Peeping Tom*, which 'flushed the dormant puritanism of the critical consensus into the open'. But neither has any-thing to say on the role of the BBFC, esp. Trevelyan, in shaping its aesthetic concerns.

26 BFPA council meeting, 2 Feb. 1955, minute 29. At the time, of course, 'exploita-tion' was invariably associated with 'X'-rated films, generally emanating from abroad. And, interestingly, the trade press noted with some pride that by the end of 1955: 'British studios are still among the least "X" conscious in the world. They made 2 "X" certificate films during 1955, a 100% rise on the previous year. The number of Amer-ican "X" films was down from 13 to 7. France, as might be expected, provided the greatest number of "X" certificates: 13 in 1955 compared with 1 in 1954. "X" certificate films from all sources totalled 31; 5 up on the previous year', *Kinematograph Weekly*, 29 Dec. 1955, p. 6.

27 BFPA council meeting, 3 Dec. 1958, minute 753.

28 See BFPA council meeting, 7 Jan. 1959, minute 767; BFPA council meeting, 6 May 1959, minute 30(a); *Kinematograph Weekly*, 14 May 1959, p. 104.

29 Robertson considers the relations between Harris and Trevelyan were particularly close and fruitful. 'Harris was almost certainly responsible for his [Trevelyan's] appointment as secretary', he believes, 'over the heads of all the full-time censors, several of whom had joined the BBFC before Trevelyan.' By contrast: 'Morrison's appointment was later to lead to friction with Trevelyan and to a clash which enabled the latter to increase the public authority of the secretary at the expense of the president.' Robertson continues: 'The root of the tension was probably Morrison's inability to adapt to a lesser public position than he had become accustomed to.' See *Hidden Cinema*, 123–4.

30 BBFC file on *Peeping Tom*: Trevelyan to Michael Powell Productions Ltd., 25 Sept. 1959.

31 Ibid., Trevelyan to Powell, 25 Feb. 1960. My interview with the scriptwriter, Leo Marks, on 13 Sept. 1991, prompted the casual if interesting remark that he was 'very surprised' at the perceptive reactions forthcoming from Trevelyan over his script for *Peeping Tom*.

32 BBFC file on *Peeping Tom*: Trevelyan to Powell, 10 Mar. 1960. Trevelyan apologized for the fact 'we are giving you so much trouble with this film but you must realise this does present censorship difficulties'. The second volume of Michael Powell's autobiography states that *Peeping Tom* had 'trouble with the censors', but does not elaborate further on the matter. However, Powell's regard for Trevelyan is clearly evident from his comments on the BBFC reaction to *They're a Weird Mob* (1966), where he compliments Trevelyan's 'generous and broad-minded approach'. See *Million-Dollar Movie* (London, 1992), 411, 485.

33 William Whitebait, 'Hold the nose', *New Statesman*, 9 Apr. 1960, and Derek Hill, 'Cheap thrills', *Tribune*, 29 Apr. 1960. See also all reviews on the microfiche for *Peeping Tom* held in the BFI Library, London. Ian Christie usefully surveys the critics' reactions in 'The Scandal of *Peeping Tom*' for his edited collection, *Powell, Pressburger and Others* (London, 1978), 53–9. Christie argues that it is fruitless 'to ridicule the reviewers of 1960 with the benefit of hindsight'. However, while sensibly stating 'the character of that near-unanimous response to *Peeping Tom* indicates that the reviewers accurately registered the unacceptability of the film when it appeared', there is yet again no evidence that Christie is aware Trevelyan played a crucial part in 'inaugurating the era of naturalistic "realism" that dominated the early 60s', and which doubtless accounted for the failure of *Peeping Tom* at the time of its initial release.

34 BBFC file on *Peeping Tom*: Trevelyan to Flintshire County Council, 23 June 1960. The major arguments advanced by Trevelyan in his letter—it was a 'well-written' script; the film-makers followed their own tack despite advice to the contrary; 'considerable cuts' were made; to have banned the film would have given it 'exploitation value'—were all subsequently refined for his autobiography. Trevelyan stated there that he thought it 'would contribute to a public understanding of mental illness, but the film seemed to be totally different. Having accepted the project at script stage we did not feel able to reject the film, so we made extensive cuts and hoped for the best. As it turned out the public did not like the film, although it was well made, and it was not a commercial success' (*What the Censor Saw*, 159–60).

35 BFPA council meeting, 5 Sept. 1960, minute 299. Subsequent meetings of the BFPA revived debate over 'exploitative' films and members expressed further concern at 'the continually rising numbers of "X" films in general release' but little was done on the matter. See e.g. BFPA council meeting, 1 Jan. 1963, minute 326. Rank chairman John Davis characteristically blamed 'new wave' films as much as anything else for the state of affairs in the British film industry and was not sorry to see them go.

At a Circuits Management Association luncheon, on 12 Dec. 1963, Davis pointed out that the five biggest box-office hits at British cinemas were *From Russia with Love*, *Summer Holiday*, *The Great Escape*, *Tom Jones*, and *The Longest Day*. 'Not one of them is the kind of dismal defeatist drama so popular with certain playwrights', he argued. 'Let the dramatists heed the public's verdict . . . Adventure and comedy, spectacle and courage are the themes that appeal now just as strongly as they ever did; Davis also repeated his traditional call for a full-scale return to 'family entertainment'. In truth, save for occasional exceptions such as producer John Woolf's 1968 film of the stage musical, *Oliver*, 'family entertainment' was more readily found on television, as audiences well recognized. Moreover by 1969, as John Trevelyan significantly noted, 'the number of "X" films was for the first time greater than the number of "U" and "A" films combined' (*What the Censor Saw*, 60).

4 Putting on the Agony

John Osborne was no stranger to controversy by the time the film script of his stage play, *Look Back in Anger*, arrived for pre-production scrutiny at the BBFC in late August 1958. When presented by the English Stage Company at the Royal Court Theatre, on 8 May 1956, the play had received a welcome and enthusiastic reception in some quarters, notably from Kenneth Tynan, but a lukewarm and occasionally hostile response in others. Most critics agreed, however, that Osborne was a dramatist to watch. Though not an instant box-office hit, the play's prospects revived after the Royal Court press officer dubbed him 'a very angry young man' and the chance remark was then turned into a catch-phrase by the press. Osborne was subsequently interviewed by Malcolm Muggeridge for BBC's *Panorama*, on 9 July, and on 16 October the BBC broadcast of an excerpt from the play was watched by nearly five million people, thereby stimulating further interest. A Granada production of the full play was networked by ITV on 28 November. This exposure, coupled with Fleet Street's increasing tendency to report or embellish Osborne's every comment, added to his notoriety. He was 'the first spokesman in the London theatre' for a generation of 'angry young men'. *Look Back in Anger* undoubtedly marked the breakthrough of 'the new drama' and 'arguably the biggest shock to the system of British theatre since the advent of Shaw'. Osborne, 'the rebel', had arrived, and his play was 'the sensation of 1956'.[1]

In fact, unsurprisingly, Osborne's play had already proved the source of much debate at the Lord Chamberlain's office when the English Stage Company first submitted it for licence earlier in the year, on 27 February. Charles Heriot, the examiner who was given the job of reading it, writing a synopsis, and drawing attention to any doubtful or offensive scenes, language, or other 'business' summarized his essentially jaundiced reaction to *Look Back in Anger* in a hastily produced report of 1 March 1956:[2]

This impressive and depressing play breaks new psychological ground, dealing with a type of man I believed had vanished twenty years ago, but which must be generally recognisable enough to write plays about. It is about that kind of intellectual that threshed about passionately looking for a cause. It usually married girls of good family, quarrelled with all their relations, and bore them off to squalor in Pimlico or Poplar where they had babies and spent all their spare time barracking Fascist meetings. In this play the venue is a large provincial town where Jimmy and Alison, his wife, share frowsty digs with Cliff, Jimmy's friend. The men run a sweet stall in the market place—both having been at a university.

Cliff is platonically loving to Alison. But Jimmy, torn by his secret daemons— his sense of social and intellectual inferiority, his passionate 'feeling' that the old order is, in some way, responsible for the general bloodiness of the world today, his determination to *épater le bourgeois* at all costs and his unrealised mother fixation for the kindly, charitable mother of one of his friends (a charwoman who married an artist, completely uneducated so that Jimmy can, quite unconsciously, patronise her while he praises her goodness)—foams at Alison, insulting her parents, teasing her about her background in an angry way and generally indulging in a grand display of tantrums that only differ from those of the nursery in having an adult sexual flavour.

'The play's interest', Heriot concluded, 'lies in its careful observation of an anteroom of hell.' Though he recommended the play for licence, he appended a list of nine specific references to be cut or altered. Once the play and Heriot's report had been read by both the Lord Chamberlain (the Earl of Scarbrough) and his Assistant Comptroller, Brigadier Sir Norman Gwatkin, six of his suggestions were endorsed and communicated to the Royal Court on 2 March 1956.[3]

Tony Richardson, the play's director and assistant artistic director of the English Stage Company, responded with Osborne's revisions. Some problems were easily, albeit reluctantly, overcome. 'Short-arsed' was changed to 'sawn off' and the line 'There's a smokescreen in my pubic hair' was altered to 'You can quit waiting at my counter, Mildred, 'cos you'll find my position closed'. Similarly, the offending couplet in one of Jimmy Porter's songs—'I could try inversion | But I'd yawn with aversion'—was amended and expanded:

> This perpetual whoring
> Gets quite dull and boring
> So avoid the python coil
> And pass me the celibate oil.

It was a significant addition because the 'python image' was related to a key speech which they had already been requested to 'tone down'. While the new-found rhyme was allowed, the proposed amendment to Jimmy's highly vituperative attack on his wife over 'the great pleasure of lovemaking', was not. In particular, the censors objected to continued talk of Alison as she 'lies back afterwards like a puffed-out python to sleep it off', and to 'the peaceful coil of that innocent-looking belly'. 'No', was their private 'blue pencil' comment: 'This is too much the same.' Richardson was duly informed of the approved revisions and the remaining reservations.[4]

Since the première of the play was less than six weeks away and rehearsals were in progress, Tony Richardson tried another attempt to win the day:

Naturally we are very disappointed that you cannot agree to the alterations we submitted. What, however, is absolutely vital to the play and I would ask you most urgently to try and help us over this, is that the 'python image'—which is central to the whole thought of the play—should be retained, though of course I appreciate the necessity for softening it a little. I am sending you therefore, the following possible amendments:

For: 'Oh, it's not that she hasn't her own kind of passion. She has that. She just devours me whole every time as if I were some over-large rabbit and lies back afterwards like a puffed out python to sleep it off.'

Read. 'Oh, it's not that she hasn't her own kind of passion. She has. The passion of a python. She just devours me whole every time as if I were some over-large rabbit.'

We would be most grateful if you could help us over this.

Three possible alternatives were also offered instead of the troublesome line 'the peaceful coil of that innocent-looking belly'. They were: 'That innocent-looking belly', 'That peaceful-looking coil', or 'That peaceful-looking belly'. Two of them were obvious attempts at circumvention and the Lord Chamberlain was not deceived. The reformulated 'python' paragraph was allowed, dropping the allusion to Alison's post-coital state. And reference to 'That peaceful-looking coil' was permitted, but with no mention of a 'belly'. Apart from a further, final proposed revision initiated by Richardson and Osborne, for a change, which recommended dispensing with 'You little existentialist' and replacing it by 'Blimey, you ought to be Prime Minister'—which was easily approved—the final manuscript was granted a licence on 28 March, and *Look Back in Anger* was given its première on 8 May.[5]

Though the Lord Chamberlain's office was ostensibly finished with this play, they had not heard the last of it. A letter was written by an irate member of the public to R. A. Butler in October 1957 urging the Home Secretary to use his 'power and influence to have the play *Look Back in*

Anger by John Osborne withdrawn both from stage and (I understand) screen'. What rankled was the fact that the New Malvern Players were staging it at the local Torquay Pavilion that week. 'Surely the complete dialogue of this production could not have been passed by the censor?', the enquirer demanded, given that 'It is the conception of a deceased and depraved mentality and the outpourings of a cesspool mind'. 'I am indeed at a loss to understand how this play should reach the English stage', he stated, as he implored finally: 'I beg of you in the interests of what is left of sanctity and sanity to give this matter your immediate and earnest attention.' 'Treat officially', noted Butler's private secretary, before passing the letter over to the Lord Chamberlain's office for a formal reply. The Assistant Comptroller took on the task. After pointing out that 'The Lord Chamberlain, of course, is only responsible for stage plays and censorship of the films is done by the British Board of Film Censors', Brigadier Sir Norman Gwatkin added, sympathetically:

The play to which you refer was submitted here some time ago and a considerable number of amendments required. When these were made the Lord Chamberlain felt that, unpleasant though the play was in many ways, it was not one that he could rightly ban in 1956. However the Lord Chamberlain is grateful to you for having troubled to write as it helps him very much in his difficult task to hear what the public's reactions are.[6]

'Tormented' of Torquay was plainly not enamoured of Mr Osborne's work. Nor, indeed, were the theatre censors exactly pleased with his efforts. Though his reputation as a new and exciting playwright soared on the basis of *Look Back in Anger*, the censors lamented the trend he had started for 'realistic plays'. The strong feelings they aroused were especially evident when it came to submission of Osborne's next piece, *The Entertainer*, in March 1957. It was given for scrutiny to Lieutenant-Colonel Sir St Vincent Troubridge, a descendant of Nelson's victorious admiral at the battle in 1797 which was used thereafter as a family name. Troubridge expressed his disapproval in no uncertain terms:

This is the eagerly awaited second play by John Osborne, whose *Look Back in Anger* was the main sensation of 1956, and who is the acknowledged head of the Angry Young Man school (or racket) of dramatists. Sir Laurence Olivier and Miss Dorothy Tutin are to appear in it in five weeks.

In the modern fashion, it has scarcely any story at all, the merest and flimsiest scaffolding, the characters, their circumstances and emotions representing the true content of the play. While the whining self-pity of Jimmy Porter in the earlier play is not here concentrated in a single character, the vitriolic negativism is now dispersed over an entire family of tatty, broken-down music hall pros, selected I should say for their suitability for the display of assorted frustrations, and somewhat Chekhovian, except that they are viewed with anger and contempt rather than an amused and tolerant pity.

Unfortunately this second play contains a good deal of verbal dirt and smart-Alec lines like 'the old church bell won't ring tonight, as the vicar's got the clappers', with traces of blasphemy and disloyalty, which I will set out for my superiors' adjudication.

'The samples' elaborated by Troubridge to show 'how Angry Young Mannery is coming along' were many and various. Most, it was agreed by Scarbrough and Gwatkin, should be cut or altered. Language, inevitably, was the greatest casualty given that 'the whole play is impregnated with sex, sexy references and half-references, and general lavatory dirt which must be debited to the bad taste account'. Some things could be permitted, of course, if not condoned. Thus, 'poke the fire' was allowed, albeit recognized as 'a double entendre on one of the words for having intercourse'. So, too, were the phrases 'a good blow through', 'pissed up', 'a couple of fried eggs' ('the lowest word for breasts'), 'take precautions', 'she needs some beef putting into her' ('intended obscenely'), and the question 'Have you ever had it on a kitchen table?' 'In drag' was allowed, once noted that it was 'the word for female dress when adopted by homosexuals'. And, after deliberation over the extent of 'permitted republican sentiment', it was agreed to pass: 'What's it all in aid of—is it really just for the sake of a gloved hand waving at you from a golden coach?' By the same token, the play's intermittent references to the Suez crisis, viewed largely through the fate of the soldier son, Mick, were the cause of some concern and discussion:

the family is informed that Mick has been killed by being shut up in a box by the 'wogs'. I think this must be accepted as historic, in spite of possible distress to Lieutenant Moorhouse's family. But Mick's death does not really affect the story, except to call for a song with couplets like "Those playing fields of Eton | Have really got us beaten'.

The banned words, predictably, included: 'ass-upwards', 'clappers', 'pouf' ('a word for a homosexual'), 'shagged', 'rogered', 'turds', and 'camp'. And exception was taken to phrases like 'Right up to the flies', 'wet your pants', 'had Sylvia', as well as, 'I always needed a jump at the end of the day and at the beginning too, usually'. The prospect of 'nude tableaux', furthermore, promising Britannia in all her natural splendour, was worrying and would require that photographs of the same be submitted in advance of production. The likely contents of 'a mimed scene' would also need to be outlined and 'submitted in full'. In this regard as in others, it was noted, Osborne was experimenting with theatrical forms: 'Though most of the scenes of family quarrelling and drinking are "realistic", the author has come under the influence of Brecht's "epic" technique which shows through strongly in the general dramaturgy, in interpolated songs, and in simultaneous cross-conversations, etc.' At the last, Troubridge added: 'Though stupid schoolboy stories beginning "A man went to Heaven and St Peter said to him . . ." are legion, I consider the whole of the one centring round the word "Balls" to be blasphemous.' He recommended the play for licence, finally, provided the appropriate amendments were made. But he did so with a considerable amount of 'aversion and disgust' and very much 'as an angry middle-aged man'.[7]

Despite the greater number of censorship strictures than on the occasion of their previous submission, Richardson responded with Osborne's proposed revisions within a day of being notified what was required. This time, however, it proved even more difficult to meet the Lord Chamberlain's demands. The requisite cuts were made. Photographs were promised of the tableaux scenes. On that front, the English Stage Company would be 'very grateful for any directions you can give us about the presentation of a nude on the stage'. 'Cockeyed' was offered and accepted as a replacement for 'ass-upwards'. So too was 'weird' for 'camp', and 'ponce' would suffice for 'pouf'. 'It's a "normal" profession at least', was the censor's blue pencil comment added in the margin of Richardson's letter (something, doubtless, by way of both a moral judgement and a pun on Archie Rice's key song, 'Thank God I'm Normal'). But 'shagged' would assuredly not do as substitute for 'screwed'. In two key respects, furthermore, Osborne was clearly unwilling to compromise and here Richardson was ready to marshal some powerful, if not wholly convincing, arguments in their defence. The first related to the use of 'clappers':

May we ask you to reconsider this word. Mr Osborne wrote the line 'the churchbells won't ring tonight because the vicar's got the clappers' solely referring to the clappers of the bell. Surely, in fact, the word 'clappers' has no other meaning and you have yourself allowed us to use the phrase later in the play (Act III, 'He just grinned like the clappers'). Naturally, as the play is in the music hall convention, Mr John Osborne, the author, wanted the pun on the word 'clap' but thought that in doing this he was avoiding any possible offence to the majority of the audience and that the pun itself would only be appreciated by the sophisticated. If it is absolutely impossible for us to have this word, would you approve 'the vicar's dropped a clanger'?

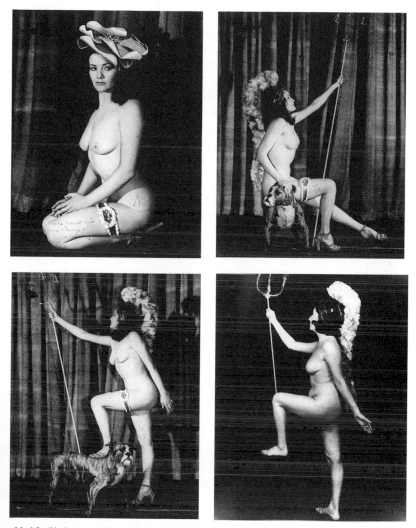

11–14. 'Nudes are allowed by the Lord Chamberlain provided they are motionless and expressionless in the face of the audience. In the case of *The Entertainer*, the nudes concerned were expressly approved in side views concealing the pudenda.' (*The Entertainer*, stage version)

The censor was not appeased, as his blue-pencil remarks emphatically and forcefully indicated. The idea that 'clappers' referred 'solely' to a bell, merited the comment: 'This is disingenuous.' Mention of the esoteric motives for Osborne's pun on the word 'clap' brought forth the rejoinder: 'Good thing if John Osborne had it—he wouldn't "pun" so much then.' Matters could only get worse, and did so when Richardson attempted his second major defence argument, in favour of retaining 'balls':

May we ask you to make a special consideration about this word. The whole effect of this story depends upon the shock effect, and in the context we would suggest that it is not in the least suggestive. This effect is meant to be a contemporary equivalent of the famous 'Not bloody likely' and there is simply no other equivalent that we can possibly find. We would beg you to make a special consideration in this case but if it is impossible to concede us the point we would suggest instead a whistle.

The precedent cited, of course, was George Bernard Shaw's notorious use of 'not bloody likely' for his character Eliza Doolittle in *Pygmalion*. This had been granted a licence in 1912 by the then Lord Chamberlain, Lord Sandhurst. The censors were not impressed, however, by the resort to case law to clinch the argument. Far from it. 'No, a thousand times no', remarked one of them, 'Who does Mr Osborne think he is?' 'Well, really, I'm astonished', added another. Richardson was informed they should find a different word for 'screwed', that 'the vicar's dropped a clanger' would have to suffice, and that 'a whistle' should indeed be substituted for 'balls'. On the matter of the nude tableaux, they were told: 'For your guidance, a nude pose should not be in any way erotic. It should be exhibited in subdued lighting only.'[8]

The saga did not end there. Though he conceded the issue of 'clanger' for 'clappers', Richardson returned with a new suggestion to replace 'balls'. He was not content with the idea of substituting a whistle and that alone. Plainly, it would not have sufficient dramatic impact. He proposed now the line: 'I am sorry ladies and gentlemen but the Censor is in tonight.' It was no doubt also intended as a wry comment, if something of an in-joke, on the whole protracted affair. Still, it was acceptable. Other amendments were not, especially when they introduced an additional sequence in which Archie Rice produces a brassière on cue to 'Lift up your Hearts' and a large pair of bloomers to accompany, 'Sunday half-hour'. What was wrong this time? When Richardson had recently visited the Chelsea Palace variety theatre, after all, the very same words and action had been used in performance there.

No matter, replied the censors, variety shows did not fall within their domain. 'We object to the tasteless gagging about religious programmes' for the simple reason that 'guying religious programmes would give offence to a number of people'. They were content, mind you, if the jokes were made at the expense of *What's my Line?* and *The Week in Westminster*. Similar niceties were expressed over the photographs of the nude Britannia tendered for their consideration and advice. Despite mention of the fact that the positions would be taken up behind a gauze screen, the warning was given that one pose could only be allowed if the model was placed 'more sideways to the audience'. The Lord Chamberlain's licence was finally issued for *The Entertainer* on 5 April 1957, just five days before the play was given its première.[9]

Norman Gwatkin actually went to see the play at the end of April and dropped a note to Troubridge afterwards, stating that 'Larry Olivier hates "The Examiner" for cutting out his best line "The vicar's got the clappers".' 'It is a very good cast', he added, 'you ought to see it if you can.' It was 'about the hottest single line I remember', Troubridge replied, 'Samuel Beckett always excepted'. The times, clearly, were not to his liking. 'It seems to me that our venerable institution of the Revels is under stronger attack at the moment than at any time since Percy Smith's Bill ten or twelve years ago', he continued plaintively, 'though perhaps it will last my remaining five years out.' He concluded, however, on a note of comforting resolve:

As I sit here hoping for rain for the garden, I rather feel that my recent evening activities have landed you rather a lot of three page reports. But *Fin de Partie*, *The Entertainer*, *Camino Real*, *Orpheus Descending* and *The Making of Moo* were all quite major affairs in their way. Provided you can take it, which I do not doubt, I prefer to examine such plays rather than this morning's arrival, *Lord Byron's Heritage*, for amateurs at Houghton Le-Spring in December.[10]

Subsequently *The Entertainer* transferred from the Royal Court to the Palace Theatre on 10 September 1957 necessitating more 'nude tableaux' photographs for the censor's consideration.[11] There followed the inevitable complaints to the Chamberlain's office from the public. While one person detected 'the merest suspicion of wit', he was adamant in wanting 'to secure the prohibition of this sort of offensive performance'. Gwatkin was called upon, yet again, to explain their reasons for allowing it to proceed at the outset. Once more, he was caught on the horns of a dilemma:

This play, which is by no means a comedy, is written by a very modern playwright in the genre of the times. It is not attractive but it is, at least, honest in its choice of word and phrase.

Plays are judged on their merits and not by rule of thumb. In order that the main character should give the impersonation which the author wishes to bring out it is dramatically essential that he should be natural and he is naturally a coarse man and a tragic one.

There are, however, limits beyond which the Lord Chamberlain cannot allow honesty of speech or action to go and it may interest you to know that over a score of alterations were requested in places where the Lord Chamberlain considered that a less violent word or passage would be adequate.

The play has been on for many months and the number of objections to it have been remarkably small. I must add that the Lord Chamberlain is grateful to you for writing to us. It is the reactions of the intelligent theatregoing public which help him in his difficult task.[12]

Despite the intermittent public criticism, however, by the end of 1957 Osborne had enjoyed considerable success with his first two plays presented on the London stage. The dramatist was very much in demand and inevitably attracted the attention of many a film producer eager to adapt his material for the cinema. Several factors contrived to prevent the likelihood of any speedy transfer from stage to screen. Though Osborne had immediately been approached with several offers for the film rights to *Look Back in Anger*, for instance, including one from John and James Woolf of Romulus Films in the autumn of 1956, he was keen on retaining a close working relationship with Richardson. Life for both of them, furthermore, was nothing if not exceptionally busy. *Look Back in Anger* transferred from the Royal Court to the Lyric Theatre, Hammersmith, on 5 November, and was then taken back to the Court, on 11 March 1957, each occasion involving extensive cast changes and further rehearsal. As noted above, *The Entertainer* had transferred to the Palace Theatre, again with cast changes. Meanwhile, the original Royal Court cast of *Look Back in Anger* was reassembled by Tony Richardson for an American production and all decisions on film matters postponed until after its Broadway première on 1 October 1957.

The acclaim which greeted the Broadway presentation of *Look Back in Anger* not only confirmed Osborne's reputation as a playwright of note but also produced an 'angel' for their film plans in the form of Harry Saltzman. Saltzman, a Quebec-born North American and 'a natural entrepreneur', capitalized on the play's new-found international reputation and Richard Burton's reported interest in playing the part of Jimmy Porter, to extract a budget of between £200,000 and £250,000 from Warner Brothers and Associated British-Pathé. Saltzman, Osborne, and Richardson formed Woodfall Films to ensure they retained artistic control and a measure of

15. Cliff (*Gary Raymond*) and Jimmy (*Richard Burton*). (*Look Back in Anger*)

16. Alison (*Mary Ure*). (*Look Back in Anger*)

independence. Given their inexperience of feature film production, however, some compromises were inevitable at the outset. Of the original cast, for example, only Mary Ure was retained for the role of Alison, and Claire Bloom, who like Burton had a cinema following, was brought in for the part of Helena. Nigel Kneale, an accomplished writer for film and television and author of BBC TV's 1953 sensational science fiction serial, *The Quatermass Experiment*, was engaged to adapt Osborne's play for the screen. Osborne provided 'additional dialogue' and received his share in the sale of the film rights of his play. Richardson, for his part, got nothing by way of a fee for directing.[13]

Kneale's draft script of *Look Back in Anger* consciously opened the play out and located several sequences outside the immediate confines of the Porters' claustrophobic flat. In particular, he added more business showing Jimmy and Cliff as they run their market stall, as well as a scene in which Alison visits a doctor to confirm her pregnancy and enquires 'Is it too late to do anything?' (In the play, this dialogue over a possible abortion is presented as confidential chat between Cliff and Alison.) Some things were sacrificed, notably Jimmy's important speech about there being 'no good brave causes left' to fight for. To make up for that omission, in particular, the script introduced a new character—an Indian stall-holder who, when threatened with racist taunts and pressure, is championed by Jimmy but finally evicted from the market-place. Jimmy's jazz background was elaborated and his relationship with Ma Tanner, the mother of his old friend, fleshed out by presenting her in person (as played by Edith Evans). For all the changes, however, Tony Richardson's purpose was clear: 'It is absolutely vital to get into British films the same sort of impact and sense of life that what you can loosely call the Angry Young Man cult has had in the theatre and literary worlds.' 'It is', he maintained, 'a desperate need.'[14]

The point was not lost on the BBFC's readers when Kneale's script was presented for their consideration at the end of August 1958. They were no more happy with it than the Lord Chamberlain's office had been with the original play. Audrey Field commented:

This sounds dull—and for a very good reason. It *is* dull. Class consciousness is a very common failing. But it has been chewed over enough, and *more* than enough, in the last few years. And all the chewing only makes people worse in this respect than they were before. I saw the play on television and I thought then that it was very mediocre, though good acting did a lot to make it seem better than it was. The film script is even less good, missing no opportunity of dragging in tendentious and irrelevant stuff about white people bullying Indians, etc. It packs less punch than the play and I find it difficult to assess from the censorship point of view. The story is basically 'A' but it is adorned with gross and violent language which serves to make it sound like an 'X'. The proper course for the company to take would be to modify the dialogue with a view to getting an 'A' certificate. But I do not think they would do this. In default of this, we could throw our previous standards overboard and give an 'A' to the film without asking for any verbal changes. But I do not think we would do this, and I hope we would not.

We have sometimes been too mealy-mouthed in the past but there is a limit to what we ought to sanction for children. And I think the limit is exceeded in certain passages of this film. The other possibility would be to allow the film uncut for 'X' and perhaps this would be politic, as many people who ought to know think John Osborne's work beyond criticism.

A long list of offending words and phrases was appended with notice of the fact that 'The bloodies are not spared in this script and are usually ugly in the context'. She took particular exception to the mention of a possible abortion and reacted to Jimmy's 'great pleasure of lovemaking speech' in precisely the same way the theatre censors had responded to it, highlighting the 'python' reference as a potential problem. This was no surprise, perhaps, given that talk of Alison's post-coital reaction—'she lies back afterwards like a puffed-out python to sleep it off'—had cannily been reinserted. Jimmy's continual vilification of his wife was frowned upon, not least his lines: 'I want to see you grovel. I want to see your face rubbed in the mud.' 'This element of sado-masochism' clearly justified an 'X' certificate, Field felt, especially 'when coupled with some fairly frank love stuff'. 'Perhaps I am off beam in even thinking it a bad "X"', she pondered, before suggesting an instant remedy for Jimmy Porter's ills: 'It's just that it seems to me such a wearisome fuss about nothing that couldn't be cured by hard manual labour or going off to the Dominions out of reach of the in-laws.''

A second script-reader, Frank Crofts, shared many of Field's misgivings and clearly felt Jimmy's masochistic streak extended beyond the bounds of his private relationship with Alison:

It is astonishing that anyone should consider this anything but trite and dreary rubbish. One can imagine Jimmy up to a point though I think he is rather a caricature. But one cannot have sympathy with him, with his self-pity, his love–hate silliness, his bullying and his masochistic wish not to take advantage of his education. As for Alison and Helena, they are unreal. Alison married Jimmy because he was sun-burnt when she first saw him and because her family (naturally) didn't like him. Helena actively disliked him till she suddenly seduced him. One simply cannot believe a well educated, reasonable girl falling for a seedy little

17. '"I want to see you grovel. I want to see your face rubbed in the mud . . ." Richard Burton's performance as Jimmy will have a considerable impact which will heighten his sado-masochistic treatment of Alison.' (*Look Back in Anger*)

twerp like him. One can put up with his boorishness, his cruelty and his stupidity, but not with his being such a bore.

Having served for a lengthy spell in the Indian civil service before joining the BBFC in 1948, Crofts was particularly upset that the script's references to India were frequently wrong when mentioning Alison's father, Colonel Redfern. 'No one from India brings a household of Indian furniture back with them', he commented, and, 'Gurkhas don't have daggers but very heavy sharp knives known as khukris.' At the last, however, for all his reservations, Crofts differed from Field in concluding: 'I don't think this is really "X". I think it should be passed for "A".'[16]

John Trevelyan, then, had to deal with a conflict of opinion among his readers. Whereas one basically felt the completed film should be given an 'X' certificate, the other believed it would probably pass for the 'A' category. His dilemma was compounded by other matters which required serious attention. The prospect of a film based on a John Osborne play

18. Jimmy and Helena (*Claire Bloom*) part. (*Look Back in Anger*)

clearly posed additional problems to the sort he had encountered earlier in his career, for instance, when confronted with the likes of Michael Croft's *Spare the Rod*. By the same token, however, it also offered more scope for his purpose. Osborne, plainly, was perceived as the spearhead of a new movement, in both theatre and literature, which threatened to invade the domain of the cinema and could hardly be treated lightly. Not that Trevelyan intended doing anything of the sort. He had, after all, his own good reasons for wanting to establish where the angry young men would fall in the canon of film censorship, and these lay largely, as we have seen, in his overall wish to promote 'adult' films of 'quality' and his desire to lend greater respectability to the 'X' category. *Look Back in Anger* like *Room at the Top*, which Trevelyan was dealing with concurrently, had just the right credentials—literary pedigree and 'realist' concerns—to accommodate such ambitions. It presented yet another opportunity to settle the critical consensus that Trevelyan wanted to see established for the 'X' certificate.[17]

Trevelyan, therefore, marshalled all the arguments he could possibly muster when seeking to persuade the film-makers of the value in accepting an 'X' on this occasion. He began by inviting Frederick Gotfurt, the scenario editor at Associated British, to his office for a discussion on the BBFC's reservations over the script, following it up the next day with a letter summarizing the major points at issue:

This script presents us with a rather unusual problem. The story is basically one which would be eligible for the 'A' category but the dialogue is not suitable for this category. The question then arises whether we work on the basis that the film will have an 'X' certificate, in which case I think we could accept this script virtually unaltered, or whether we work on the basis that the film will have an 'A' certificate, in which case there would, I think , have to be quite a number of alterations to the dialogue. I personally would be most reluctant to alter the dialogue to any extent since I think it will be difficult to establish the character of Jimmy Porter if his language is toned down. In any case this is an important play and people who have seen the play in London will expect the dialogue and characterisations to be roughly the same.

I hope therefore that the company will be prepared to accept an 'X' certificate. But I realise that they may feel that an 'X' certificate will attract not only a smaller audience but an audience which would include some who will be disappointed not to find what is all too frequently shown in this category. As I explained to you, it has always been our intention and hope that the films in the 'X' category would be largely those with adult themes and adult treatment, but I have to admit that it has not always worked out this way except in the case of certain films. I think one can claim that, although the story is one which would be suitable for the 'A' category, the theme behind the story is really adult.

Trevelyan proceeded to outline an extensive list comprising no less than twenty-four significant items which gave rise for concern. Though he welcomed a further meeting to elaborate these matters, if required, his preferred course of action was made abundantly clear—they should agree to take an 'X' certificate:

I would of course be prepared to discuss these points in detail, one by one, and we might not insist on all of those that I have listed, but I think I have given enough to show you that we would probably require a number of dialogue alterations.

I am somewhat influenced in my opinion that this would be better as an 'X' film by the fact that you have a really good cast, and I think that Richard Burton's performance as Jimmy will have a considerable impact which will heighten his sado-masochistic treatment of Alison.[18]

Gotfurt returned for another discussion two weeks later, this time bringing Harry Saltzman with him. Obviously, they were both worried about the prospect of an 'X' certificate and its likely effect on the box-office potential of their film. Trevelyan reiterated his fears about 'the forthright language used' and Jimmy's sado-masochistic treatment of Alison. It was decided they would definitely omit the word 'Christ'—'a word that we prefer not to have even in the "X" category'—and seek substitutes for 'bitch', 'virgin', and 'bastard'. In addition, they would carefully consider the 'implied references to abortion' so as to render them 'intelligible to adults and unintelligible to children'. Trevelyan, for his part, conceded that 'scripts are apt to be misleading' and that 'some of the dialogue which appears offensive on paper may well sound less offensive in the completed film'. After hearing Saltzman's ideas regarding their production plans, he was willing to accept that 'the important scenes will be treated with sincerity and restraint'. 'When we see the film', he promised, 'we will give fair consideration to your request that it should have an "A" category'. 'I cannot of course', he concluded, 'commit the Board to a category at this stage.'[19]

One can only speculate about Saltzman's reactions to the meeting: whether he believed they could provide sufficient 'sincerity and restraint' to merit an 'A'; whether he was more impressed by Trevelyan's opinion that they should settle for an 'X', or whether, quite simply, he was determined most of all upon bringing the film to fruition in a fashion that best pleased its makers. Whatever the reasons, only five of Trevelyan's list of twenty-four suggested amendments had been made when the film was completed and presented for award of a certificate in the spring of 1959. In particular, the passing reference to abortion was left precisely as in the original version. But by the start of 1959, of course, Trevelyan had already dealt with the finished film of *Room at the Top* and had pretty much resolved, to his own satisfaction at least, the thorny problem of what constituted 'adult' films and 'quality' cinema. *Look Back in Anger* was therefore given the 'X' rating it had been virtually guaranteed at the outset, and no cuts were required.

Trevelyan was doubtless much relieved at getting his way with perhaps the most controversial and publicity-prone British author of the day. The dilemma which had been highlighted by the BBFC's readers about the censorship category that best suited Osborne's material, however, soon resurfaced when the screenplay of *The Entertainer* was presented for pre-production scrutiny just three months after *Look Back in Anger* was given its première on 28 May 1959. Audrey Field, for instance, had plainly re-vised her opinion of Osborne's worth and her report on 20 August showed she was now genuinely perplexed whether this film, once finished, would merit an 'X' or 'A' certificate. After noting that 'The extensions of the play are tedious—mostly class-conscious stuff—on the same lines as the added scenes for *Look Back in Anger*', Field continued:

I still think that this young man has a cliché-ridden mind, though with real feeling, and real dramatic quality, struggling to get through. He ought to have had the kind of education which encourages people to think for themselves: all this blether about the wicked establishment is the new 'off the peg' clothing of the mind and requires neither originality nor courage. However, this is not our affair. What is our affair is that some of the language and some of the grimy gags are not suitable to the 'A' category, and if the makers of the film don't want to alter them the film should be 'X'.

An 'X' certificate can be defended, although I do not consider this a really adult story but really an adolescent story dressed up to kill. It seems to me tasteless to use a terrible private grief for purposes of entertainment in the way the story of the Suez soldier is used here; and I have the same sort of objection to references to the Prime Minister of the day (Sir Anthony Eden) 'looking like the dog down-stairs' and 'bringing people out in spots'; but neither of these items seem to be matters of censorship . . . I don't think there is anything in this script which is likely to startle the House of Lords as much as the jokes in *Look Back in Anger* but the male readers should keep their eyes skinned.

Field then provided a detailed list of cautionable words, including 'bloody', 'Christ', 'bastard', 'whore', and 'arse'. They exemplified the '*enfant terrible* language to which Mr Osborne is much addicted', she felt, and all were considered to be distinctly 'offensive'. She wondered, furthermore, whether the atmosphere of 'silly vulgarity' that the script promised, the probability of some 'near nudes', and the likelihood of an occasionally dubious scene— 'The shots of Archie and Tina together on the bunk in the caravan'— would cause problems and 'may call for a caution, even for "X"'. Nevertheless, Field concluded: 'Osborne, like Bottom, "comes but to offend", and we cannot reasonably knock the bottom out of his notion of entertaining the public.'[20]

19 and 20. 'Thank God
I'm normal'—Archie Rice
(*Laurence Olivier*). (*The
Entertainer*, film)
....

Trevelyan, however, was intent upon one course and one course alone—to have *The Entertainer* in the 'X' category. Having already won the day over an Osborne script he was determined to get his way yet again. An initial communication to Harry Saltzman promised a relatively trouble-free passage, always provided the film-makers were willing to reciprocate by settling for an 'X'. Moreover, it is noticeable that, except for requiring deletion of 'Christ' when uttered as an expletive, Trevelyan said nothing about the other potentially censorable matters which his script-reader had identified. He was doubtless keeping these cards up his sleeve should the moment arise when they might be needed:

We have now read the shooting script for *The Entertainer* and, as with *Look Back in Anger*, everything depends on the category in which the film is to be placed. As the script stands we think the film should be in the 'X' category and for this category we would want only one small alteration—the word 'Christ' as an expletive is used . . . and we would prefer to have this changed.

If you should be most anxious to get the film into the 'A' category we would do our best to help but we would want quite a number of alterations and I think that these would considerably weaken the impact of the film and might well spoil it. So I hope that we may both proceed on the assumption that this will be an 'X' film. This would certainly save censorship trouble.[21]

Saltzman, however, was less inclined to consent to Trevelyan's suggestion on this occasion. He knew, for a start, that *Look Back in Anger* had done disastrous business at the British box-office. The mixed reviews had not helped, nor, indeed, was the film aided by opening its London run during exceptionally good weather, as Saltzman noted wryly, 'in a heatwave that turned London into an outdoor city for at least a fortnight—people sleeping in the parks at night'.[22] But he must also have known that these factors did not explain why the film fared so badly outside the capital, on nationwide release. Conveniently forgetting that *Room at the Top* had turned out to be a considerable commercial success despite its 'X' rating, Saltzman, along with both Osborne and Richardson, attributed the poor box-office returns on *Look Back in Anger* to the fact that it had been landed with an 'X'. Therefore, when *The Entertainer* was finished at the end of the year and presented for a certificate, they pressed hard to have it put in the 'A' category. Trevelyan was adamant that this would not do. After viewing the completed film, he wrote to Saltzman on 29 December 1959:

We have given very careful consideration to the category problem raised by *The Entertainer*. What I anticipated at the script stage has turned out to be correct. We can give the film an 'X' certificate without asking for any cuts at all but if it is to go into the 'A' category there will have to be some cuts. As I have explained to you, we are quite reasonably open to criticism when we pass a film in the 'A' category, which enables children to see it, when it contains scenes and dialogue which are really not suitable for children. Both this film and *Look Back in Anger* are 'A' category in theme but not in treatment and dialogue.

As I said when we discussed this, we would be reluctant to have this film cut and I hope therefore that you will persuade the distributors to accept an 'X' certificate. I really believe that *Room at the Top* and *Look Back in Anger* have shown that the 'X' certificate is not a handicap to this type of film as it might well have been before these two films were shown. I think also that the general public will probably expect a John Osborne play to be in the 'X' category.

Lest Saltzman and the rest were in danger of missing the point, Trevelyan explained precisely what he would expect to see amended for the film to be seriously considered as an 'A'. Now, at last, he chose to mention the items which had already given cause for concern. They referred, as Audrey Field had noted, to language ('the words "bloody" and "bastard" are used some 15 times or more'), to jokes ('the vicar's got the clappers'), to dialogue ('take me to bed'), and to 'the bed scene in the caravan [which] must be shortened'. 'These cuts are not going to be easy to make', Trevelyan stated, 'and I hope that you will decide not to make them but accept an "X" certificate.' 'If they are to be made', he concluded ominously, 'we would want to see all the reels in which there are cuts.'[23]

It is doubtful, in fact, whether the required cuts would have been any thing like as difficult to effect as Trevelyan maintained. He was simply painting as bleak a picture as possible in order to get matters agreed to his liking and he was clearly banking on the fact that Woodfall would be reluctant to make more cuts than was absolutely necessary. If the company should prove unduly awkward, moreover, there was always the threat of discussions about the award of a final certificate becoming protracted. That much was implicit, after all, in Trevelyan's parting comment. Undaunted, Saltzman, Richardson, and Osborne held out for an 'A' certificate. 'Negotiations with the censor', Osborne records in his autobiography, 'dragged on for three months'. Since neither Woodfall nor Trevelyan were willing to relent at the last, however, the outcome was obvious. 'He hobbled us with an "X" certificate', Osborne comments, 'which ensured that it would be turned down as the entry for the Royal Film Performance, which might have helped its general release.'[24] Osborne's complaint is undoubtedly justified. The film was clearly 'hobbled' by its 'X'-certificate rating and its commercial prospects were certainly

21. Tina, the beauty queen (*Shirley Anne Field*). (*The Entertainer*, film)

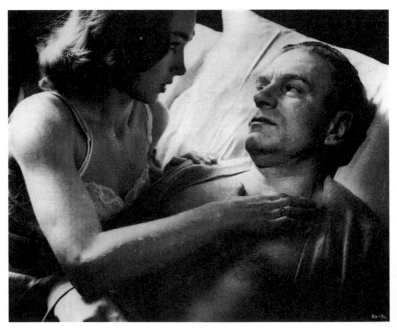

22. 'The shots of Archie and Tina together on the bunk in the caravan must be shortened.' (*The Entertainer*, film)

lessened as a result. In addition to being denied consideration for the Royal Film Performance, for example, *The Entertainer* was also discarded as the official British entry at the Cannes Film Festival in favour of the 'A'-certificate *Sons and Lovers*. The three-month hiatus spent on censorship discussions, furthermore, meant that the West End press show and première scheduled for the end of April had to be cancelled. *The Entertainer* finally opened in London on 28 July 1960 and soon turned out to be a financial flop.[25]

At the time of the film's immediate release, however, Osborne was altogether more circumspect with his comments on Trevelyan's line in virtually forcing them to take an 'X'. So, also, was Tony Richardson. Both plainly regretted that *The Entertainer* had been given an 'X' rating, 'for commercial reasons', if nothing else. Nevertheless, they were both sympathetic to Trevelyan's good intentions in attempting to redeem a category which Osborne described—in what was probably also intended as a pointed reference to films like *Peeping Tom*—as 'the licensed trademark for all kinds of sado-masochistic nastiness and perverse rubbish'. 'There has been a consistent effort by the Censor to encourage film-makers not to compromise in the treatment of serious subjects', Osborne noted, and, 'Indeed, the "X" was created for this purpose'. 'The problem', he added significantly, was that 'the distributors have not been able to keep up with the censorship'. On this occasion, in fact, Osborne reserved most of his criticism for gibes at the expense of the film distributors:

Repeatedly, one learns of instances where the Censor has begged film producers to leave their films intact and keep an 'X' certificate rather than cut it, thus damaging its style and intentions, but scraping itself an 'A', fit for the crippled imaginations of the distributors. On the whole, distributors have no interest in the problem of censorship, because it can only become a significant issue where there are serious intentions, and there are very few of these around the men who book the films for British cinemas.

Richardson, too, recognized Trevelyan's larger purpose and conceded that: 'The Censor admittedly has a difficult job.' The problem for their kind of film, as far as he was concerned, lay with unfulfilled audience expectations:

The Board of Censors is at the moment deliberately trying to establish the 'X' category as the category for adult entertainment, and consequently a number of films like *Room at the Top*, *Look Back in Anger*, *The Entertainer*, are given a brand they don't live up to. Thus one section of the audience is excluded and another is disappointed. This is placing a double burden on the problem, great enough in itself, of making this sort of realistic film.[26]

What appears to have escaped both Osborne's and Richardson's notice, however, is that perhaps Trevelyan was equally disappointed at the failure of their initial forays into film production. He set great store by Woodfall's efforts, after all, not least in trusting they would benefit his own strategy to lend greater respectability and credence to the 'X' certificate. Though *Room at the Top* had done much to rehabilitate the category, the poor public reception afforded *Look Back in Anger* and *The Entertainer* was a distinct setback, and hardly boded well for further 'realistic' British films intended as 'adult entertainment'. Moreover, the appearance of *Peeping Tom* in May 1960 and the widespread outrage it evoked—still very much in evidence at the time *The Entertainer* was given its première in July 1960—must have prompted Trevelyan to wonder whether his plans could ever be fully realized, or whether he was in for a welter of films from the critically despised lower depths of 'exploitative' commercial production, with all the hazards that might entail. Could box-office success be repeated with films on 'serious subjects' or was *Room at the Top* merely a one-off hit? Ironically, it was Woodfall Productions that provided a solution to everybody's dilemma when they expanded their horizons somewhat and turned from John Osborne to Alan Sillitoe for inspiration in their endeavours.

Notes

1 The critical and public reception afforded Osborne's first play to reach the London stage is discussed in John Russell Taylor (ed.), *John Osborne: Look Back in Anger, A Casebook* (Basingstoke, 1968), 16–21, and Ritchie, *Success Stories*, 25–31.

2 LC, file 8932/1956 on *Look Back in Anger*: reader's report, 1 Mar. 1956. Heriot tentatively suggested in a footnote: 'The prototypes of Jimmy and Alison may be Giles Romilly and his wife. Romilly was killed in the war and his biography was sketched in a book called *Friends Apart* by Philip Toynbee, published in 1954.'

3 LC, file 8932/1956 on *Look Back in Anger*: Norman Gwatkin to Michael Hallifax, 2 Mar. 1956. They agreed to allow 'lavatory' and 'homosexual' references in Act I and a reference to 'excessive lovemaking' in Act III, Scene i.

4 Ibid., Richardson to Gwatkin, 20 Mar. 1956, seen and marked with marginal comment on 21 Mar. 1956. See also ibid., Gwatkin to Richardson, 22 Mar. 1956. On another matter, incidentally, the censors selected, 'She's as rough as a night in Leicester Square and as tough as a matelot's arm', of the two options offered to replace 'She's as tough as a night in a Bombay brothel and as hairy as a gorilla's behind'. Richardson's preference was obvious: 'We really can't find any word as effective as brothel so please can we use it?' Interestingly, the 1962 edn. of the play employs the following formulation: 'She's as rough as a night in a Bombay brothel and as tough as a matelot's arm.'

5 Ibid., Richardson to Gwatkin, 26 Mar. 1956 ('This will do'), and 9 Apr. 1956 ('Allow'). The agreed speech now occurs at the end of Act I.

6 Ibid., W. Lang-Burgoyne to Butler, 6 Oct. 1957, and Gwatkin in reply, of 21 Oct. 1957.

7 LC, file 10041/1957 on *The Entertainer*: reader's report, 16 Mar. 1957; see also ibid., Gwatkin to Miriam Brickman, 20 Mar. 1957.

8 Ibid., Brickman to Gwatkin, 'on behalf of Mr Tony Richardson', 21 Mar. 1957, and marginal comments to same. See also ibid., Brickman to Gwatkin, 25 Mar. 1957. Incidentally, Johnston, *Blue Pencil*, 166–7, outlines what happened when the musical version of Shaw's play, *My Fair Lady*, was presented for consideration in 1956. Ironically, Troubridge was the reader on this occasion as well, and he commented: 'For 1956 the adaptor has sought for some equivalent *coup de foudre* that would shock without disgusting. They have found this in the Ascot scene where Eliza, having backed a horse, when watching the race with a lot of impassive socialites, adjures the horse at the top of her voice, "Move your blooming arse" . . . In fact "bloody" in 1912 is if anything more startling in relation to its date than "arse" in 1956. Though generally cut, this is a homely word, well understood by everybody.' Troubridge allowed the word and Scarbrough agreed. But, as Johnston notes, when the musical opened at Drury Lane the phrase was changed to 'move your ruddy arse' since this had a better reception. Permission was given.

9 LC, file 10041/1957 on *The Entertainer*: Brickman to Gwatkin, 19, 25, and 28 Mar., 1 and 4 Apr. 1957; Gwatkin to Brickman, 21, 27, and 29 Mar., 3 and 5 Apr. 1957. The line, 'The Censor is in tonight', and the jokey references to then current radio and television programmes were dropped in later published edns. of the play, doubtless because of the strictly contemporary nature of the allusions.

10 Ibid., Gwatkin to Troubridge, 29 Apr. 1957; Troubridge to Gwatkin, 30 Apr. 1957. E. P. Smith, a Conservative MP and author (under the name of Edward Percy) of such plays as *The Shop at Sly Corner*, had sponsored Benn Levy's unsuccessful 1949 Private Member's Bill to repeal the censorship of plays, supported by Michael Foot.

11 Ibid., Brickman to Gwatkin, 3 Sept. 1957, and reply to same of 4 Sept. 1957. Some years later, the Town Clerk of the London Borough of Sutton telephoned the Lord Chamberlain's office enquiring about the rules applied to the nude tableaux in regard to a local production of *The Entertainer*. It was stated, on 17 May 1965: 'Nudes are allowed by the Lord Chamberlain provided they are motionless and expressionless in the face of the audience. In the case of *The Entertainer* the nudes concerned were expressly approved in side views concealing the pudenda.'

12 LC, file 10041/1957 on *The Entertainer*: R. R. H. Yates to 'Chief Censor', 5 Dec. 1957; Gwatkin to Yates, 9 Dec. 1957.

13 The events surrounding the transfer from stage to screen were outlined in a radio interview with Tony Richardson for 'Frankly Speaking', 12 Dec. 1962, script held in BBC Written Archives, Caversham. See also, 'Unwanted play starts a battle', *Daily Mail*, 8 Dec. 1956; 'Osborne sells for £35,000', *Sunday Dispatch*, 13 Oct. 1957; Walker, *Hollywood, England*, 56–60. For Nigel Kneale's career in television, see George W. Brandt (ed.), *British Television Drama* (Cambridge, 1981), 14, 33. Saltzman, of course, later teamed up with Albert 'Cubby' Broccoli to produce *Dr No* (1962) and several other films in the immensely popular James Bond series.

14 Tony Richardson, 'The Man Behind an Angry-Young-Man', *Films and Filming* (Feb. 1959), 9. Penelope Houston observed Richardson at work on *Look Back in Anger* for *Sight and Sound*, 28/1 (1958/9), 31–3.

15 BBFC file on *Look Back in Anger*: reader's report, 28 Aug. 1958.

16 Ibid., reader's report, 29 Aug. 1958.

17 Note also Ian Christie's apposite comment on the notion of 'quality' cinema: 'Above all, it reflects the deep-rooted British cultural bias towards some form of "realism", and the belief that cinema can only be judged by its literary pedigree', in *Arrows of Desire*, 102.

18 BBFC file on *Look Back in Anger*: Trevelyan to Frederick Gotfurt, 4 Sept. 1958.

19 Ibid., Trevelyan to Gotfurt, 19 Sept. 1958.

20 BBFC file on *The Entertainer*: reader's report, 20 Aug. 1959. Field's comment on the House of Lords refers, of course, to Lord Amwell's intervention about 'filthy films' and *Look Back in Anger*, which was made during the Committee Stage of the Obscene Publications Bill on 22 June 1959. The BFI Library, London, holds both the final shooting-script (13 Aug. 1959) and the revised release script (25 May 1960) for *The Entertainer*.

21 BBFC file on *The Entertainer*: Trevelyan to Harry Saltzman, 25 Aug. 1960.

22 Quoted in Walker, *Hollywood, England*, 75. Josh Billings judged the film's strengths and weaknesses in his usual succinct fashion: 'Low life melodrama, adapted from John Osborne's famous play, concerning inhibited fellow whose grudge against life is vented on his wife. Story thoughtful, though squalid, characterisation first class, light relief welcome, climax moving, dialogue good and detail accurate', *Kinematograph Weekly*, 14 May 1959, p. 104. Some critics put the film's failure down to an inordinate delay between the play's initial impact in 1956 and its final 'watered-down' appearance on the screen in 1959. 'What makes it seem diluted', Isabel Quigly argued, for instance, 'is that Jimmy Porter no longer turns up as a surprise.' See her review in the *Spectator*, 5 June 1959, and other reviews on the microfiche for *Look Back in Anger* (BFI Library, London).

23 BBFC file on *The Entertainer*: Trevelyan to Saltzman, 29 Dec. 1959. The BBFC's list of final exceptions was noticeably similar to the key reservations expressed by the Lord Chamberlain's office over the original play.

24 John Osborne, *Almost a Gentleman* (London, 1991), 154. Osborne puts paid there, incidentally, to the often-quoted notion that the film was held up for re-recording purposes, reportedly because of a poor-quality soundtrack caused by the intervention of 'Morecambe seagulls'. It was 'a legend', Osborne states, 'encouraged on both sides of Wardour Street, that whole sequences of dialogue were inaudible—a calumny against deserting the studios for location shooting'.

25 Josh Billings summarized his jaundiced response in *Kinematograph Weekly*, 21 July 1960, p. 9: ' "Back and front" stage, low life comedy melodrama, adapted from John Osborne's successful play. Star brilliant, support competent and atmosphere convincing, but tale squalid, direction uneven, humour and sentiment frequently forced, and dialogue coarse. Ticklish British title and star booking.' See also the reviews on *The Entertainer* microfiche (BFI Library, London).

26 Osborne's and Richardson's views are expounded in 'Notes and Topics', *Encounter* (Sept. 1960), 64–5.

5 The Outer Limits

Karel Reisz's film of *Saturday Night and Sunday Morning* was given its première on 26 October 1960. Lewis Gilbert's *Alfie* opened on 24 March 1966. Both enjoyed considerable commercial success in Britain and also, somewhat exceptionally, in America. *Saturday Night and Sunday Morning* broke box-office records for a British film on its New York run, while one American reviewer said of *Alfie* that 'its wit and its stubborn humanity make it seem a giant of a film [for] today'. They brought instant critical acclaim for their leading actors—Albert Finney in the role of Arthur Seaton, and Michael Caine as Alfie Elkins as well as plaudits galore for a host of supporting actresses including, in the former, Rachel Roberts, Shirley Anne Field, and Hylda Baker, and, in the latter, Vivien Merchant, Jane Asher, Shelley Winters, Millicent Martin, and Julia Foster. Both films dipped in the 'proletarian pond' of British life, to borrow Alexander Walker's evocative phrase, for their subject-matter and inspiration.

There, however, the similarities end. *Saturday Night and Sunday Morning* was firmly anchored in the 'new wave' of British film-making at the turn of the 1960s with its provincial setting and hermetically sealed working-class environment, and was starkly shot in black and white. *Alfie*, by contrast, was modish, done in colour, and very much a harbinger of 'swinging London' and the 'permissive society' of the late 1960s. 'Whereas Arthur Seaton stayed rooted in the industrial milieu, against whose working-class mores he covertly offended', Walker continues, 'Alfie moved on to flamboyant open conquest of the "birds", a recognisable pretender to middle-class status with his Services badge on the breast pocket (the perfect notation mark of male solidarity allied to spivvish vanity). For Alfie, the only real life is sex life: only then can he kid himself he is living.'[1] In one key respect, moreover, the two films were vastly different. Alan Sillitoe's screenplay was denied his intended reference to a successful abortion scene, although this is present in the original 1958 novel. Bill Naughton's screen adaptation of his play—first presented on radio in 1962, on stage in 1963, and as novel in 1966—was permitted to retain its abortion scene and depict a successful abortion at that. The rigorous censorship code which appeared so obdurate and intransigent towards Sillitoe's project at the outset of the 1960s proved altogether more malleable as the decade wore on and turned out to be distinctly conducive to Naughton's purpose. Why, though, was Naughton seemingly privileged and accommodated in a way Sillitoe plainly was not? What explained this new-found permissive attitude? Was it just, as some commentators would have it, that British cinema inevitably reflected the changing attitudes and circumstances of the day? As the times changed, so the argument goes, the censors were compelled to fall in line and adapt accordingly.

Thus, *Alfie* was allowed its controversial theme precisely because, as Arthur Marwick notes, it highlighted the 'attendant horror and danger' of seeking a back-street abortion—it 'brought the situation out well enough'— and was therefore representative of a rising tide of public opinion in favour of legislative amendment on this and other fronts. Certainly, there were strong opinions on the matter and, indeed, a measure of success was subsequently achieved in reformist legislation. If proof were needed, Marwick continues, one has only to look at 1967, which was 'something of an *annus mirabilis* as far as liberal legislation in the sphere of sexual mores was concerned' since it witnessed the passing of three notable acts: the Abortion Act, the National Health Service (Family Planning) Act, and the Sexual Offences Act. If proof were needed of a consequent loosening of the censor's bonds, the British films usually cited in addition to *Alfie* are *Up the Junction* (1967), which saw the BBFC finally ending its long-upheld ban on use of the word 'bugger', or *If. . .* (1968), with its full-frontal view of female nudity. In addition, in 1968 the Theatres Act abolished the Lord Chamberlain's powers of censorship.[2]

For all that, however, the approval of *Alfie* was nowhere near as clear-cut a matter as first appears and by no means a watertight example to cite as evidence of greater liberalization in censorship. It endured exactly the same censorship strictures as *Saturday Night and Sunday Morning* had done, and comparison of the two films reveals that, while some things were permitted anew in the 'swinging sixties', British cinema was still essentially bounded and circumscribed in what it could show.

Alan Sillitoe complained long and hard about the censorship suffered by *Saturday Night and Sunday Morning* at the hands of the BBFC. Writing in the pages of the *New Left Review* in the same month, July 1960, that the completed film went before the film censors for final review and award of an appropriate certificate, he stated: 'It seems to me that censorship in the British film industry is in its own way as hidebound as that of Soviet Russia.' Looking back on the experience some twenty years later, he was convinced the pre-production amendments imposed on his script had been unduly 'harsh', 'unnecessary', and had 'distorted the tenor of the film': 'The film script of *Saturday Night and Sunday Morning* made many journeys to and from the British Board of Film Censors (no British hypocrisy about the name) before it was finally passed as fit to be made.' He had good reason to complain. Though seen initially as just another product of 'the new school of Young Writers Speaking for the People', he was soon judged to be a purveyor of nothing less than 'blatant and very trying Communist propaganda'.[3]

A scenario treatment of *Saturday Night and Sunday Morning* was first sent by Woodfall Productions to the BBFC in November 1959. In this, Sillitoe adhered quite faithfully to his original novel, though there was an inevitable compression in the number of scenes and the number of characters represented. It retained, in particular, reference to an abortion scene in which the married Brenda successfully terminates the unwanted pregnancy resulting from a love affair with her husband's workmate, Arthur Seaton. The scenario obviously did not meet with the approval of the BBFC's readers, and its potentially controversial aspects were seized upon right at the outset. Sex and violence figured prominently, of course, but the matters of 'language' and abortion were of paramount importance. One of the readers, Audrey Field, commented in a report of 20 November 1959:

I see from the accompanying compliments slip that this is the company in which John Osborne is involved; we might almost have known it from the language of the script. I imagine that the company will fully expect to have an 'X', and I fully expect that they are right. Quite apart from anything else, the language would not do for an 'A'. Neither would the love scenes, to say nothing of the discussion of abortion and the fact that the abortion is actually carried out (though not seen). As to the quality of the story, the hero is an immoral fellow who would doubtless end up in jail in real life, but I enjoyed him a lot more than the people in *Look Back in Anger* and *A Taste of Honey* (other products of the new school of Young Writers Speaking for the People), because I could believe in him, and even got to like him towards the end, when he began dimly to perceive that it was time he developed a sense of responsibility. I think most of what happens is tolerable for 'X', *but I have strong misgivings about the slap-happy and successful termination of pregnancy*, which seems to be very dangerous stuff for our younger X-cert. customers and moreover is not necessary for the story.

The reader proceeded to elaborate on precisely those incidents and lines of dialogue which gave rise to concern. A rich array of specific words is extracted to exemplify fears, for instance, over the 'language' used throughout. All are found in abundance in Sillitoe's original novel, it must be said, but then 'language', as the reader noted, 'seems to be what this school . . . really cares about and much must be conceded for the "X" category, in the case of a story which is often only "A" '. Thus, it was argued: 'I really don't think we can have "bogger", "Christ" or "sod". They ought to make do with the numerous "bleddys", "bloodies", "bleedings" and "bastards" which also adorn the script.' The remarks on that score came to a temporary halt with the statement:

I know that 'bugger' is freely used in such places as the public bars of provincial pubs, but I doubt whether the average working man uses it much in his own home in front of his wife, and that ought to be more the standard for us to adopt, even in films obviously designed for the factory worker section of society. (A great many young married men choose the films *they* want to see; their wives come with them and often don't enjoy the language, or the violence, at all.)

Subsequently, the doubtful love scenes were highlighted for further attention with comments like: 'They want love making of a *Room at the Top* directness, and should be allowed to have it, but this seems to go a bit too far.' References to the abortion were picked out, in particular: 'As I have said, I think this element dangerous stuff.' And, among other things, it was suggested that caution should be observed in the depiction of violence and 'fighting generally' since 'it will be troublesome if shot as scripted'. Problems relating to language came into the reckoning once again when the reader quoted the intended line 'I'd been knocking on wi' a married woman' then added plaintively: 'I don't know how obscene this phrase is.' Finally, it was recommended that the scenario be subjected to further scrutiny since 'much of the dialogue is of the kind which some of us find more offensive than others, and it is a pity to have to cut things which were in the script.' In the event a second reader, Frank Crofts, concluded: 'This is fundamentally an "A" story which gets its "X"-ness from being too outspoken about abortion, too revealing in love scenes and too foul-mouthed.' That examiner also compiled a list of offensive words and cited the violence as a potentially worrying factor.[4]

Both script-readers agreed, then, on the actual and likely areas of concern in the treatment presented for their consideration. And John Trevelyan proceeded to summarize their findings, and add a few more of his own, in the letter he wrote to Harry Saltzman, the film's co-producer at Woodfall

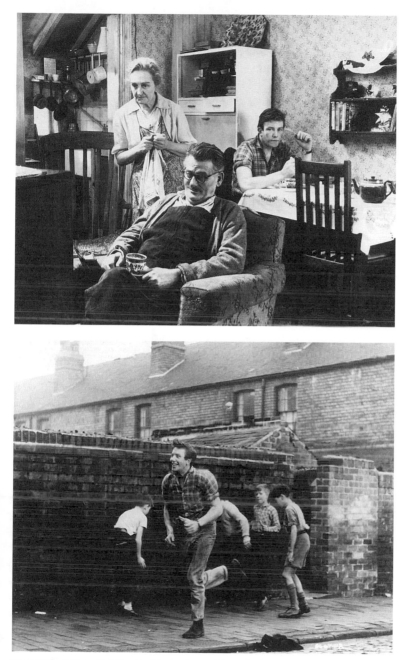

23 and 24. 'I know that "bugger" is freely used in such places as the public bars of provincial pubs, but I doubt whether the average working man uses it much in his own home in front of his wife, and that ought to be the standard for us to adopt, even in films obviously designed for the factory worker section of society.' (*Saturday Night and Sunday Morning*)

Productions, on 24 November 1959. With regard to language, especially, he asked Saltzman to note:

This script is peppered with 'language' throughout, and while for the 'X' category we would, I think, accept a reasonable number of words like 'bloody', 'bleddy', 'bleeding' and 'bastard', we would not accept 'Christ', since many perfectly reasonable people take offence at this: we would particularly dislike 'Christ Almighty' and 'Christ-all-bleeding-mighty'. Furthermore, we simply cannot accept the word 'bogger'. We have not yet accepted the use of the word 'bugger' in films and the substitution of the letter 'o' for the letter 'u' makes no significant difference: on the soundtrack the word will certainly sound like 'bugger'. I appreciate that words of this kind are normal in the speech of the type of people that the film is about but I have always found, strange though it may seem, that these are the very people who most object to this kind of thing on the screen. I hope, therefore, that this script will be revised and these words omitted.

Clearly, Sillitoe's attempt to capture the sound of the Nottinghamshire pronunciation of the word 'bugger'—a device he employed consistently throughout the novel—was lost on the censors and counted for nothing. A 'bogger' was a 'bugger' for all that, and was not allowed. This one word proved the occasion for extraordinary concern among censorship ranks, thereafter, as we shall see.

The rest of Trevelyan's letter went on to chart the censors' remaining misgivings about Sillitoe's script. 'A reasonable bed scene' would be permitted but 'it should not go too far': 'I appreciate that this relationship is entirely physical but there are limits to what we will accept.' An explanation had obviously been forthcoming to the unenlightened reader over the meaning of the phrase 'knocking on', and it was now cited as being 'a bit crude'. 'The fight should not be too brutal', and, of course, doubts were expressed about the abortion scenes:

This shows a rather casual attitude to abortion and suggests to the young that if they get into difficulties all they need is to find a kind-hearted older woman who has had a lot of children. Provided that it is not too obtrusive it would probably be acceptable, but I must ask you to bear in mind that this film is likely to be seen by a considerable number of young people of 16 to 20 years of age, and to recognise that social responsibility is called for.

In his concluding paragraph, Trevelyan explained that he had gone into a fair amount of detail in making his points because 'this is the kind of film which might well give trouble on points of detail when completed'. He reiterated that the major worries were, first, the language, and, second, the abortion, and his parting words were: 'If you can tone both of these down, there should be little other trouble.'[5]

The final draft of the shooting script, which Harry Saltzman sent for the BBFC's consideration on 26 January 1960, exercised a considerable amount of 'social responsibility'. The worrying elements were toned down all right. They were, quite simply, changed. The infamous 'bogger' gave way to the innocuous 'beggar', and the abortion turned out to be ineffective.[6] Audrey Field, the reader who had most to say on the initial scenario, now declared, with evident relief, in a report of 28 January 1960:

They have not done all we asked, but they have done what we wanted most. They have taken out 'bogger' altogether putting 'beggar' in its place, but far less frequently. They have removed all 'Christs'. They have also drastically modified the abortion element: we are told that Ada has given Brenda a very hot bath and much gin and it has not worked; later she means to go to a doctor, but decides against it and resolves to have the child after all; her husband later tells Arthur that she is 'all right', but we are left to assume that the pregnancy had been terminated without any outside interference. I am very glad that this change has been made; and their co-operation in this direction has made one hope that we can be reasonably lenient with the film as a whole (which is still a firm 'X', by reason of some very passionate physical love scenes and the several discussions of abortion).

The day was not completely won, however, and there were certain obstacles yet to be overcome. The love scenes still needed 'care', for instance, and the reader worried about lines like 'What a time we had last night', and 'Get down in bed'. Language remained a problem when there was dialogue such as 'Make room for a rabbit arse, Jack', and 'A pellet got her right on the arse'. 'Daft sod' was queried. The question was posed whether 'God all bleeding mighty' was really much better than 'Christ-all-bleeding-mighty'. And it was noted that the phrase 'I'd been knocking on wi' a married woman' was still included though this time the newly enlightened reader commented: 'I don't know if it really matters.' It was felt, however, that 'the vicious onslaught by the soldiers on Arthur may give trouble even for an "X", the repeated kicks seem to be excessive'. And last, but by no means least, there were fears about the talk of 'a hot bath and gin'. 'I believe the secretary much objects to this', Field added, 'but I don't mind, as it fails.'[7]

On 2 February 1960 Trevelyan wrote one last letter to Saltzman to tell him the outcome of the BBFC's latest deliberations. To begin with the Board expressed 'appreciation' at the way in which its comments had been taken into account, and then the points of reservation, along with further recommendations, were listed. There were fewer of them this time, of course, and they were by no means all the ones which the reader

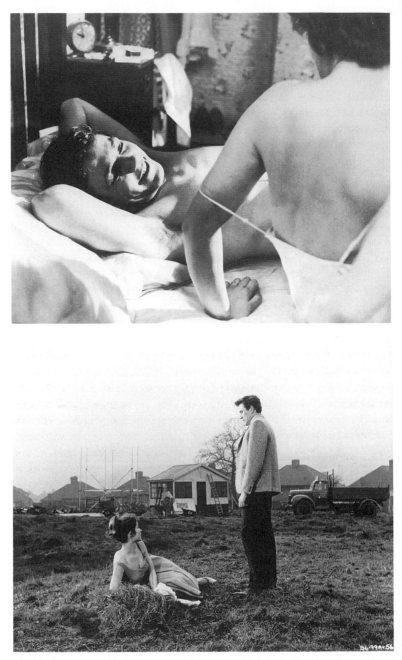

25 and 26. 'A reasonable bed scene will be permitted but it should not go too far. I appreciate that this relationship is entirely physical but there are limits to what we will accept.' (*Saturday Night and Sunday Morning*)

had outlined. Clearly, some degree of toleration was being exercised by the BBFC in view of the notable advances that had been made, and the process of negotiation continued. 'The love scenes can be passionate but should not go too far', and it was suggested that the director ought still to use 'discretion' in shooting them. The line 'Get down in bed' was thought to be 'rather direct'. The word 'sod' should be altered since it was 'a word we are trying to keep out of films', and 'God-all-bleeding-mighty' was better though 'we still do not like it'. Care should be taken over the fight scenes to avoid 'excessive brutality'. And, once again, it was hoped that the phrase 'knocking on wi' a married woman' might be changed. Indeed, Trevelyan even went so far as to suggest an alternative and wondered whether 'mucking about wi' a married woman' might not be equally good.[8]

To the last, the production company sought to reciprocate and to meet the BBFC's needs and requirements. The film went into production with a script which proved to be a characteristic mixture of compromise, outright acceptance of the BBFC's requests, and a modest amount of steadfastness. In one respect—the case of the line 'God-all-bleeding-mighty'—the script remained unchanged. But the line 'Get down in bed' was dropped altogether, the word 'sod' was changed to 'nit', and the line 'knocking on wi' a married woman' was altered to 'knocking around wi' a married woman'. The film was completed and presented to the BBFC for a certificate on 20 July 1960. The censors were obviously pleased with the changes and the final depiction of the love scenes and violence. The film was awarded an 'X' certificate.

If the BBFC was satisfied with the outcome, the trade press was overjoyed. *Kinematograph Weekly* summarized the film's prospects in its usual pithy fashion:

Down-to-earth romantic melodrama, based on Alan Sillitoe's bestseller, concerning a young Midland man who puts women and booze before his job, but finally gets permanently tied to a skirt. Story refreshingly free from moralising, acting brilliant, treatment masterly, sentiment warm, sex asides frank, dialogue fruity, and atmosphere and detail flawless.

Saturday Night and Sunday Morning, it declared, was 'Outstanding adult entertainment and an infallible box office proposition'. In the event, the distributors proved initially hostile—doubtless feeling the success which had greeted *Room at the Top* was exceptional and could not be repeated. It was only with the unexpected failure and withdrawal of a film from the Warner Theatre, Leicester Square, that a gap suddenly appeared for

Saturday Night and Sunday Morning, which opened there on 26 October 1960. It did exceptional business on its first week's run and soon few people in the film industry remained to be convinced it would prove a box-office winner. It had cost a little over £100,000 to produce, yet after just three weeks' release it had grossed more than that on the London circuit cinemas alone.[9]

However, as with *Room at the Top*, some people remained to be convinced that *Saturday Night and Sunday Morning* should have been allowed in the form finally permitted by the BBFC. On the previous occasion, it had been the Australian Board of Censorship which took offence and pressed Trevelyan hard on the matter. This time, his problems were closer to home and emanated from Warwickshire County Council, one of Britain's most powerful local authorities and, historically, one of the most intransigent over film censorship. Despite the award of the BBFC's 'X' certificate, Warwickshire required that further cuts be made before it could be exhibited throughout the county. The Cinematograph and Stage Plays Licensing Committee saw the film twice and objected to 'the whole of the bedroom scene, in which Arthur Seaton is seen in bed with Brenda, and that part of the scene at Doreen's house in which Arthur Seaton is seen on the floor with Doreen'. The distributors refused to cut the offending scenes and the film was subsequently banned, though it was shown still in Birmingham, which enjoyed its own city licensing powers, and where it played to packed audiences. Once more, predictably, Trevelyan grasped the opportunity the situation offered both to answer criticisms of the BBFC and to explain his thoughts on the Board's role:

I am sorry that you have had so much press criticism over your Committee's decision about the film *Saturday Night and Sunday Morning*. All censorship is a matter of opinion and you and your Committee have a clear right to differ from us on any matter of opinion.

The particular issue does not cause me concern, but I am somewhat concerned about one thing in a recent article in the *Birmingham Mail*. In this article a journalist . . . reports you as having said that basically you were not in favour of local authority censorship and that you suggest that the British Board of Film Censors should be replaced by another national body, without any strings attached to the cinema industry, and capable of not only putting films into categories but of banning them. This gives the impression that this Board is one that has strings attached to the cinema industry. It is true that it was set up by the industry in 1912, but the industry has always had the sense to realise that it would not command public confidence unless it was an independent body, and I can with sincerity claim that there are no such strings. We avoid the possibility of pressure being brought through finance by simply charging fees for every job we do. This avoids any question of subsidy or grant. This Board is one of the rare examples of a completely independent body. It is a curious arrangement—and rather typically British in some ways—but on the whole it works fairly well.[10]

However well the system worked in the main for Trevelyan over *Saturday Night and Sunday Morning*, it was sorely tested yet again with the arrival of Sillitoe's next script, this time a screen adaptation of the title story from his 1959 collection, *The Loneliness of the Long Distance Runner*. Though the collection won the Hawthornden Prize in 1960 for the best imaginative writing by an author under 40, Sillitoe was increasingly viewed by some BBFC examiners as a 'socially irresponsible' writer. His characterization of the anarchic, anti-authoritarian Borstal boy, Colin Smith, who deliberately throws the race he can easily win, was judged little more than the portrayal of 'a good hero of the British Soviet, in fact' and 'true party line stuff'. And, unsurprisingly, language proved a key stumbling-block in Sillitoe's efforts to transpose his story for the cinema. Audrey Field, for example, commented in her report of 1 January 1962:

I am very much disappointed in this script. I liked *Saturday Night* and, despite the hero's trying little ways, I liked him, because I felt he had the makings of becoming a sensible human being who would take people as he found them and not go on for ever taking refuge in a lot of claptrap like 'All Army officers and policemen are bad and all workers are good'. But this story is blatant and very trying Communist propaganda, and particularly worrying for us because the hero is a thief and yet is held up to the admiration of silly young thugs. If the leading citizens of Nottingham didn't like *Saturday Night* because they thought the hero was not a good representative of that city, I don't know what they will say about this epic. But basically I think we must leave this script alone (for 'X', which it must be because of the language quite apart from the moral tone) and hope that the common sense of the cinema-going public will be equal to seeing some flaws in logic. When I say that 'basically it may have to be left alone' I am not, of course, referring to the language, which must be cleaned up in accordance with our well-known rules in dealing with 'X' films.[11]

The language singled out for special attention, needless to say, included the now notorious 'bogger', as well as two newly introduced expressions which were plainly unknown to the examiner—'clapped out' ('an unsuitable connotation I suppose?') and 'caltfart' ('I view it with suspicion'). It was the question of language, moreover, which exercised Trevelyan most when writing subsequently to Woodfall Productions to express his reservations over the script. It was mixed, on this occasion, with genuine concern at the damage likely to be done to the film's commercial

27. 'This story is blatant and very trying Communist propaganda, and particularly worrying for us because the hero is a thief and yet held up to the admiration of silly young thugs.' (*The Loneliness of the Long Distance Runner*)

prospects in the potentially lucrative overseas market. But it was crucial, none the less:

The main thing that worries us is that, like Alan Sillitoe's previous script for *Saturday Night and Sunday Morning*, there is an excess of what is sometimes called 'language'. Once again he produces the word 'bogger'. This word we still find unacceptable. There are two other expletives which we also find unacceptable: these are 'Christ' (or 'for Christ's sake') and 'sod'. There are also two other expressions which we must put into the same category: these are 'clapped out' and 'caltfart'. Apart from these the word 'bloody' or 'bleedy' is used extensively— actually 32 times according to the reader whom I asked to count them. 'Bastard' is used 11 times. 'Bleeder' and 'bleeding' are used on a few occasions, but we would not worry about these. I appreciate that Alan Sillitoe wants the dialogue to be the natural speech of the kind of people shown in this film, but I would suggest that there should be some reduction nevertheless.

The question of language is likely to affect the category in which the film is placed. If there were too much 'language' used we would have to give the film an 'X' certificate. I appreciate that the film is being made essentially for the British market, but I imagine that the export market in English speaking countries is not unimportant, and I know that in a good many English speaking countries language of this kind is automatically removed regardless of its effect on the film. However, this is your problem and not mine. We are prepared to accept a reasonable degree of 'language' but, as I have already pointed out, there are certain words and phrases that are still unacceptable to us.[12]

Sillitoe, it seems, simply could not win as far as the film censors were concerned. *The Loneliness of the Long Distance Runner*, like *Saturday Night and Sunday Morning* before it, was granted an 'X' certificate at the last, on 3 August 1962. Where, previously, he had offended because of both his chosen theme and language, here, though the theme was deemed less troublesome—Trevelyan, for his part, believed it 'presents no important censorship problems'—language was still the occasion for considerable concern, and largely dictated the certificate the film would receive. While the BBFC readily conceded that Sillitoe's use of the vernacular was 'naturalist' in intent, it was also considered highly 'dubious' and not what was expected in British films. 'Quality' cinema, in short, should not include too much by way of everyday, ordinary parlance and some words— 'bogger' especially—were definitely prohibited.

But Sillitoe's saga over 'bogger' did not end there. Nor, indeed were his 'censorship problems' confined solely to adaptations of his work for the screen. What concerned the BBFC also, inevitably, worried the Lord Chamberlain's office. This much was evident when they were presented with the stage play of *Saturday Night and Sunday Morning* for consideration. Following the success of both the novel and the film (and seeking doubtless to capitalize on Sillitoe's increased prominence and high profile as a writer), the Nottingham Playhouse sought to transpose *Saturday Night and Sunday Morning* to the stage in 1964. Though not adapted in this instance by the author himself, the stage play obviously drew heavily for inspiration on Sillitoe's work. David Brett was engaged for the task and Frank Dunlop was director. Brett, in fact, reinserted characters from the novel which had been omitted in the film—noticeably, Brenda's sister, Winnie, with whom Arthur Seaton also enjoys an affair. In other respects, however, it differed somewhat from Sillitoe's original purpose, not least in its treatment of the abortion scene, where Brett seemingly sought to accommodate the difficulties which had confronted Sillitoe's film script. The Lord Chamberlain's playreader summarized Brett's script in a report of 14 March 1964:

The play of the film of the book. It is set in Nottingham. Arthur and Jack are workmates. Jack is married, Arthur is not and—unknown to Jack—whenever possible Arthur goes to bed with his wife, Brenda. The play opens with Jack

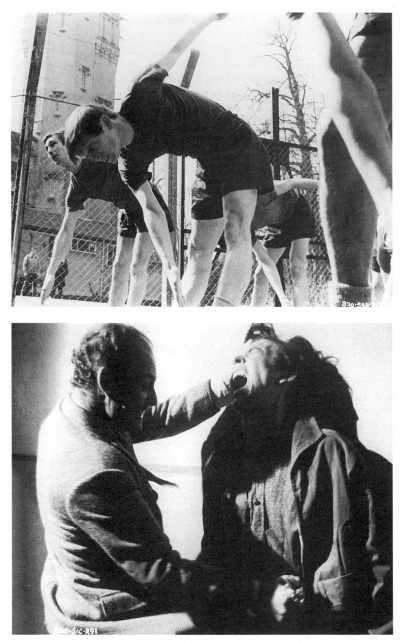

28 and 29. 'I am sure that "screws" do kick prisoners from time to time, but this kind of thing does suggest to young people who may find themselves in Borstal that this is normal treatment, and it may cause some concern to their parents.' (*The Loneliness of the Long Distance Runner*)

expected back from the races at Lincoln and with Arthur and Brenda just out of bed.

Arthur likes to feel he can do whatever he wants to do, so when Brenda introduces him to her sister Winnie—as easy virtued as Brenda is—it isn't long before he has Winnie in bed also. In the meantime, Brenda becomes pregnant by Arthur so an abortion becomes necessary. But since this is a comedy, it is the most light-hearted offstage abortion ever likely to be seen in the theatre. (Or, since it is offstage, ever likely *not* to be seen.)

By now, Arthur's promiscuity is catching up with him, for Winnie's husband has found out about Arthur bedding down with his wife, and he and some pals beat Arthur up. And when Brenda learns that she has been sharing him with her sister, she turns on him also. He begins to learn that a bachelor's lot is not altogether a happy one.

He starts going out with another girl—this time a single one, Doreen. When he discovers that she isn't eager to pop into bed with him, he becomes really interested in her, and the play ends with marriage in the offing. Arthur has had that Saturday night feeling for a long time. Now, at last, it is Sunday morning.

The long list of proposed cuts or amendments which followed would not have surprised Sillitoe one jot. By far the most frequently required alteration is to the language employed throughout. While 'daft gett', 'jumped up getts', 'ponce', and 'pox etten' would be permitted, the Lord Chamberlain simply could not condone the use of 'Christ's sake', 'Jesus', 'sod', or any of the numerous permutations of the word 'bogger' such as 'rotten bogger', 'I'll be boggered', 'bogger you', 'you smug bogger', 'knowing bogger', and you sly bogger. The Assistant Comptroller informed Nottingham Playhouse of the decision on 20 March 1964 and required that the offending words be altered or omitted altogether.[13]

Since the play's première was set for 14 April and Frank Dunlop's rehearsals with the company were in full swing, Nottingham Playhouse responsed immediately with suggested revisions. These included 'Lord's sake' (for 'Christ's sake'), 'bastard' (for 'sod') and 'hell' (for 'Jesus'). As regards 'bogger', however, they would not be deterred. Here, they resorted to a shrewd mix of 'case' law and 'common' law. Though their call upon the former was decidedly shaky, if not perhaps somewhat disingenuous—they claimed, quite simply, the word could be found in the film—their citing of the latter was based on slightly firmer ground. Nottingham Playhouse sought, in short, to enlighten the Lord Chamberlain on the word's origins and common usage:

'Bogger'. The word is widely used in Nottingham by all classes of persons in all situations. It has no indecent connotation and it ceases to be anything more than a mild swear word. It is sometimes used as a form of endearment. It is possible that this word has a completely different origin to the indecent 'bugger'. Since 'bogger' was used in the film derived from the same novel, we would like to make strong representations to keep it in this script. Should you feel unable to do this, perhaps you would consider granting us a special licence to use the word in our theatre alone. Should the play be performed in any other town, where the word might have an indecent connotation, another word might be substituted.[14]

Despite the neat compromise offered at the last, the Lord Chamberlain was not moved. Nor was he persuaded by claims that 'bogger' was used in the film of the same name. Following the policy of 'keeping in step' with the film censors' line, the BBFC was consulted. A quick check with Trevelyan's office revealed it had not been passed. All variations on 'bogger' were still banned. When Nottingham Playhouse subsequently suggested as a final solution that 'bogger' be replaced throughout by 'beggar', the Lord Chamberlain readily assented and a licence was granted for the play's presentation. This is what had already occurred in the film version of Sillitoe's novel, of course. Where the BBFC had set the course, the Lord Chamberlain's office was only too happy to fall in line.[15]

Much the same happened over other controversial matters. The censorship bodies for theatre and cinema invariably sought to 'keep in step'. When it came to the depiction of abortion, however, it was the BBFC's turn to stay abreast. What Alan Sillitoe had learned from extensive dealings with the BBFC over *Saturday Night and Sunday Morning*, moreover, Bill Naughton soon discovered from his subsequent experiences with the theatre censors over *Alfie*. Contentious issues required careful and protracted negotiation if concessions were to be won at all. And even then there was no guarantee of success.

Bill Naughton's stage play of *Alfie* was based on his radio play, *Alfie Elkins and his Little Life*, first presented on the BBC's Third Programme from 9.10 p.m. to 10.25 p.m. on 7 January 1962 in a production by Douglas Cleverdon. The radio play was much shorter than the later stage version, and the abortion scene, albeit depicting a successful termination, was also briefly dealt with and discreetly placed towards the end of the drama. None the less, audience research revealed that some listeners found it 'difficult to stomach' and there were criticisms from a minority of the sample that the programme was 'really too sordid for words'. 'Time was', one listener complained, 'when the BBC would not have considered broadcasting anything so revolting.' Another maintained it was 'not so much kitchen sink as kitchen garbage tin', while a schoolmaster who had enjoyed previous Bill Naughton plays wrote that 'after the first half-hour it became

30. Colin Smith (*Tom Courtenay*). 'A good hero of the British Soviet . . . It is true party line stuff. What the objection is to an honest-to-goodness prize openly and honestly competed for and judged, I can never see myself.' (*The Loneliness of the Long Distance Runner*)

progressively more nauseating; only curiosity as to whether it could get any worse kept me listening after the revolting abortion scene'. 'We know Mr. Naughton's gift for portraying working-class life', he concluded. 'I regret he should have become so tasteless — what happened to his sense of humour?'

But most listeners claimed to have enjoyed the broadcast, thereby producing 'an appreciation index of 73, well above the current average (63) for Third Programme features'. And audience reaction among the sample listening panel who heard all or most of the play was decidedly favourable:

A large majority of the sample had a high opinion of the programme and had evidently been completely absorbed, even fascinated; it was a memorable piece, some said, which still haunted them. Bill Naughton who continued to be 'a miraculous observer' had produced a brilliant and 'painfully acute' portrait of Alfie, a Cockney character almost impervious to all interests save hard cash and women. It seemed, many listeners said, completely authentic, a moving, spell-binding, disturbing portrayal of an immature man to whom cold self-interest had become the one value he recognised but in whom still survived (bewildering to himself) better impulses which tried to struggle to the surface. Much of what Alfie Elkins said and did was 'appalling', but yet they could not wholly dislike him, listeners sometimes said; his candour and lack of hypocrisy were redeeming features. This 'pithy analysis' was commended as unsentimental ('I liked the unemo-tional almost documentary slant'); neither did the author indulge in tedious 'moralising'. 'Richly comic' in places, the programme trod the dividing line be-tween comedy and sordid tragedy with complete assurance. It was colourful throughout and the dialogue delighted many listeners by its realism and authen-ticity ('astonishingly accurate').

Criticisms of any aspect of the production were few indeed. The vivid way in which Alfie and his life had been communicated to the listener was often warmly praised and Bill Owen was frequently spoken of in the highest terms . . .

Given the undoubted popularity the play had enjoyed, it was little wonder the BBC chose to repeat the broadcast. It was repeated twice on the Third Programme during 1962, in fact, at 6.30 p.m. on 3 February and at 8 p.m. on 11 September. On 16 September it was reviewed by 'The Critics' including Stephen Potter, Dilys Powell, and Edward Lucie-Smith, where once again it was favourably received and highly praised. It was agreed the play 'did have a very strong moral basis' though reservations were expressed about the abortion scene which some found 'excessive'.[16]

Clearly Bill Naughton must have heard enough to convince him the play was well worth expanding and adapting for full stage presentation, which he duly did. Since he was already contracted to the Mermaid Theatre for a production in March 1963 of his play *All in Good Time*, it made sense to add another to Bernard Miles's programme as part of a short Naughton season. With a first night planned for 19 June 1963, the script of Naughton's play *Alfie* was sent for licence to the Lord Chamberlain's office. Its origins as a radio play were evident in some of the dramatic techniques contem-plated for the stage. Moreover, the import of the abortion scene, now much elaborated, could not be missed. The playreader commented on 20 January 1963:

This is the study of the sexual adventures of a Cockney wide boy, Alfie Elkins. Alfie himself is the narrator and fairly long sections of the play are narrative soliloquies as Alfie tells his story to the audience. According to him, his sex life is one long struggle against his better nature, against his yearnings for domesticity— but habit dies hard and the end of the play sees him without a woman once again but looking forward to the next one.

The play is well in the fashionable rut of sordid realism—the more sordid the better—and includes an abortion on stage (though behind a screen) complete with groans and cries of pain which I cannot think can be allowed and to which I have drawn attention in the list of possible deletions and alterations below . . . This is the abortion scene, involving Lily, Alfie and the abortionist. The abortion takes place on stage, behind a screen, and little is left to the imagination. There is even a description of the foetus and Alfie's disposal of it by flushing it down the lavatory. Just how much, if any, of this scene is to be allowed I leave to you . . . It is perhaps worth mentioning that this play is by the same author as *All in Good Time* which deals with male impotence and which I returned to you a day or so ago. It seems that *Alfie* is to follow the play at the Mermaid. Is there to be a third, forming a sort of trilogy of the sex life of the mole?[17]

'Cut. Cut it all', was the Assistant Comptroller's response to the reader's query as to how much of the abortion scene might be allowed. Lt.-Col. Eric Penn was also unhappy with the play generally, and said as much in a memorandum to the Lord Chamberlain: '*Alfie* is a dull and horrid play.' 'Its only merits are the Cockney language of the script', he continued, 'and possibly the representation of life in the East End.' 'Because of the latter', he was willing to concede that 'many questionable bits of language have been let go in our recommendations.' But his unease was evident all the same and even concessions over language were grudgingly given: 'If this is really considered entertainment in 1963, perhaps it should be allowed; if so it will be interesting to see the reaction.' The abortion scene, what's more, simply could not be allowed. The Lord Chamberlain agreed and required that it be 'altered or omitted altogether'.[18]

Since they were plainly determined not to be beaten in the matter of the abortion scene, if nothing else, the Mermaid Theatre marshalled its arguments and forces accordingly. 'In view of the fact that this play was presented on the Third Programme and received magnificent press', Bernard Miles wrote in reply, 'may I bring the author and Mr Ide [the theatre administrator] along to discuss the matter in person?' So, indeed, he did. Plainly, the Lord Chamberlain's men were open to discussion, at least. But while they proved malleable on some matters, they were intransigent on others and discussions were not wholly to their visitors' liking:

At their request, Bernard Miles and Bill Naughton were interviewed by Col. Penn and Mr Hill [assistant secretary]. The cuts in this piece were agreed by them without question, except for the abortion scene, which is indeed a climacteric in Alfie's life. Our opposition to this scene was influenced by the fact that a scene revolving around the preparations for and after effects of an abortion were all in *I Am a Camera* in 1954. Mild though these were they did give offence.

It was explained to the visitors that it was accepted by the Lord Chamberlain that the play was a moral rather than an immoral one, and that it was realised that the basic facts of life were nowadays discussed freely in any company; but that in our opinion some of the clinical and practical detail in the play was of such a disgusting nature in the literal sense of the word that it was felt that to sanction it would give a precedent for action and properties which could end by blunting the sensibilities of and indeed brutalising the audience. Our viewpoint was accepted at least as a tenable one and Mr Miles read through the abortion scene which was reviewed from that aspect . . .

If the read-through which followed extracted one notable concession it also highlighted a host of potential problems. The abortion scene might just be allowed, but 'the operation ought to be conducted off stage' thereby also necessitating the removal of large amounts of vital dialogue and associated business. There should be no 'jingle of instruments' nor talk of 'scrubbing away' on the abortionist's part; and no 'cries', 'groans', 'sudden pain and winces' from Lily. 'Remember, the bed is to be off stage', it was stated, and the abortionist should 'leave the stage instead of going behind the screen'. Finally, and equally important, most references to disposal of the aborted foetus should be deleted.

Though Bernard Miles and Bill Naughton expressed a willingness to operate within these constraints and to produce a rewritten abortion scene which incorporated the new proposals, they understandably wanted some 'assurance' they would not be 'wasting their time'. They sought, in short, advance approval for their efforts since that would provide 'sufficient basis upon which to undertake the additional work'. It was a shrewd move but never likely to win the day. Inevitably, no such assurance was forthcoming. Still, the examiners were more hopeful of a successful outcome to everybody's endeavours:

It is felt that the scene even when rewritten will be a strong one and will inevitably give offence particularly to some ladies. Nevertheless the play is a straightforward depiction of what is unfortunately a real type, the facts of the play tend to social not anti-social ends, and the acceptance by most people these days of any subject for discussion—VD, homosexuality, etc.—make the scene in our opinion acceptable if not eminently desirable.[19]

In the final analysis, of course, the key decision on revisions to the script rested with the Lord Chamberlain. Moreover, the Lord Chamberlain had just changed. When *Alfie* first landed on the playreader's desk, Lord Scarbrough had been in charge. Now it was Lord Cobbold. But he was no more inclined to give advance approval than his predecessor had been. Once he had been apprised of the situation by his Assistant Comptroller, Cobbold endorsed everything the Mermaid representatives had been told:

I have read this play and attached papers and also the relevant sections of *I Am a Camera*. The latter seem to be innocuous and not to set much of a precedent for this scene. I agree that the modifications of the abortion scene proposed at your meeting with Mr Miles and the author make it a lot less objectionable: in particular I am sure that all action relating to the abortion must take place off stage. But my present feeling is that the scene, even if rewritten on the lines of the interview with Mr Miles, would still be likely to give offence to a lot of people.

I cannot give a definite decision without seeing a rewrite. Nor can I give any commitment not to ask for further alteration. If Mr Miles and the author think it worthwhile to have another shot at it on this understanding, I shall of course be very willing to look at it.[20]

'The Lord Chamberlain is still disturbed about the possible effects of this [abortion] scene', Bernard Miles was told emphatically, and 'feels very dubious about the whole of it'. 'Even with the modifications which we agreed provisionally between us', it was reiterated, 'he is still not prepared to give an unqualified assurance that the scene will be allowed.'[21]

The ball, quite simply, was back in Miles's and Naughton's court. A new script was produced on 3 May 1963. It was, they promised, 'entirely revised and rewritten'. In truth, it was nothing of the sort. If their reaction was predictable as far as the abortion scene was concerned, which was suitably toned down to meet the examiners' needs, they now proved less than willing to accommodate the other demands made of them. Hoping, perhaps, that arguments over the abortion scene had taken the new Lord Chamberlain's mind off everything else required by the readers, Naughton had quietly proceeded to forget about them. If one battle had been lost, the war was still engaged. But some examiners were ever alert. the reader of the rewritten script commented on 20 May:

The play has been considerably revised though the general outline of the plot remains unchanged. I have studied the correspondence and memoranda relating to the play and although a lot has been done to tone down the abortion scene, with the operation itself taking place off-stage, some objectionable matter remains. I notice also that no notice has been taken of the other cuts or amendments, outside the abortion scene, called for in your letter of 25 January.[22]

Although the Assistant Comptroller also admitted that the new edition had been 'considerably tidied up from the original', not least regarding the abortion, he too felt prompted to remind the Mermaid of what had previously been required by way of exceptions generally. For good measure, he added a list of exceptions to material which appeared for the first time in the revised script. Once everything had been dealt with, and not before, the play would be granted a licence. A long, carefully detailed reply from the Mermaid on 30 May with further revisions finally put paid to all the Lord Chamberlain's objections, and *Alfie* was given a licence on 5 June 1963, exactly two weeks to the day before its opening night of 19 June. Lest they be taken by surprise at the last, however, plans were made at the Lord Chamberlain's office on 17 June to ensure the finished production also met with approval: 'I see that this play by Bill Naughton containing the abortion scene etc., etc., is being presented at the Mermaid for the first time on Wednesday 19 June. In view of the contents of this play, I think that this should be inspected very early on and may arrangements therefore be made for this to happen either on the first or second night.'23

The assistant secretary was duly dispatched to watch the play on the second night of presentation and the results of his 'incognito inspection' were immediately forthcoming. While he was clearly satisfied with the staging of the abortion scene—and indeed noted the producers had done more there than had been required of them—he plainly had reservations regarding other bits of stage 'business', not to mention a profound distaste for the play generally:

I went last night to the Mermaid Theatre to see *Alfie*. I occupied stall no. D23 and I enclose the programme. The play reads better than it acts and I thought the acting, with the exception of John Neville, so bad that at times the piece instead of being tragi-comic came perilously close to bathos. Generally speaking, and for these days, there was nothing to which real objection could be taken . . .

1. Reference to 'putting your knee on the steering wheel'—still there which was prohibited.

2. A piece of 'business'—'Alfie throws back the girl's draws'—surprised we had allowed.

3. Unscripted 'business' with Alfie showing there was no hot water bottle in bed, therefore no intercourse tonight.

4. In several respects the producer has modified what the Lord Chamberlain has allowed—the reference to Lily and Alfie not taking precautions is dropped, and so is all 'business' of a clinical sort connected with the abortion. The practitioner merely calls and goes out with Lily to another room, and she comes back in a dressing gown.

5. 'Breast squeezing' . . . 'business' with Ruby in 'house coat and undies'.

We have in our strait-laced past always forbidden breast squeezing and if you admit even a short squeeze you lose complete control: lengthened squeezes, other actions, and greater degrees of breast nudity then follow and short of seeing every performance it is impossible to decide what is really impermissible and what is mildly objectionable. Personally, I would stop this act completely.[24]

If the assistant secretary was not impressed by the play or the cast apart from John Neville—it included Glenda Jackson and Gemma Jones in leading roles—a good many people were. The Mermaid was doing considerable business. And 'breast squeezing', inevitably, was sufficient cause for concern in itself. To settle his mind on that score, once and for all, the Assistant Comptroller dutifully trooped along to see the play as well. While the assistant secretary's visit had been done 'incognito' though still 'official', however, the Assistant Comptroller's visit was 'open':

We discussed this play this morning as a result of Hill's official visit (incognito) on the 20 June and my own open visit on 26 June. I phoned Bernard Miles this morning and have explained the Lord Chamberlain's rule that breasts may not be touched. I explained the reason for this is the difficulty in establishing a dividing line between brushing gently against the bosom and gripping them. Bernard Miles said that he appreciated this and will have any touching or handling of the breasts of Ruby immediately stopped. I accepted his suggestion that Alfie could outline the shape of Ruby's bosom with the hand at a safe distance away and he said that if anyone from the Lord Chamberlain's office wished to come and see this new arrangement, he hoped they would do so . . .[25]

It was, of course, hardly necessary. No more visits were required—'incognito', 'official', 'open', or otherwise. The Lord Chamberlain's office had done its job well enough. Not that everybody was satisfied: the Stage Plays Sub-Committee of the Public Morality Council, for example, sent its own 'reporter' along to view *Alfie* and felt certain some things had been slipped in after submission for licence with regard to the penultimate scene (the abortion scene) especially. 'Despite the skill demonstrated by Mr John Neville in the chief part', they commented, overall the play was 'deplorable' and 'thoroughly objectionable . . . embodying as it does seduction, abortion, adultery.'

The Lord Chamberlain was particularly well placed to respond on this occasion and assured them the play had simply not been allowed in its original form. Given the extent of scrutiny afforded *Alfie* at both the pre-production and post-production stages, in addition to the 'considerable cuts and alterations at my request', he felt confident in stating that 'the author [had] modified it radically' and 'the producer had conformed entirely to my directions'. His claim was exaggerated, of necessity, but was not too far wide of the truth. In view of the weight of damning opinion against the play expressed by his examiners throughout, however, his parting comment was nothing if not ironic: 'I think, if I may say so, without disrespect to your Committee, that the attitude of responsible critics and of the general theatregoing public towards the production confirms my judgement.'[26]

By the time, then, that the film script for *Alfie* landed in the BBFC's lap, in 1965, it had been through the censorship treadmill already and shorn of several elements. While Bill Naughton undoubtedly grasped the opportunity offered by the prospect of a film production to reinsert some of his earlier material—generally lines of dialogue which he had clearly always treasured—the plain fact of the matter is that his script stayed within the limits of what the theatre censors had allowed. Crucially, he chose not to overstep the mark when broaching contentious issues such as abortion. Changes were made, to be sure, to accommodate the demands of working on film as much as anything else. New characters and outside locations were added to flesh out the proceedings. But they were hardly substantial changes for all that. Some matters previously consigned off-stage during the abortion scene, for instance, now moved inevitably into the foreground and within view of the camera, with the abortionist plainly on show. It was done cautiously, however, without graphic or explicit depiction of any controversial aspects, and the abortion itself still took place behind a curtain. The film depended essentially upon the ingredients which had accounted for its stage success—dialogue and characterization. Most of all, Alfie's key speech about the aborted foetus of his child remained precisely as Naughton had fashioned it to meet the Lord Chamberlain's requirements. It is no surprise, in short, that the BBFC permitted an abortion scene and concluded, moreover, that it was 'the most moral' script they had encountered in some while. Nobody had ever doubted Naughton's 'moral' intent—the BBC critics had agreed it was evident in his original radio play and the theatre examiners had conceded it was present as well. The Lord Chamberlain's office had, though, added considerably to the realization of his 'moral' purpose. The BBFC, for its part, merely sought to do more of the same.

It had still to be an 'X', the script-reader thought, 'because of the abortion and the grossness of some of the sex talk'. But 'We really do not feel that the sex is dragged in to titillate the idle mind', Audrey Field concluded, and 'I think there is a case for being as lenient as possible.' John Trevelyan concurred and informed Paramount British Pictures that: 'Obviously the film could be considered only for the "X" category.' 'It is, however, a basically moral theme', he continued, 'and if it is made with integrity, as I have every reason to think that it will be, it should not give us much trouble.' As ever, his comments on precise detail ranged high and low:

We would not object to seeing dogs sniffing each other, but there might be trouble if the behaviour of the dogs was a close parallel of what was going on in the car. We are a bit concerned about the script direction '. . . adjusts his trousers and generally makes himself less uncomfortable'. Discretion should be used here. The same applies to Siddie '. . . hitching up her skirt and tidying herself up'.

We think that you should omit the shot of Alfie taking the pair of panties from his pocket and tossing them across to Siddie with his line '. . . 'Ere mind you don't catch cold'. This is more suggestive than we would like.

Although this is not a censorship point, I am doubtful whether you can get a train from Waterloo Station to Forest Hill Station. I would have thought that Victoria was more likely.

Siddie's line 'So long as you don't have to give it to him', and Alfie's reply 'I would if I were built that way', may pass, but I think that you should shoot this scene in a way that would enable these lines to be removed if necessary.

The same applies to the explicit references to menstruation. They may pass, but you should provide for the possibility that they may not . . .

I do not know whether the choice of a banana in this scene is intended to have any visual significance or not. Since it might possibly give this impression I suggest that you might well substitute an apple or something of this kind.

I would have thought that there was no need for nudity in this scene. This kind of thing has become a cliché. It will certainly be cut if nudity is clearly visible, and at most only a backview would be accepted. I hope, however, that you will omit this entirely.

Ruby's costume should be adequate and not transparent . . .

The script description reads 'Alfie and Ruby embrace with some extravagant love-making preamble'. It should not be too extravagant. We are not too happy about the phrase 'lust-box'. If you make use of this I think that you should have an alternative available.

These are strong scenes, but they will probably be acceptable in the context, since they do make a valid point against abortion. We would not want any really harrowing moans and screams.

These could be very moving scenes. Obviously we shall not see what Alfie sees in the bathroom.

We are not sure about the lines 'What, you doin' it with groups now then?' and 'Don't be disgusting'. These should be shot in a way that would enable them to be removed without difficulty if necessary.

I have one other general point. I think that the phrase 'having it off with', which is used from time to time, will probably be acceptable, but here again you might have an alternative for post-synching if it should not be.[27]

When it finally reached the screen, *Alfie* had been through a lengthy and arduous process of censorship negotiation, something which contributed substantially to its emergence as a 'basically moral' film. What Alan Sillitoe had endured, Bill Naughton was also made to suffer. Yet the film of his play was followed a year later by the 1967 Abortion Act, of course, and by a Theatres Act in 1968 which proceeded to abolish the Lord Chamberlain's powers of censorship. While social change was plainly taking place in some areas, however, it was still noticeably lacking in others.

Notes

1 Stephen Farber, '*Alfie*', *Film Quarterly*, 20/3 (1967), 42–6; Walker, *Hollywood, England*, 306–7. The release print of *Alfie* for American distribution differed slightly from the British version in that it included over the end-titles the popular song of the same name by Cher. Released on the Imperial record label (no. 66192), it entered the US 'top forty' on 20 Aug. 1966 and reached thirty-second place. It hovered around the American popular music charts for just three weeks though Dionne Warwick had a bigger hit with it there on 27 May 1967, achieving fifteenth position and lasting for nine weeks with her Sceptre label recording (no. 12187). The song was a hit in Britain for Cilla Black, on the Parlophone label (no. 5427): it entered the UK 'top twenty' pop charts on 9 Apr. 1966, made it to ninth position, and survived for twelve weeks.

There was no song, however, in the original British version of the film: Burt Bacharach and Hal David composed it only after the London première of the completed print on 24 Mar. 1966. The original British copy contained a musical score specially commissioned from tenor sax player, Sonny Rollins, and that alone. Cilla Black made the first recording of the Bacharach and David song; Cher covered it for the American market. The dubbing of her version on to the US soundtrack qualified it to be nominated for the Best Song Oscar at the 1966 Academy Awards (for details see Alan Warner, *Who Sang What on the Screen* (London, 1984), 59). Ironically, the American version of *Alfie* is the one invariably preferred for regular repeat showings of the film on British television. Michael Caine's experiences on the film are amusingly recounted, in his usual inimitable style, in his autobiography (and audio-cassette of the same), *What's It All About?* (London, 1992).

2 Marwick, *British Society since 1945*, 147–9. Trevelyan broadly outlined the reasons for the BBFC relenting over the key words of 'bad language'—'bloody', 'bugger', and 'fuck'—in *What the Censor Saw*, 178–9. When it came to *If . . .*, the BBFC broke with precedent by permitting the glimpse of Mrs Kemp's pubic hair as she wanders naked down a school dormitory corridor. 'There is nothing erotic in the scene', Trevelyan maintained: 'In the context there's nothing offensive about it.' Though 'as compensation', to borrow director Lindsay Anderson's own words, the censor 'demanded the substitution at the start of the shower scene, of an alternative take in which the discreet use of towels prevented an equivalently frank look at the boys'. See his 'Notes for a Preface' to the film-script found in Lindsay Anderson and David Sherwin, *If . . .* (London, 1969), 9–13. *If . . .* is explored at greater length by Jeffrey Richards in his chapter, 'The

Revolt of the Young', for Jeffrey Richards and Anthony Aldgate, *Best of British: Cinema and Society, 1930–1970* (Oxford, 1983), 147–61.

3 Alan Sillitoe, 'What Comes on Monday?', *New Left Review*, 4 (1960), 58–9; id., 'Writing and Publishing', *London Review of Books*, 1–14 Apr. 1982, pp. 8–10. Sillitoe's original novel was first published in 1958 by W. H. Allen. It sold 8,000 in a hardback edition over two years before being published in paperback (as a 'tie-in' with the forthcoming film) by Pan Books in 1960. The first Pan printing was for 150,000 copies and it was expected by Aug. that sales would reach the quarter-million mark 'within a few months'. By Oct. 1960, the month of the film's release, sales had already topped the 300,000 mark and were described by Pan as 'absolutely phenomenal'. By Dec. some 600,000 copies had been printed. By Feb. 1961 750,000 had been sold and another impression for 125,000 was forthcoming. Within a year of publication by Pan, *Saturday Night and Sunday Morning* had become one of the first million-selling paperbacks in Britain, along with *Lady Chatterley's Lover*, *The Dam Busters*, *Peyton Place*, and the Penguin *Odyssey*. The book has been regularly reprinted ever since. For further publication details, see J. A. Sutherland, *Fiction and the Fiction Industry* (London, 1978), 176; and for invaluable exposition on Sillitoe, see Ritchie, *Success Stories*, 184–219. My own initial survey of BBFC reaction to Sillitoe's work, 'The Seeds of Further Compromise', is found in Richards and Aldgate, *Best of British*, 131–45.

4 BBFC file on *Saturday Night and Sunday Morning*: readers' reports, 20 Nov. 1959.

5 Ibid., Trevelyan to Saltzman, 24 Nov. 1959.

6 Sillitoe, 'What Comes on Monday?', 58–9, recounts: 'For reasons of censorship the "bringing it off" scene of Brenda in the bath is not shown, but only referred to. It was also thought best, because of possible censorship complications, to make the attempted abortion fail. The only advantage of having it fail was that in the film the climax centres around a more complex situation than in the book.' In 'Writing and Publishing', p. 8, Sillitoe notes that 'In the novel the main female character has an abortion. In the film, the attempt could be indicated, but not shown as successful. This ruling had to be accepted . . . The contract had been drawn up and signed, and the £90,000 which the film cost had already been invested, so we had to accept the cuts.' Director Karel Reisz is reported as saying that he 'never regretted making those changes' to the abortion scene, in the reprint of Boleslaw Sulik's 1961 essay on the film in John Russell Taylor (ed.), *Masterworks of the British Cinema* (London, 1974), 349.

The extent to which the production company willingly applied the requisite amounts of 'social responsibility' and perhaps even benefited from BBFC intervention—not least in regard to Sillitoe's first proposal to set the film's ending in a registry office, as outlined in his scenario treatment—is explored in Aldgate, 'Seeds of Further Compromise', 140–1. The phrase is redolent of the public rebuke by Giulio Andreotti—responsible for film censorship in his own right—of director, Vittorio De Sica, and scriptwriter, Cesare Zavattini, for their 1951 film of *Umberto D*, which he felt did 'wretched service to the fatherland'. It came in the form of a long open letter first published in *Libertas*, the Christian Democrat weekly, on 24 Feb. 1952, where he admonished De Sica for failing to take account of the government's programmes for economic reconstruction and social welfare, and urged: 'We ask only of a man of culture to feel his social responsibility, which cannot be limited to describing the vices and miseries of a system and a generation but must help to conquer them.' Quoted in Anthony Aldgate, 'The Italian Neo-realist Cinema', in id., *Liberation and Reconstruction: Politics, Culture and*

Society in France and Italy, 1943–1954 (Milton Keynes, 1990), 51. Tony Richardson for one, co-producer on *Saturday Night and Sunday Morning*, acknowledged his admiration for De Sica in 'The Man Behind an Angry-Young-Man', 9.

7 BBFC file on *Saturday Night and Sunday Morning*: reader's report, 28 Jan. 1960. Despite fully realizing that Brenda 'resolves to have the child after all' and noting that her husband tells Arthur she'll be 'all right', the reader plainly misunderstood the script's intentions when thinking that the pregnancy is finally 'terminated without any outside interference'. It is difficult to fathom how this could be construed. It is abundantly clear from the different scripts for the film (held at the BFI Library, London: S329, undated, and S330, July 1960), as well as the finished production, that Brenda tells Arthur she cannot go through with another attempt at abortion when she says: 'I've decided to have it and face whatever comes of it.' However, the BBFC script-reader was hardly alone in her thinking on this score. Even after the film's release, the critics differed noticeably in their opinions on whether the pregnancy was terminated or not, and that despite the fact that the attempted abortion was reported a failure. By the same token, there were differing interpretations of the film's ending, with some critics arguing it was 'a surrender' and others maintaining that Arthur Seaton was only 'half-tamed'. See reviews of the film held on the microfiche at the BFI, London, and the commentary provided in Aldgate, 'Seeds of Further Compromise', 137–42.

8 BBFC file on *Saturday Night and Sunday Morning*: Trevelyan to Saltzman, 2 Feb. 1960.

9 *Kinematograph Weekly*, 27 Oct. 1960, p. 10; Walker, *Hollywood, England*, 88.

10 BBFC file on *Saturday Night and Sunday Morning*: Clerk of Warwickshire County Council to Trevelyan, 25 Jan. 1961; Trevelyan to Clerk of the Council, 8 Feb. 1961. For an outline of Warwickshire's traditionally uncompromising line over film censorship generally, see Hunnings, *Film Censors and the Law*, 111–13, 126, 134, 143.

11 BBFC file on *The Loneliness of the Long Distance Runner*: examiner's report, 3 Jan. 1962. The script-reader felt the 'socially irresponsible' aspects were particularly evident in dialogue like 'We should be working for each other, not working against each other', which prompted the remark: 'This sort of high-souled talk is the reason why young people are liable to think that Colin is a Good Man. It is true party line stuff. What the objection is to an honest-to-goodness prize openly and honestly competed for and judged, I can never see myself. People are always competing, and the secret, unacknowledged competitions are far more bitter and deadly. (Particularly in Communist countries, where the loser commonly gets shot.)' It also prompted wry comment at the expense of the Board of Directors at Woodfall Productions and, indeed, the Royal Family: 'I don't think messrs. Sillitoe, Osborne, Richardson (or the other Englishmen with the funny-sounding names on the letter-heading [presumably Oscar A. Beuselinck and Walter T. Strich]) would feel so sure of their ground if Colin were a real thief of their own acquaintance who had taken away their lovely Jaguars or whatever . . . One could do rather an interesting short parody of this film: a recent well-remembered Grand National Loser (Devon Loch) who, it will be remembered, stopped short a few yards from the post for no reason that anybody could discover, did it to spite the Queen Mother and all the Royal Family.' By contrast, 'except [for] violently intemperate and wrong-headed social sentiments', the script-reader felt 'there is not a lot of violence in this film'.

12 BBFC file on *The Loneliness of the Long Distance Runner*: Trevelyan to Michael Holden, 9 Jan. 1962. While Trevelyan thought 'the theme of this script presents no important censorship problems' he expressed concern that 'some of the ideas' it contained might be the cause of excessive violence or offensive dialogue: 'I appreciate that the film wishes to show the inhumanity of "authority", and that this is the reason why the "screws" are shown kicking Stacey, but I wonder whether this really adds anything to the story. I am sure that "screws" do kick prisoners from time to time, but this kind of thing does suggest to young people who may find themselves in Borstal that this is normal treatment, and it may cause some concern to their parents. Perhaps this is intended . . . The same kind of thing applies to the dialogue in this scene. We are not out to protect the police or prison service from criticism, but since this picture is clearly localised in Nottingham, the local police force may feel that it is being unfairly criticised.' Thereafter, the completed film was viewed by two examiners, Trevelyan and the BBFC president, on 20 July 1962, whereupon the secretary was asked to take up certain points with Woodfall and endeavour to obtain alterations: '(i) The behaviour of the police detective when visiting the house, and one line of dialogue, produced somewhat unfair criticism of the police. The line of dialogue threatened brutality at the police station, and the detective tore the bottom off the chair when hunting for stolen money. (ii) One of the masters in the Borstal used bad language to the boys. This will invite criticism of Borstal masters.' As the result of a subsequent telephone conversation between Trevelyan and Tony Richardson, a further line of dialogue was dropped. The film's editor, Tony Gibbs, confirmed he had removed: 'If we get you down to the nick you will get a few bruises for your trouble.' See BBFC file on *The Loneliness of the Long Distance Runner*: Gibbs to Trevelyan, 1 Aug. 1962. Trevelyan's handwritten note to the same states that after further discussion with the president, the film was passed with an 'X' certificate on 3 Aug. 1962.

13 LC, file 4112/1964 on *Saturday Night and Sunday Morning*, reader's report, 14 Mar. 1964; E. Penn, Assistant Comptroller, to P. Stevens, Theatre Administrator, 20 Mar. 1964. Alan Sillitoe's *The Loneliness of the Long Distance Runner* was also adapted for the stage by Big Arts Productions and presented at The Grove Theatre, Kensington Park, Ladbroke Grove, London in October 1990.

14 Ibid., Stevens to Penn, 25 Mar. 1964, with handwritten amendment its to same, by Lord Chamberlain's office regarding consultation with BBFC. The situation was reversed a year later when Nottingham Playhouse once again cited the precedent of the BBFC allowing a word on film which the Lord Chamberlain's office were forbidding in the theatre. This time they were undoubtedly correct and rewarded accordingly. As first presented at the Duchess Theatre in 1960, Harold Pinter's play, *The Caretaker*, was not allowed to include the phrase 'piss off'. But the BBFC allowed it for Clive Donner's film of the play in 1963. Thus, for their 1965 production of *The Caretaker*, the Nottingham Playhouse asked for the phrase to be reinstated on the grounds that it had been used in the recent film. John Johnston, then Assistant Comptroller, recounts what happened thereafter in *Blue Pencil*, 194–5: 'I checked with John Trevelyan . . . who confirmed that, whereas customarily they did not allow such language, they had done so in this case. In view of our policy of keeping in step with the Film Board, we agreed.' Trevelyan takes credit for the change in *What the Censor Saw*, 212.

15 LC, file 4112/1964 on *Saturday Night and Sunday Morning*: Penn to Stevens, 6 Apr. 1964, and reply by Stevens, 9 Apr. 1964. The licence was issued on 13 Apr. 1964.

Ironically, when the play was presented in 1966 at the Prince of Wales Theatre, London, the Assistant Comptroller informed the producer that the word 'beggar' which had previously been allowed was now 'disallowed': 'The Lord Chamberlain felt it was putting too great a strain upon the actors and actresses if he allowed the continued use of closely related euphemisms.' See the attachment of 9 Feb. 1966 to licence no. 1442 (13 Apr. 1964), and the letter from J. Johnston to M. White, 10 Feb. 1966. Thus, it was the theatre censors who initially lifted the long-imposed ban on the word 'bogger', and the BBFC followed suit in 1967 when they allowed 'bugger' for the first time in a British film in the dialogue for *Up the Junction*.

16 BBC Written Archives Caversham: *Alfie Elkins and his Little Life*, Audience Research Report, 30 Jan. 1962 IR / 62 / 58; *The Critics*, 16 Sept. 1962, transcript. The original radio play was repeated by the BBC yet again, during 1992, as part of a tribute to Bill Naughton, following his death on 9 Jan., which comprised a short season of his plays. My own observations on the genesis and evolution of Bill Naughton's *Alfie* from radio play to film script were presented in a BBC Radio 5 programme, 'What was it all about, Alfie? Censorship in the Swinging Sixties', which was produced by Angela Jamieson and broadcast on 30 May and 6 June 1993.

17 LC, file 3492/1963 on *Alfie*: reader's report, 20 Jan. 1963, and handwritten amendments to same by E. Penn, Assistant Comptroller.

18 Ibid., memorandum from Penn to Lord Chamberlain, 24 Jan. 1963; letter from Penn to P. Ide, Administrative Director, Mermaid Theatre, 25 Jan. 1963.

19 Ibid., Bernard Miles to Comptroller, 28 Jan. 1963; Gwatkin's report of meeting, 7 Feb. 1963.

20 Ibid., Cobbold to Penn, 11 Feb. 1963.

21 Ibid., Penn to Miles, 14 Feb. 1963.

22 Ibid., Ide to Comptroller, 3 May 1963; reader's report, 20 May 1963.

23 Ibid., Penn to Ide, 24 May 1963; Ide to Penn, 30 May 1963; memorandum from Penn to R. Hill, assistant secretary, 5 June 1963.

24 Ibid., Hill's report of 'incognito inspection', 21 June 1963.

25 Ibid., Penn's memorandum to Lord Chamberlain, 27 June 1963.

26 Ibid., letter from Public Morality Council, 12 Sept. 1963; Lord Chamberlain's reply, 25 Sept. 1963. Gwatkin, the Comptroller, added by way of cryptic marginal comment to the Lord Chamberlain's letter: 'I particularly like this last sentence and I hope they will appreciate the word "responsible". They make occasional sallies in order that they may say that they have done so in the book being produced now and again to wheedle subscriptions from gullible old ladies.' Another letter from the Public Morality Council on 9 Oct. 1963 makes it clear they were not assuaged, and letters from members of the public on 24 Sept. and 18 Oct. 1963 bear out continued animosity to the play. In 1964, furthermore, Mary Whitehouse embarked upon her 'Clean-up TV' campaign and, as Arthur Marwick notes, 'a running battle between the advocates of permissiveness and tolerance and those of purity and censorship was joined'. 'That battle in itself', Marwick continues, 'served to publicize the fact that change indeed was taking place', *British Society since 1945*, 125.

Alfie was also presented in New York, where it opened at the Morosco Theatre on 17 Dec. 1964 after a short tour of New Haven and Washington. The up-and-coming

Terence Stamp, who played Alfie, expected great things and thought 'My Broadway debut appeared to be placing me in the right place at the right time'. But the production ran for just twenty-one performances. Stamp maintains: 'After a splendid tour with packed, laughing houses we hit a stolid first-night house at the Morosco Theatre. A devout Catholic critic who was reputedly offended by the abortion scene, but too smart to mention the fact, found other ways of making the play seem unwatchable', *Double Feature* (London, 1990), 147. Jean Shrimpton cites other factors for its lack of success: 'The audience did not understand the Cockney rhyming slang; in fact they did not understand the play at all. Terry was dynamic enough, but this near-monologue from him in an East End accent was baffling the audience. It seemed to me it was not going to work, and it didn't. The applause at the end was polite, and the critics delivered the *coup de grâce* the next morning. The play was a flop', *An Autobiography*, 127.

Whatever the reasons for the failure of the 1964 New York production, Stamp, according to his old friend, Michael Caine, 'now wanted nothing more to do with it'. So, when Lewis Gilbert offered Stamp the part of Alfie in the film version, he declined the role. 'To my astonishment, Terry turned it down, and I actually spent three whole hours trying to talk him into accepting it', Caine says. 'I still wake up screaming in the middle of the night as Terry takes my advice and accepts the role.' Caine, of course, who had failed an audition to take over from John Neville in the original stage production, jumped at the offer of the film role and made it a huge success in both Britain and America. Although, interestingly, he notes: 'The film, as I later learned, was turned down by many British actors because it contained an abortion scene, and stars in those days did not want to be associated with anything of that kind, in case it ruined their image' (*What's It All About?*, 163, 180).

27 BBFC file on *Alfie*: examiner's report, 28 Apr. 1965; Trevelyan's letter to Paramount British Pictures, 4 May 1965. Two of Bill Naughton's other plays were also adapted for the screen. *All in Good Time* appeared as a Boulting Brothers' production, *The Family Way*, with Hywel Bennett and Hayley Mills in 1966, while *Spring and Port Wine* was filmed under the same title by Memorial Enterprises with James Mason and Susan George in 1970.

6 **A Woman's Lot**

Shelagh Delaney, Salford born, was almost 19 years old when her play *A Taste of Honey* was first presented on 27 May 1958 at the Theatre Royal, Stratford-atte-Bowe, London E15, in a production for Theatre Workshop which was directed by Joan Littlewood. Rita Tushingham enjoyed her nineteenth birthday on 14 March 1961, the day that Walter Lassally set up his Arriflex camera by the docks of the Manchester Ship Canal and, at 7.31 a.m. precisely, started shooting Tony Richardson's film of Delaney's play.[1] Their youthfulness was the cause of much comment on each occasion. Kenneth Tynan, for example, considered it an asset and said of the stage production:

There are plenty of crudities in Miss Delaney's play: there is also, more importantly, the smell of living. When the theatre presents poor people as good, we call it 'sentimental'. When it presents them as wicked, we sniff and cry 'squalid'. Happily, Miss Delaney does not yet know about us and our squeamishness, which we think moral but which is really social. She is too busy recording the wonder of life as she lives it. There is plenty of time for her to worry over words like 'form', which mean something, and concepts like 'vulgarity', which don't. She is nineteen years old; and a portent.

Alan Brien, by contrast, was less pleased and his initial reaction more guarded. He worried about the dramatist's apparent display of 'adolescent contempt for logic or form or practicability upon a stage' and believed: 'Twenty, ten, or even five years ago, before a senile society began to fawn upon the youth which is about to devour it, such a play would have remained written in green longhand in a school exercise book on the top of the bedroom wardrobe'. Delaney was variously dubbed 'teenager of the week' by the *Evening News*, 'an angry young woman' by *Theatre World*, and 'the Françoise Sagan of Salford' by the *News Chronicle*.[2]

Tushingham's youth, furthermore, allied to her distinctly modest amount of professional acting experience, were popularly held to account both for landing the leading role in the film, in the first place, and for some of the acclaim which greeted its première on 14 September 1961. A Liverpool grocer's daughter, she was chosen from a band of 2,000 'young hopefuls' by Richardson, who reportedly rejected the offer of American finance provided he would cast Audrey Hepburn in the part. 'None of the accepted actresses, stage or film, could possibly look a teenager on screen', he stated. Tushingham possessed 'a natural talent'. 'The antithesis of a traditional movie actress', Boleslaw Sulik noted, 'her face is real and expressive and the performance, in spite of an apparent lack of formal training, is most effective'. She had 'the sort of face and quality', Penelope Gilliat felt, 'that one has pined for through all the years of Surrey-rose ingenues'. Tushingham was 'an astounding find', the critics agreed, an opinion that was endorsed with an award from the British Film Academy for the 'Most Promising Newcomer' of 1961.[3]

For all the attendant publicity which inevitably harped upon the youth of Delaney and Tushingham, however, the more significant and enduring features of *A Taste of Honey*, as both play and film, have been sufficiently acknowledged. 'The appearance of motherhood as subject matter', Michelene Wandor states, 'breaks an unspoken taboo on theatrical content, which in the vast majority of plays is defined by issues of direct concern to men.' 'The gender bias', she adds, 'is also reversed from that of most other plays, in that it is the women we follow from scene to scene. The men come and go according to the needs of the women characters.'[4] Wandor's assessment of the play's impact was echoed in Stuart Laing's comments on the film: 'it was the only "New Wave" film to give the central place to a woman character; a woman isolated, independent by force of circumstances and clearly not dependent on a strong male character'.[5] *A Taste of Honey*, then, proved a major departure for both British theatre and cinema by virtue of the fact that its concerns were female-centred and that women were the instigators of its dramatic action. It celebrated, essentially, female sexuality and motherhood. Ironically, if somewhat predictably, what occupied the censor's minds most, theatre and film alike, was not so much Delaney's depiction of women but rather her representation of another issue, homosexuality.

Delaney's playscript was submitted for licence to the Lord Chamberlain's office on 2 May 1958. Though some critics have long puzzled just how many changes were made to Delaney's original text in rehearsal as a result of Joan Littlewood's highly improvisatory techniques, the play-reader's synopsis suggests that Delaney's plot essentials, at least, remained pretty fixed from first to last:[6]

A Woman's Lot

31. Helen (*Dora Bryan*) has 'a gypsy-like reluctance to tie herself down and wanders from lodging to lodging always taking her half educated daughter along with her.' (*A Taste of Honey*)

Helen is a freelance tart and Josephine is her teenage daughter. Between the two of them exists a very real bond, though it expresses itself in mutual recrimination. Helen is half-Irish and was born in the Catholic faith. She has a gypsy-like reluctance to tie herself down and wanders from lodging to lodging always taking her half-educated daughter along with her. The latter is due to leave school and get a job—it is clear that she despises her mother's way of life without openly criticising it. Peter appears, a wealthy man ten years younger than Helen, a constant swain who proposes marriage. Helen agrees and then discovers that Jo has fallen for a nice young coloured merchant seaman. She shrugs off her responsibility and goes off with her new husband, leaving Jo to fend for herself.

The seaman goes off and what we thought was the real thing turns out to be the old story. Jo is pregnant with no immediate hope (or desire) of a husband. Then she finds and brings Geof home. Geof has the reputation of being a pervert—and he confesses that there is a little flame to the immense amount of smoke. But he explains that he is really quite a normal young man, only not very strongly sexed, and with a real desire to marry and settle down to have a family. He remains with Jo, taking a far more intense interest in her pregnancy than Jo herself—who loathes the idea of having a baby especially as Helen has told her that her father was 'mentally retarded'.

Helen and Peter reappear and offer a home for Jo and her child. Peter, too, is fond of children and would be glad to adopt his step-daughter's child. Reluctantly and defiantly Jo more or less accepts the offer. Her pains come on and she is whisked off to hospital. Helen remains to tell Geof what has happened and what is going to happen. His dreams of marrying Jo and being, even by proxy, a father, crash about his ears. The curtain falls and we are left with the slightest hint that this is the end for him and that he will never get another chance to prove himself normal.

Charles Heriot's comments followed. 'This is a surprisingly good play', he stated, 'though God knows it is not to my personal taste.' 'The people are strangely real and the problem of Geof is delicately conveyed', he felt, though he wished to see some things excised, not least the scenes where Geof 'explains his position in society to Jo' and Helen 'calls him a pervert and a castrated little clown'. 'These can easily come out', he argued, and Heriot, at least, was of the opinion it should be allowed:

The point I wish to make is that this play is balanced on a knife edge. It is the perfect borderline case, since it is concerned with the forbidden subject in a way that no one, I believe, could take exception to. In my opinion, therefore, it is recommended for licence but I think that the Comptroller and the Lord Chamberlain should both read the play carefully themselves.[7]

So, indeed, they did. Until 1957, after all, the Lord Chamberlain had maintained an absolute ban on homosexuality as a stage theme. Before the publication in September 1957 of Sir John Wolfenden's Report of the Committee on Homosexuality and Prostitution, however, the Lord Chamberlain had requested a meeting with the Home Secretary of the day, R. A. Butler, at which he raised among other things the question of plays with homosexual themes. After this meeting, on 4 June 1957, Lord Scarbrough noted 'it was bound to appear absurd to quite sensible people to disallow any attempt to deal seriously with a subject which had now become, unfortunately, one of the problems of life'. The ban on homosexual subjects was lifted later in the year. This decision may well have marked, as John Johnston states, 'a milestone in the history of the theatre censorship'. But it was tardily achieved, not easily forthcoming, nor readily welcomed in all quarters. Furthermore, while it was agreed 'it can no longer be held that a complete ban should be maintained', the point was made that the Lord Chamberlain could still not allow 'complete liberty on the subject'. There remained conditions attached to its portrayal:

(a) Every play will continue to be judged on its merits and only those dealing seriously with the subject will be passed;

(b) Plays violently homosexual will not be passed;

(c) Homosexual characters will not be allowed if their inclusion in the piece is unnecessary to the action or theme of the play;

(d) Embraces between homosexuals will not be allowed.[8]

A Taste of Honey, in short, was the first important test of how far the theatre censors had really changed their outlook regarding the depiction of homosexuality. Not surprisingly, it was the cause of considerable deliberation among their highest ranks. Norman Gwatkin was distinctly unhappy with it: 'I've read it and think it revolting, quite apart from the homosexual bits. To me it has no saving grace whatsoever. If we pass muck like this it *does* give our critics something to go on.' Lord Scarbrough endorsed Heriot's suggestions in wishing to see the word 'castrated' removed and Geof's self-revelatory speech toned down to lessen 'the suggestion of homosexuality'. The licence was issued 'on the understanding the omissions are made' on 15 May, just five days before the proposed date of production. In the event, *A Taste of Honey* opened on 27 May 1958.[9]

Since, however, Joan Littlewood's rehearsal methods had plainly made some changes to Delaney's script, Theatre Workshop felt compelled to return to the Lord Chamberlain's office with the reworked version, after the play had commenced its run. 'The differences are caused by cutting and re-shaping', it was remarked, but 'a certain amount of new material' had also been introduced. 'The plot remains unchanged', Heriot noted, though 'the character of Geof has been toned down in accordance with the Lord Chamberlain's instructions.' He was not impressed with the additional material: 'The lover, Peter, has been given a silly drunken scene to indicate that his life with Helen is not all it should be. This is, in my opinion, a mistake and coarsens the play.' 'Is this possible?' Gwatkin queried sarcastically. Still, apart from requiring that one of the new lines be dropped ('Worn out but still a good few pumps left in her'), the play was passed yet again. *A Taste of Honey* was revived at Stratford East on 21 January 1959 and transferred by the impresarios, Donald Albery and Oscar Lewenstein, to Wyndham's Theatre on 10 February.[10]

Before it transferred, however, the Lord Chamberlain was taken severely to task by an irate member of the public, and held to account for his action in allowing the play:

I feel compelled to draw your attention to a play entitled *A Taste of Honey* now playing at the Theatre Royal, Stratford E15, and shortly to be transferred, I am told, to a West End theatre. I attended a performance of this play on Wednesday 28 instant and understood that it was a modern play on a sordid theme. What I did not and cannot understand was the appalling use of blasphemy in the dialogue. One appreciates that plays of this type are said to present realistically a side of 'modern' life but that is no excuse whatever for permitting blasphemous dialogue to be added to the general filth and I can only conclude that the production has escaped the vigilance of your office.

The country is still, nominally at least, Christian and we owe allegiance to our Sovereign who is sworn to uphold the Faith. To permit language of this kind to be used at a public theatre simply cannot be reconciled with this position. We are rightly appalled when we read of militant atheism in Communist countries and yet our responsible authorities permit public blasphemy in the name of theatre or drama presented presumably as entertainment. The hypocrisy of the position is shattering and I trust, Sir, you will give fresh consideration as to the duties of your office towards plays of this type.

Gwatkin was directed by the Lord Chamberlain to reply:

After some misgivings the Lord Chamberlain gave this play a licence but not before he had insisted upon certain alterations and deletions. From what is left you will, I am sure, realise that the original could hardly have been licensed. It is especially difficult with a play of this type to delete all passages which may give offence. If the actors are to perform the play in the spirit in which it is written they have, within bounds, to speak and act in accordance with the author's conception of the mentality and outlook of the characters.

The Lord Chamberlain feels that whilst there are passages which will be objectionable, as they have proved to you, they are in character in this sordid and melancholy play. To live the theatre must be a mirror to contemporary life in its good and bad aspects, and the Lord Chamberlain is of the opinion that because it depicts such a sad collection of undesirables it will not do the public any harm. I am to add that the Lord Chamberlain is grateful to you for troubling to write.[11]

A Taste of Honey ran for nearly a year in the West End, winning the Foyle's New Play Award and an Arts Council bursary for Shelagh Delaney in the process. By the time it opened in America, however, at the Biltmore Theatre in Los Angeles on 6 September 1960, there had been several changes to production personnel. Joan Plowright and Angela Lansbury had supplanted Frances Cuka and Avis Bunnage in the roles of Jo and her mother, and Tony Richardson had taken on the task of co-director. The considerable critical and popular acclaim the play received there, especially after its Broadway presentation on 4 October at the New York Lyceum where it ran for 376 performances and won the award of a 'Tony' for Plowright as Best Actress of 1960, merely stiffened Richardson's resolve

A Woman's Lot

32. Jo (*Rita Tushingham*) and her merchant seaman lover (*Paul Danquah*): 'I have said nothing about the black lover. This is because he is quite all right. The physical contacts of the two in frame seem to be pretty demure.' (*A Taste of Honey*)

to turn *A Taste of Honey* into a film. He had always been intent upon doing so, in fact, even before taking on the American stage production, and had already prepared a screenplay with Delaney by May 1960 which was lodged straight away with the BBFC. But several factors conspired to prevent him getting further with the project at that point.[17]

For one thing, Richardson was heavily involved with censorship and distribution problems over *The Entertainer*. For another, this had proved a box-office flop, which did not exactly help in raising finance for new ventures, especially since Harry Saltzman considered *A Taste of Honey* 'too provincial and too English'. Besides, after opening *A Taste of Honey* on Broadway—a move intended, anyway, to assist the chances of a wider distribution for any subsequent film of the play—Richardson immediately became engaged upon his first Hollywood film, *Sanctuary*. By the end of 1960, however, the situation had improved considerably. Woodfall were riding the crest of a wave after the huge success of *Saturday Night and Sunday Morning*. Saltzman had quit Woodfall, furthermore, and his place

127

had been taken by Oscar Lewenstein, who already had a vested interest in Delaney's play. Richardson was now able to contemplate returning to the film production of *A Taste of Honey*, which he did in earnest at the beginning of 1961. Although it was doubtless frustrating, the delay between completing the screenplay and embarking upon its filming had clearly aided his purpose: finance was now available. In addition, Richardson was able to formulate a detailed response to the concerns raised by the BBFC over the project, not least since they, like the Lord Chamberlain's office, had been greatly exercised at the outset by the intended depiction of homosexuality.

In large measure, of course, the BBFC's reaction to the screenplay of *A Taste of Honey*, when it was first presented in May 1960, was helped by the fact that the play had survived the scrutiny of the Lord Chamberlain's office some two years earlier. The changing climate of opinion which led both to publication of the Wolfenden Report in September 1957 and the partial lifting of the stage ban on homosexuality in the same year, not to mention the considerable public debate which ensued in the press and on television, must also have played their part in determining the film censors' response. Early in 1959, for example, Trevelyan maintained: 'In our circles we can talk about homosexuality, but the general public is embarrassed by the subject, so until it becomes a subject that can be mentioned without offence it will be banned.'[13] Later that year he demonstrated a certain willingness to accommodate the 'subject' by permitting the film of Philip King's play, *Serious Charge*. Crucially, in that instance, the plot revolved around a vicar who is falsely accused of making sexual advances to a male teenager and is finally exonerated of the charge. There was 'no suggestion of real homosexuality' and it remained merely a 'shadow' concern. Thus the film was allowed, but given an 'X' certificate.[14]

Trevelyan, in short, continued to regard homosexuality as a contentious issue and clearly shared many of Lord Scarbrough's reservations about granting free and unfettered licence to its presentation. If public opinion was changing, went their argument, it was changing ever so slowly on the matter of homosexuality. In this regard, the censors merely echoed the reason advanced by the Conservative government for shelving the Wolfenden Report or even allowing time for parliamentary discussion of its recommendations. It was the opinion of R. A. Butler, for example, that there remained 'at present a very large section of the population who strongly repudiate homosexual conduct and whose moral sense would be offended by an alteration of the law which would seem to imply approval or tolerance of what they regard as a great social evil'.[15] Over a year

passed before the Wolfenden Report was finally debated in the House
during November 1958, whereupon its proposals over prostitution were
quickly incorporated in the 1959 Street Offences Act. But legislation
regarding homosexuality, of course, had to wait until 1967.

Still, by 1960 homosexuality was at least on the agenda as a topic for
cinematic representation. And if May 1958 had proved a test of the Lord
Chamberlain's intentions in the matter, this was as nothing compared to
the test which confronted John Trevelyan in May 1960. In that month
alone, he witnessed not only the release of two completed films about the
life of Oscar Wilde (Ken Hughes's *The Trials of Oscar Wilde* and Gregory
Ratoff's *Oscar Wilde*) but also the submission for pre-production scrutiny
of a first draft screenplay for *A Taste of Honey* and, just a few days later,
a synopsis for *Victim*. The first two films posed few problems, since they
comfortably cushioned their theme within the generic confines of period
reconstruction and costume drama, though they still merited 'X' certificates. But the two latter films promised contemporary settings and rendi-
tions for the subject of homosexuality. The profound reservations which
the BBFC shared with their theatre colleagues soon became apparent. In
addition, these two films brought out all the film censors' latent, if strongly
felt and distinctly élitist, concerns about the nature and character of the
audience that constituted the average cinema-goer. These films, in short,
tested their notions of the kind of 'entertainment' fit for 'the masses'.

No less than three censors tendered their comments on *A Taste of Honey*
for Trevelyan's consideration. Audrey Field's report of 8 May 1960 began
immediately by comparing the screenplay with the stage production she
had seen:

Extended by scenes on the hockey field, at Blackpool, in a graveyard (between Jo
and her West Indian lover); softened in language —to its advantage—here and
there, but basically the same situation. I think it is more credible now but I still
don't feel it comes from the heart; more like a semi-poetic fancy concocted by
someone young and inexperienced (which indeed Shelagh Delaney is). Anyway,
from our point of view it seems a fairly straightforward 'X'. It must be 'X', because
of the extreme youth of the central character who finds herself expecting a black
baby; because of the character of Geoffrey (still presumably a 'queer'); and still
(though less forcibly than in the play) because of some of the language. *The main
essential is that Jo should not be too young.*

Her reservations over 'language' were enumerated, with directions to
drop the use of words like 'Christ': 'This expression should not be used
here or elsewhere.' And Field requested that several of Peter's lines should

be toned down, including 'Who's got a bun in the oven?', 'bubble belly', and 'a couple of grapefruit on a thirty-two bust, rich, young and juicy'. Apart from noting they were 'a bit crude', however, she felt that 'Peter's language is at least much less offensive than it was in the play'. What concerned Field, in large measure, was the age of the leading character and the depiction of Geof's homosexuality. The scene between Jo and Geof, in particular, which had so perturbed the theatre censors, was highlighted for special attention:

Here we have some rather tasteless hints at Geoffrey's sexual bent. I don't think we can help his character being 'betwixt and between': the young man in *I Am a Camera* was much the same, and that was before we had opened our doors to 'homos'. But casting and playing will be important in this role and in the others: we don't want Geoffrey too 'sissy' or Jo *too young in appearance*.

By contrast, as Field made clear, she was not in the least worried about the fact that Jo had a coloured merchant seaman as a lover. Her reader's report concluded on that score: 'Looking back, I see that I have said nothing about the black lover. This is because he is quite all right. The physical contacts of the two in frame seem to be pretty demure. We could not ask for anything much less if the theme is to be allowed and we have agreed to it already—rightly, as I think.'[16]

Field was correct, of course. The question of interracial love had been broached, although in muted fashion, during the course of *Sapphire* (1959), a film which utilized the conventions of both the classic detective story and the social problem genre—the murdered woman turns out to be of mixed ethnic origin—to explore current attitudes towards racial prejudice. When news first leaked out of the film's impending production, in autumn 1958, it was the cause of much concern. The Council of the Citizens of East London wrote to the Rank Organization on the matter, and the Mayor of Kensington followed up with a note to the BBFC. In the wake of the Notting Hill riots in September 1958, they were understandably worried about press reports that the film proposed to include 'scenes of riot between white and coloured people'. Both sought a postponement or abandonment of the project. 'If they are going ahead', was the handwritten BBFC comment appended to the Lord Mayor's letter, 'the sooner we are consulted the better'. Plainly, consultation and discussion ensued. Though it is difficult for once to fathom the precise nature of these negotiations, Trevelyan was clearly relatively happy by the time the completed film was viewed for certification on 13 February 1959. Scriptwriter Janet Green, director Basil Dearden, and producer Michael Relph had done enough to assuage the censors. The only problems that remained were twofold:

1. We question the desirability of showing the escaping negro being beaten up by 'Teddy Boys'. I understand that you are re-editing and shortening these sequences to give them less emphasis. This will be satisfactory to us.
2. The first interrogation of the negro by Inspector Hazard and Sergeant Learoyd. We feel that this scene might cause some coloured people to be afraid that if they fell into the hands of the police, even for a minor offence, they would be bullied and shouted at. I understand that you are prepared to reduce the volume on the soundtrack and that this will have the effect of lessening the impact of the scene. This will be satisfactory to us.[17]

The producers responded as the BBFC required and *Sapphire* was given an 'A' certificate. The critical reaction to the film centred largely upon its success in combining the formulaic elements of popular entertainment with serious subject matter—a traditional 'whodunnit' with the question of 'colour prejudice'. 'Though the majority of reviewers lauded the film's achievements', Carrie Tarr notes, 'a significant minority were disturbed by its apparently unconscious racism, drawing attention to the stereotyping of the characters, especially some of the black cameo roles, and to a *mise-en-scène* which equates colour with "tomtoms, slums, rackets, zooty suits, taffeta petticoats". The film was therefore perceived by some as failing to confront the real social issues.' And, as William Whitebait put it in a contemporary review for the *New Statesman*: 'Notting Hill, we may feel, deserves serious handling or none. As it is, Colour provides the red herring to keep us from spotting the murderer too soon.'[18]

Plainly, *A Taste of Honey* contemplated dealing with the theme of inter-racial love in an altogether different fashion to *Sapphire*. But, like Audrey Field, the remaining BBFC script-readers saw little to worry about on that front. Newton K. Branch, for instance, reiterated Field's fears regarding the importance of playing and casting. He also proceeded to explain, for the benefit of those who did not know, a piece of Delancy's slang:

'to goose' means to put a stick or umbrella or what not between someone's legs who is walking away from you and is generally considered very comical. On looking back to this play, I think what I remember most vividly was its curious atmosphere of whimsy, make-believe, almost of innocence. This was due mostly to playing (much of it, again, curiously naïve) and direction. *Very* much will depend on casting here.[19]

The last reader, Frank Crofts, took exception to much of the dialogue, though he found it 'unseemly rather than censorable'. He noted the use

33. Peter (*Robert Stephens*): 'a wealthy man, younger than Helen, a constant swain who proposes marriage.' (*A Taste of Honey*)

of 'bitch', 'whore', 'Christ', and ten examples of 'bloody', in addition to Peter's objectionable line 'A couple of grapefruit on a thirty-two bust'. 'Peter's drunken outburst' was unreasonable, in part, as was 'Jo's interest in Geoffrey's homosexuality'. Crofts concluded:

It is a scathing comment on current taste that scribbling of this sort should be considered entertainment, even a masterpiece. The most important thing is to impress on the director that Jo should be at least 16: she falsifies her age as 18 and is obviously leaving school rather young, but there are no more definite clues. In the same way, Geoffrey should not be an exaggerated nancy boy.[20]

Armed with his script-readers' reports, Trevelyan proceeded to arrange a meeting with Tony Richardson in late May 1960 to talk over outstanding issues. The meeting did indeed take place. But since Richardson indicated he was now shelving the project for the moment, Trevelyan settled for conveying the gist of their reservations by word of mouth and was spared the need to summarize them in writing. Although *A Taste of Honey* had suddenly, if temporarily, disappeared from view, however, the subject

34. Jo 'loathes the idea of having a baby especially as Helen has told her that her father was mentally retarded.' (*A Taste of Honey*)

of homosexuality had not. And Trevelyan was immediately preoccupied thereafter with his readers' reactions to the prospect of *Victim*.

The synopsis for *Victim* (which first appeared under the working title of 'Boy Barrett') emanated from the same team which had been responsible for *Sapphire*: director Basil Dearden, producer Michael Relph, and scriptwriter Janet Green. As with their earlier film, they proposed a mix of the popular and the serious, a film set solidly within the conventional crime format once again but dealing, in this instance, with the question of homosexual blackmail. Dirk Bogarde was set to star as a successful barrister who risks both career and marriage by revealing his own homosexual inclinations in an attempt to expose the blackmailers of other covert homosexuals. The synopsis for *Victim* arrived within a few days of the BBFC receiving the screenplay for *A Taste of Honey*. Audrey Field's comments followed just one week after she had reviewed Delaney's script.

'The synopsis reads perfectly all right', she found, because 'it is a sympathetic, perceptive, moral and responsible discussion of a problem which can be dealt with on paper as much as the writing fraternity wishes—which will probably be a very great deal, as the world of the arts is full of inverts.' The prospect of a film on the subject, though, was a different matter and likely to be 'very oppressive'. It could prove 'somewhat startling no doubt on celluloid', not least since it promised to confront audiences 'with a world peopled with practically no one but "queers" '. Field believed: 'Great tact and discretion will be needed if this project is to come off, and the "queerness" must not be laid on with a trowel.' In short, she argued: 'The more we can see of the various characters going about their daily life in association with other people who are *not* queers, and the less we need have of "covens" of queers lurking about in bars and clubs, the better.' What Field sought, essentially, was 'to let a little much needed normality and light and shade into this very sombre world'.[21]

Trevelyan conveyed the BBFC's formal response in a letter to Michael Relph on 18 May 1960, at precisely the same moment as he was arranging the meeting with Tony Richardson over *A Taste of Honey*. Trevelyan must have been very relieved to find that Richardson's film was postponed, at least, in view of the profound problems which remained to be sorted out over *Victim*. Though he acknowledged that Green's synopsis presented 'a sympathetic, perceptive and responsible discussion of a real problem', he could not escape the feeling that:

This kind of analysis presents no difficulties in a book but it does produce difficulties when translated to a medium of public entertainment for the masses. I do not say that the theme is impossible for an 'X' certificate film but I do think that great tact and discretion would be needed if the film is to be acceptable not only to us but also to the general public. As you know, public reaction on this subject tends to be strong. For the most part, intelligent people approach it with sympathy and compassion, but to the great majority of cinemagoers homosexuality is outside their direct experience and is something which is shocking, distasteful and disgusting. This argues that public education is desirable and indeed it may be, but it also suggests that a film-maker should approach the subject with caution.

This synopsis suggests to us that the film may give an impression of a world peopled with no one but 'queers' since in the story there are few characters who are not of this kind. It also suggests that the 'queerness' may be rather strongly emphasised. To balance this we feel that the more we can see of the characters going about their daily lives in association with other people who are not 'queers', the less we have of groups of 'queers' in bars, and clubs and elsewhere the better. There is plenty of scope for the police, Barrett's employers, etc., to let a little normality and light and shade into this very sombre world. Mel, the central character, is very different from the others and the more the film can favour him the better . . . Our view is that the normal sex, such as it is in this story, will need to be handled with more discretion than usual.[22]

When Janet Green's full script was offered for consideration at the end of June 1960, it was judged 'a good script, but may well be tricky'. If anything, the censors' consternation was increased by the introduction of 'an added complication'—'a good deal of nasty violence on the lines of that practised by the East End "vice gangs" who are flourishing just now'. 'I really am rather nervous of this script', commented Audrey Field, 'Messrs. Relph and Dearden are not sensational film-makers, but a lot of the material here is in itself pretty sensational; and the public may be getting a bit tired of exaggerated plain speaking on the subject.' She felt that 'Important questions of policy are involved'. John Trevelyan outlined precisely what they were, at length, in his reply to Green of 1 July 1960. His letter was straightforward, businesslike, and showed a real concern for the film's commercial prospects, not least in America. Initially, however, he was also somewhat disingenuous about the BBFC's attitude towards homosexuality. While, strictly speaking, the BBFC may not actually have 'banned' the subject from the screen hitherto, it was certainly true to say, as Audrey Field had noted, that they had only recently 'opened the doors' to its screen depiction:

We have never banned the subject of homosexuality from the screen but we have not until recently had very much censorship trouble with it, partially because American film producers were prevented from dealing with the subject by the inflexible ruling of the [Motion Picture Association of America Production] Code and because British film producers knew that the subject was not one of general discussion in this country and was one that would probably not be acceptable to British audiences. Recently the situation has changed in this country due on the one hand to the Wolfenden Report, which was followed up by a good deal of free discussion in the press and on radio and television, and on the other hand to the Lord Chamberlain making a public announcement in the press that he was now willing to accept homosexuality as a theme for stage plays. As far as the film is concerned, we have so far only had the problem as presented in the two films about Oscar Wilde. These films dealt with something that was historical fact about a real person and the real details relating to homosexuality appeared very largely in the clinical atmosphere of the Court. When we passed these films we had no idea what the reaction of the critics and the public would be. Fortunately we were not criticised, and I gather that the two films are doing good business, which suggests that the public accepts them, although it is possible that the publicity which resulted from the rivalry of the two companies and Court actions may have heightened public interest in the films. As you know on the subject of homosexuality there is a division of public opinion, and, if this week's debate in the

House of Commons is anything to go by, it appears that there is still a majority opposed to any compassionate treatment of it. In these circumstances a film-maker dealing with this subject is treading on dangerous ground and will have to proceed with caution. It is, I think, most important that the division of public opinion should be reflected in this, or any other film dealing with the subject, and I think it would be wise to treat the subject with the greatest discretion. Further-more, I think it is really important that a film of this subject should be one of serious purpose and should not include any material which might lead to sensationalism and would lessen its claim to seriousness.[23]

Trevelyan warned, finally, that he 'must submit this project at the appropriate time to Lord Morrison, our new President'—a prospect which worried Michael Relph, at least, who feared that with a new president might come a hardening of BBFC policy. In fact, as James Robertson has stated, 'there is no clear indication that Lord Morrison ever viewed the film'; but then, of course, there was hardly need for him to do so. Trevelyan had set out the BBFC's stall clearly enough over the depiction of homosexuality on the screen. All that remained was for the producers to fall in line and follow the detailed strictures laid down for them, which the makers of *Victim* duly did. Once a few feet had been cut from the completed print by the BBFC, their film was finally awarded an 'X' certificate on 1 June 1961. 'Although some reviews commented upon short snatches of pro-homosexual dialogue', Robertson notes, '*Victim* was on the whole surprisingly uncontroversial after its September 1961 British release following a showing at the Venice film festival of that year.' In truth, however, it is no surprise that *Victim* proved uncontroversial given, as Robertson himself rightly concludes, that 'the BBFC had significantly influenced the final shape of the film'.[24]

Moreover, in the intervening period between the tendering of a revised script for *Victim* in August 1960 and submission of the finished film for certification purposes in May 1961, *A Taste of Honey* had resurfaced once again for consideration, thereby presenting Trevelyan with an admirable opportunity to cement the policy he had lately formulated. The arguments he marshalled and presented to Woodfall Productions—to play down any potential sensationalist aspects and to bear in mind marketing factors—were very similar to his views regarding *Victim*. He advised the company, on 2 March 1961:

After we had read this script last May I had talks with Tony Richardson about it and it seemed unnecessary at that time to put our comments into writing. I understand, however, that production is starting very shortly and I am therefore prepared to do this now.

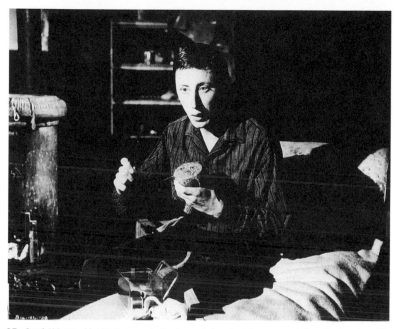

35. Geof (*Murray Melvin*) 'seems to be less obviously a homosexual than in the play. We would not refuse to accept him as a homosexual, but I think it would be desirable to show this by inference rather than by direct treatment.' (*A Taste of Honey*)

36. 'We hope that in appearance Jo will not be less than about 16. In view of what happens to her we would not want to have a possible complication of what I might perhaps describe as a "Lolita element".' (*A Taste of Honey*)

First let me say that it seems likely that a film based on this script would be basically suitable for the 'X' category. For this category I have two general points to make and some comments in detail.

The two general points are as follows:

1. We hope that in appearance Jo will not be less than about 16. In view of what happens to her we would not want to have a possible complication of what I might perhaps describe as a 'Lolita element'. Since Jo tells Jimmy that she is nearly 18 it would be unconvincing if she looked younger than 16, so perhaps I am raising a point which is unnecessary to raise.

2. Geoffrey seems to be less obviously a homosexual than in the play. We would not refuse to accept him as a homosexual, but I think it would be desirable to show this by inference rather than by direct treatment, particularly since you may have in mind extensive distribution in the USA under a Code Seal. The film certainly needs to establish that Geoffrey is a person who does not make sexual demands on Jo, but this can be treated with reasonable discretion . . .

The detailed comments which followed covered familiar ground. All usage of the expletive 'Christ' should be omitted: 'This word we try to keep out of films in this sort of context.' And lines like 'Who's got a bun in the oven?', 'bubble belly', and 'a couple of grapefruit on a thirty two bust' were considered 'a bit crude', albeit that the language was 'already toned down from the play script'. No nudity would be allowed on the script direction where 'Jo pulls everything off and flops into bed' and 'Helen's description of the comparative pleasures of the act of love is pretty direct'. 'It might possibly pass', Trevelyan noted, 'but I think it would be wise for you to have an alternative take with modified dialogue.'

The remaining exceptions were reserved, however, for those scenes and dialogue broaching the matter of Geof's homosexuality. Thus, the key lines between Jo and Geof—'I've always wanted to know about people like you' and 'I want to know what you do. I want to know why you do it'—were singled out especially. So, too, was Helen's reference to 'that pansified little freak' ('We just want to keep out unnecessarily pointed comments on Geoffrey being a queer'), and the visual intention to have 'a child imitating Geoffrey's walk' ('It might be rather unpleasant if it is markedly mincing in a homosexual way'). Trevelyan, in fact, required cuts in the screenplay which had already been passed for the stage version of Delaney's play. His reasons for doing so were explained at the last and highlighted, once again, his genuine interest in commercial prospects and his élitist concern about the mass cinema-going audience:

You may think that I have made too much of a point about Geoffrey's homosexuality. I think it would be in your interest to take this into account, not only because of the position in the USA, but also because there is some evidence that the cinemagoing public here is not attracted by homosexuals on the screen. I am told that films dealing with homosexuality have not been a great success commercially. We have never had any ban on homosexuality on the screen but, bearing in mind that the cinemagoing public is in the main very different from the theatre audiences, we usually suggest that where it is not a main theme but is incidental, it should be suggested rather than directly shown.

The give-and-take attitude which generally distinguished the ensuing process of censorship negotiations produced some concessions, as always. Besides, Woodfall were on firmer ground when seeking the retention of those aspects which had at least been allowed by the Lord Chamberlain's theatre censors. So, while several of Peter's comments to Jo were cut ('bubble belly', 'a couple of grapefruit'), other remarks addressed to Geof were allowed ('Mary Ann', 'It's all right, luv, I know the district'); and if Helen's calling Geof a 'pansified little freak' was thought to be going too far for cinema audiences and banned along with any visual imitation of his 'markedly mincing walk', Jo's open questioning of Geof's sexuality, by contrast, was allowed. The result was a typical compromise between the film-makers and the censors.[25]

Although *Kinematograph Weekly* reported that *A Taste of Honey* did not have as big an impact on the box-office as *Saturday Night and Sunday Morning* had enjoyed, it pleased the critics well enough winning the 1961 British Film Academy Awards for 'Best British Film', 'Best British Screenplay', 'Best British Actress' (Dora Bryan), and, 'Most Promising Newcomer' (Rita Tushingham). Amid the widespread praise for Delaney's contribution, however, it was the writer's lot invariably to see one feature of her work singled out for attention above all else. The critics' perception proved as selective as the censors' had been. Moreover, when Dilys Powell expressed a fervent hope 'soon to feel the moment has come to stop congratulating the British cinema on its ability to mention homosexuality', she did so with an unconscious irony which must have struck a sympathetic note among the BBFC's ranks.[26]

Notes

1 The BFI Library, London, holds the daily continuity reports on the film's progress (14 Mar.–1 May 1961, S2694) as well as the final screenplay (3 Mar. 1961, S328), and post-production script (Sept. 1961, S4658). Walter Lassally's thoughts on the film were recorded in interview with Barbara White for *The Journal of the University Film Association*, 26/4 (1974), 61–2, 79–80.

2 Kenneth Tynan, *Observer*, 1 June 1958; Alan Brien, *Spectator*, 6 June 1958, p. 729; Mary Watson, *Evening News*, 30 May 1958; *Theatre World* (July 1958), 37; *News Chronicle*, 5 Dec. 1958.

3 Julian Holland, *Evening News*, 15 Mar. 1961; Boleslaw Sulik, *Tribune*, 22 Sept. 1961; Penelope Gilliat, *Observer*, 17 Sept. 1961.

4 Michelene Wandor, *Look Back in Gender: Sexuality and the Family in post-war British drama* (London, 1987), 40.

5 Laing, *Representations of Working-Class Life*, 127.

6 See Howard Goorney, *The Theatre Workshop Story* (London, 1981), 109, where he quotes Frances Cuka and Avis Bunnage to the effect that much was changed in rehearsal, but esp. John Russell Taylor, *Anger and After* (London, 1988), 134–5, where on comparison of the original and final scripts, he concludes the original was 'not so radically different from the version finally performed as most published comment on the subject would lead one to believe'.

7 LC, file 1017/1958 on *A Taste of Honey*: reader's report, 5 May 1958.

8 Quoted in Johnston, *Blue Pencil*, 171–2 and 177–8. Nicholas de Jongh also usefully surveys the depiction of homosexuality on stage in *Not In Front of the Audience* (London, 1992).

9 LC, file 1017/1958 on *A Taste of Honey*: handwritten additions to reader's report. Also, Gwatkin to Gerald C. Raffles, 8 May 1958, and Raffles to Gwatkin, 14 May 1958.

10 Ibid., Raffles to Gwatkin, 5 June 1958; reader's report and marginal comments to same, 6 June 1958; Gwatkin to Raffles, 10 June 1958. Interestingly, on the latter occasion, Gwatkin questioned whether the whole of the new version had been tendered for consideration, given that it ran to only 47 pp. of script. He was assured it was complete. Taylor, *Anger and After*, 134–6, analyses the revisions and also notes the 'far-reaching changes' concerning Peter's character. Taylor plainly feels the changes were for the better since 'Peter, originally, is a complete seventeen-year-old's dream figure of cosmopolitan sophistication . . . [who] . . . reveals a child's loving heart of gold beneath the cynical exterior'. In contrast with the Lord Chamberlain's Senior Examiner, Charles Heriot, Taylor concludes: 'The play is obviously much superior in its final version.'

11 LC, file 1017/1958 on *A Taste of Honey*: E. L. Norton to Lord Chamberlain, 29 Jan. 1959; Gwatkin to Norton, 2 Feb. 1959.

12 Tony Richardson, 'The Two Worlds of the Cinema', *Films and Filming* (June 1961), p. 7. Laurence Olivier elaborates on Joan Plowright's American success in *Confessions of an Actor* (London, 1984), 247–9.

13 Quoted in Robinson, 'Trevelyan's Social History', 71.

14 It was doubtless allowed production, finally, for the same reason the Lord Chamberlain had allowed the play to proceed, albeit some six years earlier. On that occasion the reader, Charles Heriot, had noted: 'The play is strong and sensible. We are in no doubt at any time that the vicar is innocent of the "serious charge". Therefore, though the forbidden topic of homosexuality shadows this play, it does so in an inoffensive manner.' On being asked by Norman Gwatkin, 'How can you recommend this if we are to be at all consistent?', Heriot replied: 'But I am being consistent. Here there is no suggestion of real homosexuality, it is all lies.' The playreaders agreed: 'This is where we want the Solomon Touch.' And the Lord Chamberlain was asked to adjudicate on the script.

Lord Scarbrough responded: 'I am not convinced by the retort that because the accusation was untrue no question of propriety can arise. But neither am I convinced that the relevant part of the play should be cut or altered. It is a straight play and though it is conceivable that some embarrassment might be caused, I think on the whole no great harm will be done and that the play should be licensed.' Gwatkin wrote to Heriot: 'There you are. The judgment of Solomon has been given. And may God have mercy on your soul.' See the reader's report and memoranda contained in LC, file 5355/1953 on *Serious Charge*. Terence Young's 1959 film, of course, starred Anthony Quayle as the vicar and Andrew Ray as the teenager, and introduced Cliff Richard to the screen.

15 Quoted in Brian Masters, *The Swinging Sixties* (London, 1985), 118. For further discussion of the Wolfenden Committee's proposals see Jonathan Dollimore, 'The Challenge of Sexuality', in Alan Sinfield (ed.), *Society and Literature 1945–1970* (London, 1983), 61–2.

16 BBFC file on *A Taste of Honey*: reader's report, 8 May 1960.

17 BBFC file on *Sapphire*: correspondence of 23 Oct. 1958, 25 Oct. 1958, with marginal comment to same, and 13 Feb. 1959.

18 Carrie Tarr adds: 'However, the murder mystery itself constitutes a further red herring to keep us from spotting that the film in fact turns about the investigation of a woman's sexuality.' See her article, '*Sapphire, Darling* and the Boundaries of Permitted Pleasure', *Screen*, 26/1 (1985), 34, which includes brief reference to Whitebait's review. The same edn. of *Screen* contains further exposition on the film by John Hill, 'The British "Social Problem" Film: *Violent Playground* and *Sapphire*', 34–49. Neither author, however, explores the film's treatment at the hands of the BBFC.

19 BBFC file on *A Taste of Honey*: note from examiners, 11 May 1960.

20 Ibid., 17 May 1960.

21 BBFC file on *Victim*: reader's report, 16 May 1960.

22 Ibid., Trevelyan to Relph, 18 May 1960.

23 Ibid., reader's report, 29 June 1960, and Trevelyan to Green, 1 July 1960.

24 James C. Robertson's astute analysis of the BBFC documentation on *Victim* is found in *Hidden Cinema*, 119–26.

25 BBFC file on *A Taste of Honey*: Trevelyan to Holden, Woodfall Productions Ltd., 2 Mar. 1961.

26 See *Kinematograph Weekly*, 14 Sept. 1961, p. 10, which noted curtly that *A Taste of Honey* was an 'Outstanding British title booking for other than strictly family halls' and commented: 'Low life melodrama adapted from famous play, dealing with uneasy relationship between "good time" Lancastrian and her young daughter. Story shapeless, but kaleidoscopic approach effective, salient situations sharply contrasted, verbal exchanges candid, backgrounds authentic, and camera work impressive.' Also ibid., 14 Dec. 1961, p. 6, where it was reported the film had not done as well as *Saturday Night and Sunday Morning* but was still 'no mean hit'. Dilys Powell's review appeared in the *Sunday Times*, 17 Sept. 1961.

7 **The Party's Over**

In the authors' production notes for a published edition of the 1960 play, *Billy Liar*, Keith Waterhouse and Willis Hall were perfectly precise about their intentions and how best to achieve them. 'A production in which Billy is directed purely for laughs in the first two acts', they maintained, 'will find its audience unprepared to accept the serious content of the third act when Billy, for a time, sheds his final skins of make-believe.' 'The play should be directed for reality rather than comedy', they continued, 'and with subtlety rather than with the heavy hand which would take it dangerously near to farce.' 'Naturalism' was the watchword they advocated in regard to staging or characterization, and nowhere more so than over the language employed. Their advice to prospective directors was that the humour of the dialogue should be tempered by awareness of its serious purpose: 'On first reading of the text it will be seen that many of the lines are very funny—it must be appreciated however that the same lines are carefully naturalistic.' Intentions apart, though, Waterhouse and Hall were plainly also aware of the problems this posed in production and the possibility of adverse audience reaction to their work. The word 'bloody', they noted especially, 'may give some trouble if it is used as an expletive and not as an unconscious punctuation mark'. And they allowed that: 'where the use of the word at all is likely to give offence, the authors give permission for it to be deleted completely—but not for the substitution of euphemisms such as "ruddy", "blooming", etc.'[1]

While sensibly protecting the prospects for widespread production of their play, Waterhouse and Hall had genuine cause for worry. Both had been alerted to the likelihood that difficulties might arise by their prior experiences at the hands of the theatre censors. Ironically, on each occasion, they had escaped the worst possible strictures over 'language' simply because some ground had been conceded, albeit reluctantly, to their 'naturalistic' themes and concerns. In most other respects, however, they had encountered the usual array of intractable demands made of their original texts and suffered inevitable deletions or requests for revision as a consequence.

When Willis Hall submitted his solo-scripted play of *The Long and the Short and the Tall* in 1958, for example, he found that a fair amount was permitted which might not otherwise have been condoned in view of its distinctly male-dominated and wartime army setting. The Lord Chamberlain's reader admitted as much in his report:

Yet another lost-patrol-in-the Malayan-jungle play, and not a very good one as it lacks action. There is nothing whatever . . . except the constant quarrels of five regional types, which gets boring . . . Then we have another usual gambit in these plays, the capture of a Japanese prisoner of war and the different reactions to killing him as it will be impossible to get him back to base . . . The main characters are a strong Sergeant and Corporal of no pronounced region, a Scottish Lance Corporal, two Cockneys, one a barrack room lawyer, spiv and acid grouser, a Welshman, and a weak Newcastle radio operator. The psychological surprise is that it is the hard-boiled and cynical Cockney who makes the strongest protest at the killing of the prisoner of war. I have given the soldiers' talk some latitude and what I have set out is mostly of excretory reference as so much soldiers' talk is, regrettably.[2]

Subsequently, the jointly-authored playscript of *Billy Liar*, which was based on Waterhouse's successful 1959 novel, also won concessions on language as a result of grudging recognition being afforded their evident attempt to render characters and dialogue in a naturalistic fashion. But the reader was hardly enamoured of the play's dramatic potential, and commented:

This is a motionless portrait of a psychopathic liar. I call it that because the authors merely present the character, who does not develop. They offer no explanation for his behaviour, nor do they offer any solution for his problems. This is all right in a novel but it makes a very poor play since there is no drama. Billy Fisher is the 19-year-old son of a well-to-do garage proprietor in a North Country industrial town. It is the usual set-up: vulgar furniture in a villa with the semi-senile grandmother living with her daughter and her husband. The father is a well-meaning but stupid man who still uses 'bloody' as his only adjective. Billy is their only son, lazy, dirty, unshaven, employed slightly in an undertaker's, and living in a world of fantasy in which he tells lies for no reason except that they are always more interesting than the truth . . . All this is served up with carefully observed and loutish slang. There is a deal of petulance masquerading as emotion—but the play adds up to nothing because, I suspect, the authors can describe people but they do not yet understand their motives.[3]

'I have left all father's "bloodies" in since this is a part of his "character"',
the reader concluded, 'but there is a lot of nasty stuff that must come out.'
Among the offending 'nasty stuff' were words and phrases such as 'Christ',
'naffing', 'frigging', 'bint', 'bugger', 'bog off', 'stuffy black pudding', and
the line, 'You'll be as randy as an old ram'. And two scenes in particular,
both highlighting Billy's relations with his girlfriends, were required to be
extensively rewritten or omitted completely. In one, Billy tries to dose
Barbara, 'a plain girl given to eating oranges', with tablets which he has
been assured will serve as an aphrodisiac. This, the reader felt, was plainly
intended as 'The great joke of the first act' because it has 'no connection
with the plot and is never referred to afterwards in the play'. 'I find it
disgusting', he noted. The other scene foregrounds Liz. Here, the reader
was more circumspect since he recognized the character as 'a former
sweetheart who can get nearer to reality with Billy than anyone else, and
who is sensible enough to allow him to indulge his fantasies and thus, she
hopes, discharge them'. Despite that, however, the reader would not allow a passage of Billy's dialogue which alluded to contraceptives ('What
do you think we ought to do about—you know, babies? | I haven't got—
you know . . .'). Nor, indeed, was he especially pleased at Liz's telling
response: 'Billy . . . Do you know what *virgo intacta* means?'

Once informed of the Lord Chamberlain's misgivings, the play's producer, Oscar Lewenstein, marshalled his defences accordingly:

I have now discussed your letter's contents with my colleagues, Willis Hall and
Keith Waterhouse, who wrote the play, and Lindsay Anderson, who is directing
it. Certain of the Lord Chamberlain's requirements have come as a complete
shock to us all and we are wondering if this is as a result of some misunderstand-
ing of the nature of the play and perhaps also of the way we wish to present it.

Although *Billy Liar* may fairly be described as a comedy, it is in no sense a farce
and we feel it is most important that Billy himself should appear a real human
being, presented with understanding and subtlety, and calling for as much pity as
laughter. He is a boy who seeks continually to escape from an unsympathetic
reality through his fantasies, and this leads him to continually falsify his personal
relationships, sometimes in an absurdly naïve way.

Viewed from this point of view, we do not feel that the episode of the 'Passion
Pills' can possibly cause offence. There is never the slightest question that Billy
would *actually* seduce Barbara—or that the pills can have any effect on her whatsoever—and it is with this accentuation that we intend the scene should be played.
In other words, this is primarily a character situation: it is certainly not our aim
to exploit it for any vulgar or offensive effect . . .

We feel that the objections to the lines between Liz and Billy . . . may spring
from a similar misconception. This is designed to be the most moving scene in the

play, and to be played with great tenderness. Billy is at last brought face to face with reality (in the person of Liz) and of course he is revealed by it as nothing more than a shy and sensitive schoolboy. There is nothing 'jokey' about his talk with Liz here, and her reference to 'virgo intacta' is characteristic of her plain, direct, blunt (but not unkindly or vulgar) Northern personality. Honesty is the keynote of this girl's personality and we feel that these lines are necessary to convey this in the situation.

We should be grateful if you would reconsider these points in the light of our intentions in presenting this play as a serious study of character—based on one of the most highly praised novels of last year—and in line with such recent plays as *The Long and the Short and the Tall* by Mr Hall, *The Hostage*, and *A Taste of Honey*.[4]

Despite the reservations expressed about the play generally, the Lord Chamberlain's office willingly contemplated the arguments offered in mitigation by Lewenstein. Mere assurances about the company's seriousness of purpose, however, were hardly enough to win the day. The theatre censors remained to be convinced of everybody's earnest intentions and required changes, still, to make their case. In regard to the 'Passion Pills' episode, for instance, which all agreed was 'not a subject for laughs', it was felt 'We could meet the authors by asking them to resubmit in a version without the [present] farcical ending.' The numerous instances of offensive language, moreover, had yet to be resolved. And though the Lord Chamberlain was willing perhaps 'to stretch a point' and permit Liz's mention of 'virgo intacta', for the reasons advanced, he was assuredly not ready to allow even the slightest hint of contraceptives—'the contraceptive references must come out'. Lewenstein replied with a list of Waterhouse and Hall's proposed revisions. 'Bugger' was dropped, along with 'randy', 'bint', and 'stuffy black pudding'. 'Christ' would be replaced by 'cripes', 'frigging' by 'fizzing', and 'bog off' by 'rot off'. Each was passed. So, too, was a newly written scene set to follow the 'Passion Pills' sequence in which Billy escapes into yet another fantasy-ridden reverie. Any allusions to contraceptives, of course, were dutifully omitted. Now, when Billy asked what should be done about 'you know, babies?', Liz replied: 'Have them. Lots and lots of them.' When Billy persisted simply with 'No, I mean tonight', Liz responded with just 'It's all right'. The note of original concern had been replaced, of necessity, by bland reassurance.[5]

The play of *Billy Liar*, like the novel before it, was an immediate success and enjoyed a London run of 600 performances lasting from September 1960 well into 1962. Its undoubted popularity marked it out as an obvious candidate for filmic treatment. Waterhouse and Hall, moreover, soon showed they were the ones best suited to the task. Following fast upon their stage success, for instance, they had been engaged to adapt various writers' work for the cinema and had earned considerable praise in the industry for screenplays of *Whistle Down the Wind* (1961, from Mary Hayley Bell's novel) and *A Kind of Loving* (1962, based on Stan Barstow's book). If it was no surprise that they finally landed the job of translating their own work to the screen, it was also no surprise that they sought to re-store much that had previously been denied them by way of treatment and dialogue. They found that things were no less difficult with the film censors than they had been with the stage censors.

The BBFC's reaction to their adaptation of Stan Barstow's *A Kind of Loving*, in the autumn of 1961, should have alerted Waterhouse and Hall to the fact they would encounter problems once again. The lines were strictly drawn at the outset and the point was made that 'In general terms you must take it that what we have accepted in such films as *Room at the Top* and *Saturday Night and Sunday Morning* represents the limit of what we would accept at the present time.' 'There are several things in ordinary human life and in normal conversation that would be unacceptable for a film shown under the conditions of public entertainment', John Trevelyan commented, and 'one real danger, both to censor reaction and to audi-ence reaction, is the possibility of embarrassment'. Predictably, 'the cru-dity of dialogue' was singled out for special attention, with repeated requests 'to modify the language' used throughout. 'It does not seem really necessary to have "bloody" every tenth word or so', the scriptwriters were told, and words like 'mucking', 'cowing', and 'God Almighty' should be dropped entirely. 'I am surprised that any scriptwriter should think that he could get away with "Bugger the neighbours" ', Trevelyan added, while 'Vic's line "Do you think I had to tie her down to do it?" would be less offensive if the words "to do it" were omitted'. Inevitably, warnings were issued that 'the scenes involving sexual relations must be shot with extreme care', and the producer was advised 'to have alternative versions of these scenes so that if they prove to be unacceptable you have replace-ment material'.

But it was the occasional references to contraceptives which appeared to worry the film censors most of all. 'We would not be prepared to have any talk or action about the purchase of contraceptives', Trevelyan stated emphatically on 23 October 1961. A consultation with the producer, Joseph Janni, did little to put his mind readily at ease, 'I am worried about the introduction of contraceptives into films', he reiterated on 3 November: 'You think this can be done in a way that is quite acceptable and inoffen-sive, and you may be right, but, after further discussion with our Examiners,

I think it is likely that we shall find this material unacceptable.' Nor, indeed, did the subsequent revision to the script by Waterhouse and Hall settle the issue, as Trevelyan made abundantly clear on 30 November 1961:

This, as you told me, takes out all the conversation about contraceptives, with the exception of Vic's lines 'Well, you know all about it. You give me some good advice' followed by Jeff's lines 'Go on, you're alright. It's a bloke' which are said against the background of a chemist's shop at night. This is obviously important from our point of view. Of course, much would depend on the subsequent scene in the chemist shop which I cannot recollect in detail.[6]

Given that Trevelyan had the BBFC reader's copious comments as well as the film script at his disposal, it would have been a simple matter to recap what particular scenes entailed, but this was his usual course of action in correspondence with producers. It was hardly necessary in this instance, though, since he chose more direct means to achieve his ends, visiting Shepperton Studios and observing for himself how Joseph Janni and the director, John Schlesinger, were progressing on 8 December 1961. After further negotiation and viewing of 'rushes', Trevelyan felt altogether happier. 'I think the picture may cause us less trouble than we anticipated', he reported. By the time his fellow examiners got to see the completed film, on 6 February 1962, they were all inclined to agree that *A Kind of Loving* was 'an exceptional British picture; the characterisation never fails in any part; the camerawork, and the atmosphere created by this in some outdoor sequences, and the story itself, make the film memorable'. Some anxiety was expressed about the love scenes ('It *is* very adult') and a view of Ingrid's 'naked back'. There were reservations still about mention of contraceptives and 'the chemist shop incident'. But in the latter case, crucially, what was originally intended to have a serious purpose was now presented largely to comic effect. The BBFC was clearly satisfied in the main. And one examiner was sufficiently moved as to feel 'absolutely certain' that 'the Moral Welfare Council would highly approve this film'.[7]

In view of the cordial relationship which ultimately developed between the film company and the BBFC over *A Kind of Loving*, Waterhouse and Hall must have fancied their chances somewhat when the same producer, Joseph Janni, subsequently tendered their script of *Billy Liar* for consideration. John Schlesinger, furthermore, was director yet again and he had worked hard at cultivating friendly contacts with Trevelyan during the pre-production stage. Doubtless, also, the critical and commercial success achieved with *A Kind of Loving* helped explain the amount of 'language' permitted by the BBFC for a cinema treatment of *Billy Liar* (not least from Billy's father, who was allowed his ubiquitous 'bloody', and Billy's own use of 'cowing'). Certainly, while the former film landed an 'X' certificate, the latter was granted an 'A'. That said, however, there were losses to be sustained as well as gains made: although the 'Passion Pills' episode was permitted, on the one hand, Liz's mention of *'virgo intacta'*, which had been passed for the theatre, was considered distinctly taboo as far as cinemagoers were concerned (it was replaced by the line 'You know there have been others, don't you?'). And when it came to their attempts to reinstate the contraceptive references which had already been excised by the theatre censors, Waterhouse and Hall soon realized there were no concessions to be won from the BBFC on that score. What they proposed was to insert their original dialogue, once more, with Billy asking 'What do you think we ought to do about—you know, babies?', followed up by his line 'I haven't got—you know'. What they were allowed was merely Billy enquiring 'Are you sure?', greeted by Liz's response 'Yes', and followed by his mumbling 'Err—well—what . . .' with the direction 'They kiss'. On matters such as contraception, in short, obfuscation was distinctly preferable to clarity as far as the BBFC was concerned.[8]

The BBFC's marked preference for obscuring the details of controversial subjects was a factor which John Schlesinger encountered again thereafter, but was compelled to accept in order to ensure he retained in his films those elements that the BBFC would otherwise have wished to see totally discarded. In the case of *Darling*, for instance, the lengthy discussions which took place between September 1964 and June 1965, from pre-production to final completion, revolved increasingly and principally around one potentially 'notorious' aspect—voyeurism. A BBFC reader stated at the outset that Frederic Raphael's screenplay raised the prospect of a film which would be likely to be realized in 'the Dolce Vita manner':

I suppose this is, in the main, well done in a Dolce Vita-ish sort of way, though I think it has flashes of being too jolly smart. No one will expect it to be to my taste and it is not. I might have said once 'too dry for my taste' but in fact as time goes on I find I like things reasonably dry. But I don't care for flat tonic water, and to me, the things people like this see fit to do with their lives seem about as good a choice for a film as flat tonic water for a drink. Anyway, that is by the way. And I feel in no doubt about it censor-wise. Most of it will get by for 'X' (done in the 'classy' way these people no doubt intend to do it). But our rules on 'X' love scenes and 'X' nudity will be contravened here and there if they don't look out, and there will be no justification for us allowing any more in this line than we usually do. And we *should* not (and I hope won't) allow the episode of the tart waiting in a bedroom for a man who is to make love to her and all these raffish layabouts assembling (with the camera at the ready) and waiting for the show to begin. This is vicious stuff.

Albeit acknowledged as an 'admittedly competent' screenplay, it was felt there was too much that hinted of the 'smart-Alec' and 'the sort of thing that vitiates this script as a work of art'. 'I shouldn't be surprised if somewhere behind this project', the reader pronounced, 'there were some poor fellow venting personal spleen—usually a shaky foundation.' Even the evident promise of better-than-average production values prompted fears: 'I do hope I am right about the "classy treatment". In the hands of some of our bright boys the film could be quite troublesome."[9]

Though most of the major detailed points of criticism were subsequently resolved to the censors' satisfaction, the question of the voyeuristic opening to a Parisian party scene dogged production from start to finish. On 29 September 1964, for example, Trevelyan informed Joseph Janni of the basic problems. His notes were sent 'as a basis for a verbal discussion' since he was certain that 'with you and John making this film I would not expect any lapses of taste'. Nevertheless, Trevelyan obviously felt the need to advance some positive suggestions on how best to proceed:

Here we get the 'Dolce Vita' type scenes . . . [which] appear to represent a 'voyeurism' party, and their acceptability will depend on how they are treated. If it comes clearly from the screen that these people are there to watch a young man and a girl copulating, I think that we would be very uneasy about them, but I think it not unlikely that you will take refuge in obscurity as Losey did in the final scenes of *The Servant*. Indeed in *La Dolce Vita* there were somewhat obscure hints at unusual perversions, but the obscurity was sufficient to allay our worries. These scenes may present a serious problem, and I hope that you will have alternatives in case they do.

By 26 May 1965, on first viewing the film, Trevelyan proposed more detailed amendments:

We cannot accept even the suggestion that the group of people in Paris are watching a couple copulating. It is true that the actual copulation is not seen, but there is absolutely no doubt about what is happening. I suggest that you cut the episode from before the hostess says that a young man will soon arrive and remove the whole of the rest of the episode. You may have some other way of dealing with this, and we are prepared to consider any alternative that you wish to put to us, but I must make it clear that we shall not accept anything which suggests the nature of the 'entertainment'.

At the last, on 22 June 1965, Trevelyan made his final intervention with yet further proposals:

The cuts that John has made certainly render the incident more obscure than it was, perhaps even to the point of making it rather incomprehensible, but we feel that to the percipient viewer the nature of the 'entertainment' is still obvious, and we decided that we must repeat our request for its complete removal. We feel that the continuity could be maintained by moving from the conversation between Miles and the sculptress to the starting of the movie projector. We appreciate the point that John makes about the disintegration of the girl in these scenes but feel that this point is adequately made during the party sequence which follows; indeed we felt that it is made more strongly and clearly in the party sequence than in the one which we want you to remove.[10]

Janni and Schlesinger conceded the issue in the end. Though they retained as much of the voyeuristic 'entertainment' as possible, what remained at the last were essentially mere vestiges of their former purpose. In their attempts to keep, yet trim, the episode to meet the censor's dictates, moreover, they had undoubtedly rendered it 'obscure'; indeed, It was well-nigh 'incomprehensible', as Trevelyan had rightly spotted. In one respect, of course, this hardly mattered. None of the BBFC's strictures prevented *Darling* from turning out to be a worldwide commercial success. And despite their script-reader's misgivings, Frederic Raphael won the 1965 Oscar for 'best original screenplay' while Julie Christie also received an Oscar for 'best actress', and was the first British actress to do so. But one thing is certain. *Darling* was not the film that Raphael, Schlesinger, or Janni had originally intended.[11]

As it was in 1955 and 1960, so it was in 1965. Voyeurism, like nudity, 'language', homosexuality, sex, abortion, contraception, and various other subjects which exercised the censors minds, was not considered fit entertainment to put before the British cinema-going public in undiluted or unsanitized form, if it was to be mentioned at all. Yet changes took place throughout these years, to be sure, and many of the strictures traditionally laid down by the censors were relaxed in time. Where Lindsay Anderson found that he was denied shots of nude males for *This Sporting Life* in 1963, and again in 1968 for *If . . .* , Ken Russell discovered that by 1969 he was allowed a full-frontal view of men wrestling for *Women in Love*. What had been denied to Alan Sillitoe and Karel Reisz, in 1960, by way of mention of the word 'bugger' and reference to successful abortion, was permitted for the film of *Up the Junction* in 1967.[12]

Censorship was neither fixed nor immutable, uncompromising or unyielding. It depended for its interpretation and application upon a number of key individuals, several of whom showed they were genuinely liberal in outlook and more than willing to engage in mutually beneficial bouts of give-and-take. The scriptwriters and film-makers were, of necessity, complicit in this bargaining. It was 'a curious arrangement' to repeat John Trevelyan's words, and, as he aptly described it, 'rather typically British in some ways'. The demise of theatre censorship in 1968, furthermore, was a notable advance. If the fruits of this permissiveness were perhaps most evident in the latter half of the 1960s, the 'swinging sixties', the decade from 1955 to 1965 undoubtedly proved crucial in the slow, complex, and fraught process of liberalization for British cinema and theatre alike.

To suggest, however, as some have done, that permissiveness was rife would be misleading. A new generation of playwrights, including David Edgar, David Hare, Howard Brenton, and Howard Barker, certainly enjoyed a degree of freedom of choice in speech or subject which had clearly been denied their predecessors such as John Osborne and Shelagh Delaney. By the same token, the likes of Ken Russell and Stanley Kubrick savoured a greater measure of licence in theme or presentation for their early 1970s films, *The Devils* and *A Clockwork Orange*, that would plainly not have been possible a decade earlier—although on release both endured a barrage of hostile criticism from some quarters, which so confounded Kubrick that he later withdrew *A Clockwork Orange* from British circulation.

What British cinema and theatre gained from the swings of censorship, in short, was almost lost on the roundabouts of reaction and repression. The forces aligned against the liberalizing tendency and in favour of purity and censorship—more vocal and better organized than ever with the advent of the National Viewers' and Listeners' Association, and the Festival of Light—fiercely contested the notion that 'the permissive society was the civilized society'. They soon set forth their ideologically charged reading of the 1960s as 'an illiberal decade'. It is this jaundiced vision which subsequently prompted Thatcherites to damn the decade for being riddled with 'permissive claptrap' and worse. It is mythologizing of a high order. Mythologizing, moreover, which serves to curtail the public domain, silence specific areas of discourse, and erode the meaning of language itself. So too, indeed, does censorship.

Notes

1 Keith Waterhouse and Willis Hall, *Billy Liar* (London, 1966), 96–7.

2 The documentation on *The Long and the Short and the Tall* is found under its original title, *The Disciplines of War*, as first presented by Oxford Theatre Group at the 1958

Edinburgh Festival Fringe. LC, file 1203/1958: reader's report, 26 July 1958. Peter Dews's production was staged at the Nottingham Playhouse on 1 Sept. 1958 and Lindsay Anderson's production for the English Stage Company opened on 7 Jan. 1959 at the Royal Court Theatre, London, before transferring to the New Theatre on 8 Apr. Subsequent proposed alterations to the script before London presentation, however, elicited the following censor's comment: 'I don't see why we should allow any of this. They are only dirtier additions to a dirty play.' See LC, file 1203/1958: Gwatkin to the Lord Chamberlain, 31 Dec. 1958. Few of these new suggestions were finally allowed. The London cast included Ronald Fraser, Alfred Lynch, Peter O'Toole, Bryan Pringle, and Robert Shaw.

3 LC, file 1012/1960 on *Billy Liar*: reader's report, 6 Aug. 1960.

4 Ibid., letter from Oscar Lewenstein, 13 Aug. 1960.

5 Ibid., Gwatkin to Lewenstein, 17 Aug. 1960; reply by Lewenstein with amendments, 22 Aug. 1960; approval was granted in a letter from Gwatkin, 27 Aug. 1960, and the play was stamped for licence on 15 Sept. 1960. Further addition of one line to the 'Passion Pills' scene was passed for inclusion in the licensed manuscript on 9 Sept. 1960. The play opened at the Cambridge Theatre on 13 Sept. 1960, with Albert Finney in the lead role, and ran for eighteen months.

6 BBFC file on *A Kind of Loving*: Trevelyan to Janni, 23 Oct. 1961, 3 Nov. 1961, and 30 Nov. 1961, with Trevelyan's handwritten notes to same of 8 Dec. 1961.

7 Ibid., note from examiners, 6 Feb. 1962, with amendments. The production company had already done many of the things required of it by the BBFC including 'toning down' the language and dropping, at Trevelyan's suggestion, the words 'to do it' in Vic's line 'Do you think I had to tie her down to do it?' In addition, unsurprisingly, the phrase 'bugger the neighbours' was omitted from the script and film entirely at the last. The BFI Library holds the release script for *A Kind of Loving* (S4684). Josh Billings considered the film a 'British box office certainty' and added: 'Story very true-to-life, characterisation flawless, treatment sensitive and shrewd, sex angle frank, comedy apt, feminine appeal compelling, dialogue sharp and atmosphere vividly realistic.' It turned out to be one of Anglo-Amalgamated's 'biggest successes of the year'. See *Kinematograph Weekly*, 19 Apr. 1962, p. 9, and 13 Dec. 1962, p. 7.

A *Kind of Loving* was also subsequently adapted for stage production though written this time by Stan Barstow himself, with Alfred Bradley. It was presented at the Sheffield Playhouse in 1965 and at York Theatre Royal in 1968. Their stage version reinstituted the complete line, 'Do you think I had to tie her down to do it?' but still dropped 'Bugger the neighbours', which was replaced by 'To hell with the neighbours'. See Stan Barstow and Alfred Bradley, *A Kind of Loving* (London, 1970), 72–3.

8 For Schlesinger's relations with the BBFC over *Billy Liar* and other films see Trevelyan, *What the Censor Saw*, 107, 178, 208–9, where he notes that Schlesinger was one of those directors, along with Joseph Losey, who 'used to like me to come to the studio while their films were being shot. I think they realised that by doing this I could get the "feel" of the production'. 'This, in retrospect, I regard as the greatest compliment that a film-maker could pay me', he stated with some pride, since 'It implied that I cared about their films, and that they regarded me more as an adviser or consultant than a censor.'

There is for once little documentation of substance in the BBFC's files relating to *Billy Liar*, although there are sufficient sources elsewhere to help fill in the censorship picture. The differences between the scriptwriters' intentions and what was realized in the finished film may be accurately gauged from materials housed in the BFI Library, which holds both the final draft screenplay (S12075) and the post-production script (S4642), as well as detailed comparison with the texts of the original novel, the subsequent play, and the Lord Chamberlain's play file.

9 BBFC file on *Darling*: examiner's report, 24 Sept. 1964.

10 Ibid., Trevelyan to Janni, 29 Sept. 1964, 26 May 1965, and 22 June 1965. It would have been very difficult, anyway, for Schlesinger to contemplate much more work on the film since he was heavily involved at the time in directing the Royal Shakespeare Company's production of *Timon of Athens*. And, in fact, Trevelyan's June correspondence was already being copied and addressed to him in Stratford. That said, Schlesinger did not wholly agree with Trevelyan's feeling that there would be no loss in continuity due to the latest cuts. Thus, he inserted a brief superimposition of neon signs to serve as a bridge for the move from the 'voyeurism' incident to the subsequent party sequence. The BBFC files and the scripts held in the BFI Library (Frederic Raphael's screenplay (S1438) and a post-production script (S4634)) reveal another interesting facet of the production. The 'voyeurism' prelude to the party was itself originally preceded by scenes depicting a film-star's wedding in which gendarmes, while controlling the attendant milling crowd, are observed 'practically killing an Algerian who is shouting something offensive'. The BBFC had issued a caution about this matter from the start and it, too, was eventually discarded.

11 The *Kinematograph Weekly* stressed much the same 'good life' theme as the BBFC in its potted preview: 'Modern drama of a girl's self-destructive search for "fulfilment" with savage side kicks at the social and commercial dolce vita. Story compelling, direction and camerawork intelligent, acting of stars distinguished. Sex scenes frank but moral proper . . . The film is a cruel but perhaps just indictment of an aspect of modern life.' *Darling* topped £4,700 in box-office returns from the first three days of release at the Plaza, Piccadilly Circus, alone, when it opened on 16 Sept. 1965. See *Kinematograph Weekly*, 12 Aug. 1965, p. 10, and ibid., 23 Sept. 1965, pp. 6–7.

12 In fact David Storey's screenplay of his 1960 novel, *This Sporting Life*, was first tendered for BBFC consideration in Aug. 1961 with Karel Reisz lined up as director. The BBFC objected to various matters, not least—despite its obvious sporting setting in rugby league football—the problems likely to be posed by scenes of men in showers and changing-rooms: 'We do not want any considerable nudity, and even full length back shots should be few and discreet.' In the event, the film was not made for another year or so, with Reisz as producer and Lindsay Anderson now brought in as director. After viewing the finished film on 11 Jan. 1963 the BBFC reiterated its earlier warning: 'It was agreed that an "X" certificate could be issued subject to the removal of visuals showing male genital areas.' For which, see the details found in BBFC file on *This Sporting Life*: 4 Aug. 1961–14 Jan. 1963. Again, in the case of *If . . .*, while the BBFC broke with precedent by allowing a glimpse of female pubic hair, it would not allow any explicit male shower scenes, preferring instead an alternative take in which 'the discreet use of towels prevented an equivalently frank look at the boys'. Interestingly, the American censors passed Anderson's original version, though American film distributors still cut the nude scenes, at least initially, for release outside of New York. See the director's preface to Anderson and Sherwin, *If . . .*, 11. Unfortunately, no substantial or well-documented account of American film censorship during this period has yet been forthcoming. It is obvious, however, that e.g. the easing of film censorship in America from 1967, the year of *Bonnie and Clyde*, undoubtedly had a more widespread effect on the content of motion pictures, esp. in Britain.

Sources

Individual Works

Alfie

RADIO PLAY
First broadcast on 7 Jan. 1962, 9.10–10.25 p.m., BBC Third Programme, under the title *Alfie Elkins and His Little Life*. Produced by Douglas Cleverdon, with Bill Owen as Alfie.

STAGE PLAY
Mermaid Theatre, London, 19 June 1963. Directed by Donald McWhinnie and designed by David Myerscough Jones. The cast included John Neville (Alfie), Glenda Jackson (Siddie), and Gemma Jones (Gilda). *New York première*: Morosco Theatre, 17 Dec. 1964.

PUBLISHED
London: Samuel French, 1963.

NOVEL
London: MacGibbon & Kee, 1966.

FILM
1966. *Production company*: Sheldrake. *Distributors*: Paramount. *Producer–director*: Lewis Gilbert. *Screenplay*: Bill Naughton, from his play. *Photographer*: Otto Heller. *Editor*: Thelma Connell. *Art director*: Peter Mullins. *Music*: Sonny Rollins. *Certificate*: X. *Running-time*: 114 minutes.

Cast: Michael Caine (Alfie), Shelley Winters (Ruby), Millicent Martin (Siddie), Julia Foster (Gilda), Jane Asher (Annie), Shirley Anne Field (Carla), Vivien Merchant (Lily), Eleanor Bron (Doctor), Denholm Elliott (Abortionist), Alfie Bass (Harry), Graham Stark (Humphrey), Murray Melvin (Nat), Sydney Tafler (Frank).

Unpublished Documentation
Lord Chamberlain's Office, file no. 3492, 20 Jan. 1963–30 Sept. 1964.
British Board of Film Censors file, 28 Apr. 1965–4 May 1965.

Billy Liar

NOVEL
London: Michael Joseph, 1959.

Sources

STAGE PLAY
Cambridge Theatre, London, 13 Sept. 1960. Directed by Lindsay Anderson, with décor by Alan Tagg. The cast included Albert Finney (Billy Fisher), George A. Cooper (Geoffrey Fisher), Mona Washbourne (Alice Fisher), Ethel Griffies (Florence Boothroyd), Trevor Bannister (Arthur Crabtree), Ann Beach (Barbara), Juliet Cooke (Rita), Jennifer Jayne (Liz).

PUBLISHED
London: Blackie, 1966.

FILM
1963. *Production company*: Vic–Waterhall. *Distributors*: Anglo-Amalgamated–Warner Pathé. *Producer*: Joseph Janni. *Director*: John Schlesinger. *Screenplay*: Keith Waterhouse and Willis Hall, from the novel by Keith Waterhouse and play by Keith Waterhouse and Willis Hall. *Photographer*: Denys Coop. *Editor*: Roger Cherrill. *Art director*: Ray Simm. *Music*: Richard Rodney Bennett. *Certificate*: A. *Running-time*: 98 minutes.

Cast: Tom Courtenay (Billy Fisher), Julie Christie (Liz), Wilfred Pickles (Geoffrey Fisher), Mona Washbourne (Alice Fisher), Ethel Griffies (Florence Boothroyd), Finlay Currie (Duxbury), Rodney Bewes (Arthur Crabtree), Helen Fraser (Barbara), Gwendolyn Watts (Rita), Leonard Rossiter (Shadrack), George Innes (Eric Stamp).

Unpublished Documentation
Lord Chamberlain's Office, file no. 1012, 6 Aug.–9 Sept. 1960.
British Film Institute scripts: final draft screenplay (S12075); post-production script, domestic version (S4642).

Darling

FILM
1965. *Production company*: Vic–Appia. *Distributors*: Anglo-Amalgamated–Warner Pathé. *Producer*: Joseph Janni. *Director*: John Schlesinger. *Screenplay*: Frederic Raphael. *Photographer*: Ken Higgins. *Editor*: James Clark. *Art director*: Ray Simm. *Music*: John Dankworth. *Certificate*: X. *Running-time*: 127 minutes.

Cast: Dirk Bogarde (Robert Gold), Laurence Harvey (Miles Brand), Julie Christie (Diana Scott), Roland Curram (Malcolm), Alex Scott (Sean Martin), Jose-Luis de Villalonga (Prince Cesare), Basil Henson (Alec Prosser-Jones), Helen Lindsay (Felicity Prosser-Jones), Tyler Butterworth (William Prosser-Jones), Pauline Yates (Estelle Gold), Peter Bayliss (Lord Grant).

NOVEL
New York: New American Library, 1965.

Unpublished Documentation
British Board of Film Censors file, 24 Sept. 1964–22 June 1965.
British Film Institute scripts: screenplay/shooting-script, Sept. 1964 (S1438); post-production script, UK version, July 1965 (S4634).

Entertainer, The

STAGE PLAY

Royal Court Theatre, London, 10 Apr. 1957. Directed by Tony Richardson with décor by Alan Tagg. The cast included Laurence Olivier (Archie Rice), Brenda de Banzie (Phoebe Rice), George Relph (Billy Rice), Dorothy Tutin (Jean Rice), and Richard Pasco (Frank Rice). *New York première*: Royale Theatre, 12 Feb. 1958.

PUBLISHED

London: Faber & Faber, 1957.

FILM

1960. *Production company*: Woodfall–Holly. *Distributors*: British Lion–Bryanston. *Producer*: Harry Saltzman. *Director*: Tony Richardson. *Screenplay*: John Osborne and Nigel Kneale, from John Osborne's play. *Photographer*: Oswald Morris. *Editor*: Alan Osbiston. *Art director*: Ralph Brinton. *Music*: John Addison. *Certificate*: X. *Running-time*: 96 minutes.

Cast: Laurence Olivier (Archie Rice), Brenda de Banzie (Phoebe Rice), Roger Livesey (Billy Rice), Joan Plowright (Jean Rice), Alan Bates (Frank Rice), Daniel Massey (Graham), Shirley Anne Field (Tina), Thora Hird (Mrs Lapford), Miriam Karlin (Soubrette).

Unpublished Documentation

Lord Chamberlain's Office, file no. 10041, 16 Mar.–9 Dec. 1957.

British Board of Film Censors file, 20 Aug.–29 Dec. 1959.

British Film Institute scripts: final shooting-script, 13 Aug. 1959 (S324); revised release script, 25 May 1960 (S322).

Kind of Loving, A

NOVEL

London: Michael Joseph, 1960.

FILM

1962. *Production company*: Vic–Waterhall. *Distributors*: Anglo-Amalgamated. *Producer*: Joseph Janni. *Director*: John Schlesinger. *Screenplay*: Willis Hall and Keith Waterhouse, from the novel by Stan Barstow. *Photographer*: Denys Coop. *Editor*: Roger Cherrill. *Art director*: Ray Simm. *Music*: Ron Grainer. *Certificate*: X. *Running-time*: 112 minutes.

Cast: Alan Bates (Vic), June Ritchie (Ingrid), Thora Hird (Mrs Rothwell), Bert Palmer (Mr Brown), Gwen Nelson (Mrs Brown), Malcolm Patton (Jim Brown), Pat Keen (Christine), David Mahlowe (David), Jack Smethurst (Conroy), James Bolam (Jeff), Michael Deacon (Les), Leonard Rossiter (Whymper), Patsy Rowlands (Dorothy).

STAGE PLAY

Adapted by Stan Barstow and Alfred Bradley; published London: Blackie, 1970.

Unpublished Documentation

British Board of Film Censors file, 23 Oct. 1961–6 Feb. 1962.

British Film Institute script: release script (S4684).

Loneliness of the Long Distance Runner, The

NOVEL
London: W. H. Allen, 1959.

FILM
1962. *Production company*: Woodfall. *Distributors*: BLC–British Lion–Bryanston. *Producer–director*: Tony Richardson. *Screenplay*: Alan Sillitoe, from his short story. *Photographer*: Walter Lassally. *Editor*: Antony Gibbs. *Art director*: Ted Marshall. *Music*: John Addison. *Certificate*: X. *Running-time*: 104 minutes.

   Cast: Tom Courtenay (Colin Smith), Michael Redgrave (Governor), Avis Bunnage (Mrs Smith), James Bolam (Mike), Alec McCowan (Brown), Dervis Ward (Detective), Topsy Jane (Audrey), Julia Foster (Gladys), James Cairncross (Jones), Philip Martin (Stacey).

STAGE PLAY
Adapted by Big Arts, The Grove, Kensington Park, London, 27 Oct. 1990; adapted by Paul Brennan and Stephan Jameson, Octagon Theatre, Bolton, 7 May 1991.

Unpublished Documentation
British Board of Film Censors file, 3 Jan.–1 Aug. 1962.

Look Back in Anger

STAGE PLAY
Royal Court Theatre, London, 8 May 1956. Directed by Tony Richardson with décor by Alan Tagg. The cast included Kenneth Haigh (Jimmy Porter), Alan Bates (Cliff Lewis), and Mary Ure (Alison Porter). *New York première*: Lyceum Theatre, 1 Oct. 1957.

PUBLISHED
London: Faber & Faber, 1957.

FILM
1959. *Production company*: Woodfall. *Distributors*: Associated British–Pathé. *Executive producer*: Harry Saltzman. *Producer*: Gordon L. T. Scott. *Director*: Tony Richardson. *Screenplay*: Nigel Kneale, with additional dialogue by John Osborne, from John Osborne's play. *Photographer*: Oswald Morris. *Editor*: Richard Best. *Art director*: Peter Glazier. *Music*: Chris Barber and his band. *Certificate*: X. *Running-time*: 101 minutes.

   Cast: Richard Burton (Jimmy Porter), Claire Bloom (Helena Charles), Mary Ure (Alison Porter), Edith Evans (Mrs Tanner), Gary Raymond (Cliff Lewis), Glen Byam Shaw (Colonel Redfern), Donald Pleasance (Hurst), George Devine (Doctor), Phyllis Neilson-Terry (Mrs Redfern), S. P. Kapoor (Kapoor), Walter Hudd (Actor).

Unpublished Documentation
Lord Chamberlain's Office, file no. 8932, 1 Mar. 1956–21 Oct. 1957.
British Board of Film Censors file, 28 Aug.–19 Sept. 1958.

Peeping Tom

FILM

1960. *Production company*: Michael Powell Productions Ltd. *Distributors*: Anglo-Amalgamated. *Producer–director*: Michael Powell. *Associate producer*: Albert Fennell. *Screenplay*: Leo Marks. *Photographer*: Otto Heller. *Editor*: Noreen Ackland. *Art director*: Arthur Lawson. *Music*: Brian Easdale and Wally Stott. *Certificate*: X. *Running-time*: 109 minutes.

Cast: Carl Boehm (Mark Lewis), Anna Massey (Helen Stephens), Maxine Audley (Mrs Stephens), Moira Shearer (Vivian), Brenda Bruce (Dora), Esmond Knight (Arthur Baden), Martin Miller (Dr Rosen), Michael Goodliffe (Don Jarvis), Shirley Anne Field (Diane Ashley), Bartlett Mullins (Mr Peters), Jack Watson (Inspector Gregg), Nigel Davenport (Sergeant Miller), Pamela Green (Milly), Miles Malleson (Elderly Gentleman), Michael Powell (Mr Lewis).

Unpublished Documentation
British Board of Film Censors file, 25 Sept. 1959–23 June 1960.

Room at the Top

NOVEL
London: Eyre & Spottiswoode, 1957.

FILM

1959. *Production company*: Remus. *Distributors*: British Lion–Independent Film Distributors. *Producers*: John and James Woolf. *Director*: Jack Clayton. *Associate producer*: Raymond Anzarut. *Screenplay*: Neil Paterson, from the novel by John Braine. *Photographer*: Freddie Francis. *Editor*: Ralph Kemplin. *Art director*: Ralph Brinton. *Music*: Mario Nascimbene. *Certificate*: X. *Running-time*: 117 minutes.

Cast: Laurence Harvey (Joe Lampton), Simone Signoret (Alice Aisgill), Heather Sears (Susan Brown), Donald Wolfit (Mr Brown), Ambrosine Philpotts (Mrs Brown), Donald Houston (Charles Soames), Raymond Huntley (Mr Hoylake), John Westbrook (Jack Wales), Allan Cuthbertson (George Aisgill), Hermione Baddeley (Elspeth), Mary Peach (June Samson), Richard Pasco (Teddy).

Unpublished Documentation
British Board of Film Censors file, 1 Oct. 1958–7 Apr. 1959.
British Film Institute script: release script, Dec. 1958 (S925).

Sapphire

FILM

1959. *Production company*: Artna. *Distributors*: Rank. *Producer*: Michael Relph. *Director*: Basil Dearden. *Screenplay*: Janet Green and Lukas Heller. *Photographer*: Harry Waxman. *Editor*: John Guthridge. *Art director*: Carmen Dillon. *Music*: Philip Green. *Certificate*: A. *Running-time*: 92 minutes.

Cast: Nigel Patrick (Superintendent Hazard), Yvonne Mitchell (Mildred), Michael Craig (Inspector Learoyd), Paul Massey (David Harris), Bernard Miles (Ted Harris), Olga Lindo (Mrs Harris), Earl Cameron (Dr Robbins), Gordon Heath (Paul Slade), Harry Baird (Johnny Fiddle).

Unpublished Documentation
British Board of Film Censors file, 23 Oct. 1958–13 Feb. 1959.

Saturday Night and Sunday Morning

NOVEL
London: W. H. Allen, 1958.

FILM
1960. *Production company*: Woodfall. *Distributors*: British Lion–Bryanston. *Producers*: Harry Saltzman and Tony Richardson. *Director*: Karel Reisz. *Screenplay*: Alan Sillitoe, from his novel. *Photographer*: Freddie Francis. *Editor*: Seth Holt. *Art director*: Ted Marshall. *Music*: Johnny Dankworth. *Certificate*: X. *Running-time*: 89 minutes.

Cast: Albert Finney (Arthur), Shirley Anne Field (Doreen), Rachel Roberts (Brenda), Hylda Baker (Aunt Ada), Norman Rossington (Bert), Bryan Pringle (Jack), Edna Morris (Mrs Bull), Frank Pettitt (Mr Seaton), Elsie Wagstaffe (Mrs Seaton), Avis Bunnage (Blousy Woman), Robert Cawdron (Robboe), Colin Blakeley (Loudmouth), Irene Richmond (Doreen's Mother).

STAGE PLAY
Adapted by David Brett and directed by Frank Dunlop; Nottingham Playhouse, 15 Apr. 1964. Published by Michael White Productions, London, 1966.

Unpublished Documentation
British Board of Film Censors file, 20 Nov. 1959–14 Feb. 1961.
Lord Chamberlain's office, file no. 4112, 14 Mar.–13 Apr. 1964.
British Film Institute scripts: scenario (S329); post-production script, July 1960 (S330).

Spare the Rod

NOVEL
London: Longman, Green, and Co., 1954.

FILM
1961. *Production company*: Weyland. *Distributors*: British Lion–Bryanston. *Producer*: Victor Lyndon. *Director*: Leslie Norman. *Screenplay*: John Cresswell, from the novel by Michael Croft. *Photographer*: Paul Beeson. *Editor*: Gordon Stone. *Art director*: George Provis. *Music*: Laurie Johnson. *Certificate*: A. *Running-time*: 93 minutes.

Cast: Max Bygraves (John Sanders), Donald Pleasance (Mr Jenkins), Geoffrey Keen (Arthur Gregory), Betty McDowall (Ann Collins), Peter Reynolds (Alec Murray), Jean Anderson (Mrs Pond), Eleanor Summerfield (Mrs Harkness), Richard O'Sullivan (Fred Harkness), Mary Merrall (Miss Fogg), Aubrey Woods (Mr Bickerstaff), Claire Marshall (Margaret), Jeremy Bulloch (Angell), Annette Robinson (Doris), Michael Craze (Thatcher), Brian Love (Hoole).

Unpublished Documentation
British Board of Film Censors file, 4 Oct. 1954–15 Feb. 1961.

Taste of Honey, A

STAGE PLAY

Theatre Royal, Stratford, London, 27 May 1958. Directed by Joan Littlewood with settings by John Bury. The cast included Avis Bunnage (Helen), Frances Cuka (Jo), Nigel Davenport (Peter), Clifton Jones (The Boy) and Murray Melvin (Geoffrey). *New York première*: Lyceum Theatre, 4 Oct. 1960.

PUBLISHED

London: Methuen, 1959.

FILM

1961. *Production company*: Woodfall. *Distributors*: Bryanston. *Producer–director*: Tony Richardson. *Screenplay*: Shelagh Delaney and Tony Richardson, from Shelagh Delaney's play. *Photographer*: Walter Lassally. *Editor*: Antony Gibbs. *Art director*: Ralph Brinton. *Music*: John Addison. *Certificate*: X. *Running-time*: 100 minutes.

Cast: Dora Bryan (Helen), Rita Tushingham (Jo), Robert Stephens (Peter), Murray Melvin (Geoffrey), Paul Danquah (Jimmy), David Boliver (Bert), Moira Kaye (Doris).

Unpublished Documentation

Lord Chamberlain's Office, file no. 1017, 5 May 1958–2 Feb. 1959.
British Board of Film Censors file, 8 May 1960–2 Mar. 1961.
British Film Institute scripts: final screenplay, 3 Mar. 1961 (S328); daily continuity reports, 14 Mar.–1 May 1961 (S2694); post-production script, Sept. 1961 (S4658).

This Sporting Life

NOVEL

London: Longman, 1960.

FILM

1963. *Production company*: Independent Artists. *Distributors*: Rank. *Producer*: Karel Reisz and Albert Fennell. *Director*: Lindsay Anderson. *Screenplay*: David Storey, from his novel. *Photographer*: Denys Coop. *Editor*: Peter Taylor. *Art director*: Alan Withy. *Music*: Roberto Gerhard. *Certificate*: X. *Running-time*: 134 minutes.

Cast: Richard Harris (Frank Machin), Rachel Roberts (Mrs Hammond), Alan Badel (Weaver), William Hartnell (Johnson), Colin Blakely (Maurice Braithwaite), Vanda Godsell (Mrs Weaver), Anne Cunningham (Judith), Jack Watson (Len Miller), Arthur Lowe (Slomer), Harry Markham (Wade), George Sewell (Jeff), Leonard Rossiter (Phillips).

Unpublished Documentation

British Board of Film Censors file, 4 Aug. 1961–14 Jan. 1963.
British Film Institute script: screenplay (S272).

Victim

FILM

1961. *Production company*: Parkway. *Distributors*: Rank. *Producer*: Michael Relph. *Director*: Basil Dearden. *Screenplay*: Janet Green and John McCormick. *Photographer*:

Otto Heller. *Editor*: John Guthridge. *Art director*: Alex Vetchinsky. *Music*: Philip Green. *Certificate*: X. *Running-time*: 100 minutes.

Cast: Dirk Bogarde (Melville Farr), Sylvia Syms (Laura Farr), Dennis Price (Calloway), Nigel Stock (Phip), Peter McEnery (Jack Barrett), Donald Churchill (Eddy Stone), Anthony Nicholls (Lord Fulbrook), Hilton Edwards (P. H.), Norman Bird (Harold Doe), Derren Nesbitt (Sandy), Charles Lloyd Pack (Henry), John Barrie (Inspector Harris).

Unpublished Documentation
British Board of Film Censors file, 12 May 1960–12 Sept. 1961.

OTHER PRIMARY SOURCES

BBC Written Archives, Caversham

Alfie Elkins and his Little Life, Audience Research Report, 30 Jan. 1962, IR/62/58.
'Broadcasting Reviewed', *The Critics*, 16 Sept. 1962.
Lee Thompson, J., 'Who Shall Censor the Censor?', *Talking of Films*, 15 Apr. 1958.
Richardson, Tony, 'Frankly Speaking', 12 Dec. 1962.
Source, copyright, and contributors' files (various) on: Lindsay Anderson, Stan Barstow, John Braine, Shelagh Delaney, Willis Hall, John Osborne, Frederic Raphael, Karel Reisz, Tony Richardson, John Schlesinger, Alan Sillitoe, David Storey, John Trevelyan, and Ted Willis.
Trevelyan, John, 'Answering J. Lee Thompson's Criticisms', *Talking of Films*, 13 May 1958.

British Film Producers Association, Executive Council Minute Books

7 Jan. 1953–2 Dec. 1954
5 Jan. 1955–6 Mar. 1957
3 Apr. 1957–18 Mar. 1959
1 Apr. 1959–5 Apr. 1961
3 May 1961–3 Mar. 1964
7 Apr. 1964 –1 Mar. 1966
5 Apr. 1966–21 Oct. 1969

British Library, London

Lord Chamberlain's Office, Play Censorship Correspondence
Federation of British Film Makers
Miscellaneous papers, in the possession of Roy Boulting.

SECONDARY SOURCES

ALDGATE, ANTHONY, and RICHARDS, JEFFREY, *Britain Can Take It* (Oxford: Basil Blackwell, 1986; 2nd edn. Edinburgh University Press, 1994).

ANDERSON, LINDSAY, and SHERWIN, DAVID, *If . . .* (London: Lorrimer, 1969).

ARMES, ROY, *A Critical History of British Cinema* (London: Secker and Warburg, 1978).

BARR, CHARLES, *Ealing Studios* (London: Cameron and Tayleur/David and Charles, 1977).

—— (ed.), *All Our Yesterdays* (London: British Film Institute, 1986).

BERGONZI, BERNARD, *Wartime and Aftermath* (Oxford: Oxford University Press, 1993).

BETTS, ERNEST, *The Film Business* (London: George Allen & Unwin, 1973).

BOGARDE, DIRK, *Snakes and Ladders* (Harmondsworth: Penguin, 1988).

BOX, MURIEL, *Odd Woman Out* (London: Leslie Frewin, 1974).

BRANDT, GEORGE W. (ed.), *British Television Drama* (Cambridge: Cambridge University Press, 1981).

BROWN, GEOFF, *Launder and Gilliat* (London: British Film Institute, 1977).

—— with ALDGATE, TONY, *The Common Touch: The Films of John Baxter* (London: British Film Institute, 1989).

BYGRAVES, MAX, *I Wanna Tell You a Story* (London: W. H. Allen, 1976).

CAINE, MICHAEL, *What's It All About?* (London: Century, 1992).

CAMERON, IAN (ed.), *Movie Reader* (London: November Books, 1972).

CHRISTIE, IAN (ed.), *Powell, Pressburger and Others* (London: British Film Institute, 1978).

—— *Arrows of Desire* (London: Waterstone, 1985).

COOK, CHRISTOPHER (ed.), *The Dilys Powell Film Reader* (Manchester: Carcanet, 1991).

CURRAN, JAMES, and PORTER, VINCENT (eds.), *British Cinema History* (London: Weidenfeld & Nicolson, 1983).

DE JONGH, NICHOLAS, *Not in Front of the Audience* (London: Routledge, 1992).

DE LA ROCHE, CATHERINE, 'Don't Shoot the Censor', *Films and Filming* (Apr. 1955), 12.

DICKINSON, MARGARET, and STREET, SARAH, *Cinema and State* (London: British Film Institute, 1985).

DURGNAT, RAYMOND, *A Mirror for England* (London: Faber & Faber, 1970).

EDGAR, DAVID, *The Second Time as Farce: Reflections on the Drama of Mean Times* (London: Lawrence & Wishart, 1988).

—— *That Summer* (London: Methuen, 1988).

ELLIS, JOHN, 'Art, Culture and Quality', *Screen*, 19/3 (1978), 9–49.

ELSAESSER, THOMAS, 'Between Style and Ideology', *Monogram*, 3 (1972), 2–11.

EVES, VICKI, 'Britain's Social Cinema', *Screen*, 10/6 (1969), 51–66.

—— 'The Structure of the British Film Industry', *Screen*, 11/1 (1970), 41–54.

FARBER, STEPHEN, 'Alfie', *Film Quarterly*, 20/3 (1967), 42–6.

FIELD, SHIRLEY ANNE, *A Time for Love* (London: Bantam, 1991).

FINDLATER, RICHARD, *Banned: A Review of Theatrical Censorship in Britain* (London: MacGibbon & Kee, 1967).

FORBES, BRYAN, *Notes for a Life* (London: Collins, 1974).

—— *A Divided Life* (London: Mandarin, 1993).

GASTON, G. M. A., *Jack Clayton: A Guide to References and Resources* (Boston, Mass.: G. K. Hall, 1981).

GIFFORD, DENIS, *The British Film Catalogue 1895–1985* (Newton Abbot: David and Charles, 1986).

GOORNEY, HOWARD, *The Theatre Workshop Story* (London: Eyre Methuen, 1981).

GRAHAM, PETER, *The Abortive Renaissance* (London: Axle Publications, 1963).

HACKER, JONATHAN, and PRICE, DAVID, *Take Ten: Contemporary British Film Directors* (Oxford: Oxford University Press, 1991).

HICKEY, DES, and SMITH, GUS, *The Prince* (London: Leslie Frewin, 1975).

HIGSON, ANDREW, 'Space, Place, Spectacle', *Screen*, 25/4–5 (1984), 2–21.

—— 'The Concept of National Cinema', *Screen*, 30/4 (1989), 36–46.

HILL, DEREK, 'The Habit of Censorship', *Encounter* (July 1960), 52–62.

HILL, JOHN, 'The British "Social Problem" Film: *Violent Playground* and *Sapphire'*, *Screen*, 26/1 (1985), 34–48.

—— *Sex, Class and Realism: British Cinema 1956–1963* (London: British Film Institute, 1986).

HOUSTON, PENELOPE, 'Look Back in Anger', *Sight and Sound*, 28/1 (1958/9), 31–3.

—— *The Contemporary Cinema, 1945–1963* (Harmondsworth: Penguin, 1963).

HUNNINGS, NEVILLE MARCH, *Film Censors and the Law* (London: George Allen & Unwin, 1967).

HUSTON, JOHN, *An Open Book* (London: Macmillan, 1981).

HYDE, H. MONTGOMERY (ed.), *The Lady Chatterley's Lover Trial* (London: Bodley Head, 1990).

JOHNSTON, JOHN, *The Lord Chamberlain's Blue Pencil* (London: Hodder & Stoughton, 1990).

KELLY, TERENCE, with NORTON, GRAHAM, and PERRY, GEORGE, *A Competitive Cinema* (London: Institute of Economic Affairs, 1966).

LAING, STUART, 'Room at the Top: The Morality of Affluence', in Christopher Pawling (ed.), *Popular Fiction and Social Change* (Basingstoke: Macmillan, 1984), 157–84.

—— *Representations of Working Class Life 1957–1964* (Basingstoke: Macmillan, 1986).

LANDY, MARCIA, *British Genres: Cinema and Society 1930–1960* (Princeton, NJ: Princeton University Press, 1991).

LASSALLY, WALTER, *Itinerant Cameraman* (London: John Murray, 1987).

LEE THOMPSON, J., 'The Censor Needs a Change', *Films and Filming* (June 1958), 8.

LEJEUNE, ANTHONY (ed.), *The C. A. Lejeune Film Reader* (Manchester: Carcanet, 1991).

LOVELL, ALAN, 'The British Cinema: The Unknown Cinema' (London: British Film Institute Education Department Seminar Paper, 1969).

—— and HILLIER, JIM, *Studies in Documentary* (London: Secker and Warburg/British Film Institute, 1972).

LOVELL, TERRY, 'Landscapes and Stories in 1960s British Realism', *Screen*, 31/4 (1990), 347–76.

MCFARLANE, BRIAN, *Sixty Voices* (London: British Film Institute, 1992).

MANVELL, ROGER, *New Cinema in Britain* (London: Studio Vista, 1969).

MARWICK, ARTHUR, 'Room at the Top, Saturday Night and Sunday Morning, and the "Cultural Revolution" in Britain', *Journal of Contemporary History*, 19/1 (1984), 127–51.

—— 'The 1960s: Was There a "Cultural Revolution"?', *Contemporary Record*, 2/3 (1988), 18–20.

—— (ed.), *The Arts, Literature and Society* (London: Routledge, 1990).

—— *British Society since 1945*, 2nd edn. (Harmondsworth: Penguin, 1990).

—— *Culture in Britain since 1945* (Oxford: Basil Blackwell, 1991).

MASTERS, BRIAN, *The Swinging Sixties* (London: Constable, 1985).

MEDHURST, ANDY, 'Victim: Text as Context', *Screen*, 25/4–5 (1984), 22–35.

Monopolies Commission, *Report on the Supply of Films for Exhibition in Cinemas* (London: HMSO, 1966).

MORGAN, KENNETH, *The People's Peace: British History 1945–1989* (Oxford: Oxford University Press, 1990).

MURPHY, ROBERT, *Sixties British Cinema* (London: British Film Institute, 1992).

OAKLEY, CHARLES, *Where We Came In* (London: George Allen & Unwin, 1964).

OLIVIER, LAURENCE, *Confessions of an Actor* (London: Coronet, 1984).

OSBORNE, JOHN, *Almost a Gentleman* (London: Faber & Faber, 1991).

PARK, JAMES, *British Cinema: The Lights That Failed* (London: Batsford, 1990).

PERRY, GEORGE, *The Great British Picture Show* (Frogmore, St Albans: Paladin, 1975).

—— *Movies from the Mansion: A History of Pinewood Studios* (London: Elm Tree Books, 1976).

PETRIE, DUNCAN J., *Creativity and Constraint in the British Film Industry* (Basingstoke: Macmillan, 1991).

PHELPS, GUY, *Film Censorship* (London: Victor Gollancz, 1975).

Political and Economic Planning, 'The British Film Industry, 1958', *Planning*, 24 (1958), 424.

POWELL, DILYS, *The Golden Screen* (London: Pavilion, 1989).

POWELL, MICHAEL, *Million-Dollar Movie* (London: Heinemann, 1992).

RAPHAEL, FREDERIC, *Two for the Road* (London: Jonathan Cape, 1967).

RICHARDS, JEFFREY, 'New Waves and Old Myths: British Cinema in the 1960s', in Moore-Gilbert, Bart, and Seed, John (eds.), *Cultural Revolution? The Challenge of the Arts in the 1960s* (London: Unwin Hyman, 1992), 218–35.

—— and ALDGATE, ANTHONY, *Best of British: Cinema and Society, 1930–1970* (Oxford: Basil Blackwell, 1983).

RICHARDSON, TONY, 'The Man Behind an Angry-Young-Man', *Films and Filming* (Feb. 1959), 9.

—— 'The Two Worlds of the Cinema', *Films and Filming*, (June 1961), 7.

RITCHIE, HARRY, *Success Stories: Literature and the Media in England, 1950–1959* (London: Faber & Faber, 1988).

ROBERTSON, JAMES C., *The Hidden Cinema: British Film Censorship in Action, 1913–1972* (London: Routledge, 1989).

ROBINSON, DAVID, 'Trevelyan's Social History: Some Notes and a Chronology', *Sight and Sound*, 40/2 (1971), 70–2.

SHRIMPTON, JEAN, *An Autobiography* (London: Sphere, 1991).

SILLITOE, ALAN, 'What Comes on Monday?', *New Left Review*, 4 (1960), 58–9.

—— 'Writing and Publishing', *London Review of Books*, 1–14 Apr. 1982, pp. 8–10.

SINFIELD, ALAN (ed.), *Society and Literature 1945–1970* (London: Methuen, 1983).

SINFIELD, ALAN, *Literature, Politics and Culture in Postwar Britain* (Oxford: Basil Blackwell, 1989).

SINYARD, NEIL, *The Films of Richard Lester* (London: Croom Helm, 1985).

—— *The Films of Nicolas Roeg* (London: Charles Letts, 1991).

SPRAOS, JOHN, *The Decline of the Cinema* (London: George Allen & Unwin, 1962).

STAMP, TERENCE, *Stamp Album* (London; Grafton, 1988).

—— *Coming Attractions* (London: Grafton, 1989).

—— *Double Feature* (London: Grafton, 1990).

STONE, PAULENE, with EVANS, PETER, *One Tear is Enough* (London: Michael Joseph, 1975).

Structure and Trading Practices of the Film Industry: Recommendations of the Cinematograph Films Council (London: HMSO, 1964).

SUSSEX, ELIZABETH, *Lindsay Anderson* (London: Studio Vista, 1969).

SUTHERLAND, J. A., *Fiction and the Fiction Industry* (London: Athlone Press, 1978).

SUTHERLAND, JOHN, *Offensive Literature: Decensorship in Britain, 1960–1982* (London: Junction Books, 1982).

TARR, CARRIE, '*Sapphire, Darling* and the Boundaries of Permitted Pleasure', *Screen*, 26/1 (1985), 50–65.

TAYLOR, JOHN RUSSELL (ed.), *John Osborne: Look Back in Anger, A Casebook* (Basingstoke: Macmillan, 1968).

—— (ed.), *Masterworks of the British Cinema* (London: Lorrimer, 1974).

—— *Anger and After* (London: Methuen, 1988).

THUMIM, JANET, 'The "Popular", Cash and Culture in the Postwar British Cinema Industry', *Screen*, 32/3 (1991), 245–71.

TREVELYAN, JOHN, 'Censored: How and Why We Do It', *Films and Filming* (July 1958), 8.

—— *What the Censor Saw* (London: Michael Joseph, 1973).

WALKER, ALEXANDER, *Hollywood, England: The British Film Industry in the Sixties* (London: Michael Joseph, 1974).

WALKER, JOHN, *The Once and Future Film* (London: Methuen, 1985).

WANDOR, MICHELENE, *Look Back in Gender: Sexuality and the Family in Post-war British Drama* (London: Methuen, 1987).

WARNER, ALAN, *Who Sang What on the Screen* (London: Angus & Robertson, 1984).

WARREN, PATRICIA, *Elstree: The British Hollywood* (London: Elm Tree Books, 1983).

WHITEBAIT, WILLIAM, 'This Nanny', *New Statesman*, 9 July 1960, p. 48.

—— 'This Censorship', *New Statesman*, 30 July 1960, pp. 153–4.

WILLIAMSON, WILLIAM, *The Temper of the Times: British Society since World War II* (Oxford: Oxford University Press, 1990).

WILLIS, TED, *Evening All* (Basingstoke: Macmillan, 1991).

WOOD, LINDA (ed.), *British Film Industry* (London: British Film Institute, 1980).

Index

Index

Index